Palgrave Macmillan Studies in Family and Intimate Life

Series Editors
Graham Allan
Keele University
Keele, UK

Lynn Jamieson
University of Edinburgh
Edinburgh, UK

David H.J. Morgan
University of Manchester
Manchester, UK

'The Palgrave Macmillan Studies in Family and Intimate Life series is impressive and contemporary in its themes and approaches'—Professor Deborah Chambers, Newcastle University, UK, and author of *New Social Ties*.

The remit of the Palgrave Macmillan Studies in Family and Intimate Life series is to publish major texts, monographs and edited collections focusing broadly on the sociological exploration of intimate relationships and family organization. The series covers a wide range of topics such as partnership, marriage, parenting, domestic arrangements, kinship, demographic change, intergenerational ties, life course transitions, step-families, gay and lesbian relationships, lone-parent households, and also non-familial intimate relationships such as friendships and includes works by leading figures in the field, in the UK and internationally, and aims to contribute to continue publishing influential and prize-winning research.

More information about this series at
http://www.palgrave.com/gp/series/14676

Alexandra Macht

Fatherhood and Love

The Social Construction of Masculine Emotions

Alexandra Macht
Oxford Brookes University
Oxford, UK

Palgrave Macmillan Studies in Family and Intimate Life
ISBN 978-3-030-20360-3   ISBN 978-3-030-20358-0   (eBook)
https://doi.org/10.1007/978-3-030-20358-0

© The Editor(s) (if applicable) and The Author(s), under exclusive licence to Springer Nature Switzerland
AG 2020
This work is subject to copyright. All rights are solely and exclusively licensed by the Publisher, whether
the whole or part of the material is concerned, specifically the rights of translation, reprinting, reuse of
illustrations, recitation, broadcasting, reproduction on microfilms or in any other physical way, and transmission or information storage and retrieval, electronic adaptation, computer software, or by similar or
dissimilar methodology now known or hereafter developed.
The use of general descriptive names, registered names, trademarks, service marks, etc. in this publication
does not imply, even in the absence of a specific statement, that such names are exempt from the relevant
protective laws and regulations and therefore free for general use.
The publisher, the authors and the editors are safe to assume that the advice and information in this book
are believed to be true and accurate at the date of publication. Neither the publisher nor the authors or
the editors give a warranty, express or implied, with respect to the material contained herein or for any
errors or omissions that may have been made. The publisher remains neutral with regard to jurisdictional
claims in published maps and institutional affiliations.

This Palgrave Macmillan imprint is published by the registered company Springer Nature Switzerland AG.
The registered company address is: Gewerbestrasse 11, 6330 Cham, Switzerland

To my family
Larisa, Răzvan and Olivia

It is good to love many things, for therein lies true strength.
And whosoever loves much performs much, and can accomplish much,
and what is done in love, it is well done!

—Van Gogh

Acknowledgements

In no specific order, I would like to extend my warm gratitude to Lynn Jamieson and Mary Holmes, for providing me with invaluable support in the process of writing the thesis on which this book is based and for convincing me to hold on and finish it. I would also like to thank Gillian Ranson for providing advice on an earlier version of the second chapter, as well as Julie Brownlie for offering insightful suggestions on how to improve the concept of emotional bordering. I'd like to thank Oksana Shmulyar Gréen alongside the Sociology and Social Work Group at the University of Gothenburg for inviting me to present the book in their seminar series and for providing me with constructive criticism. Finally, to the 47 fathers I interviewed for this project and their family members—thank you so much for your time and stories! It has been an emotionally transforming process to live with your words for this long and to distil meaning from your life experiences.

Contents

1 Changing Fathers and Changing Emotional Selves   1

2 Doing Love: Fathers' Emotions in Relation to Their Children   35

3 Memories of Love: Fathers' Emotions in Relation to Their Own Parents   71

4 Love and Power: Fathers' Emotions in Relation to Their Romantic Partners'   109

5 Discussion   145

List of Participants   161

References   169

Index   185

1

Changing Fathers and Changing Emotional Selves

© The Author(s) 2020
A. Macht, *Fatherhood and Love*, Palgrave Macmillan Studies in Family and Intimate Life, https://doi.org/10.1007/978-3-030-20358-0_1

Who taught you to love? The inscription welcomed me on the door of a Toronto-based apartment as I returned from giving a presentation on fatherhood and love to a small, yet enthusiastic, audience at the International Sociological Association's 2018 Conference. The question seemed apt, as it mirrored some of the thoughts I was investigating as part of my research on paternal love: 'Is love something we learn or is it an instinct? Why do we gender it? Why is romantic love so socially prominent? And why are other forms of love obscured in the analysis of everyday life?' You are about to engage with a sociological analysis on love, which attempts to provide some answers to these questions, filtered as they shall appear through the narratives of a specific group of European fathers. Why is it important to explore paternal love in the realm of family relationships? One reason is that, so far, there are no extensive accounts of paternal love in sociology. While accounts of romantic love abound (Illouz 2012; Beck and Beck-Gernsheim 2014; Seebach 2017; Engdahl 2018), paternal love continues to remain curiously absent. Another reason could be a 'blanket' effect, whereby lesser-studied European populations such as Scottish and Romanian involved fathers are usually overlooked because, in the first case, Scottish fathers tend to be grouped under the definition of 'British men', while accounts of Romanian fatherhood are categorized under the literature termed 'Eastern-European studies'. These are reasons for studying specific groups of fathers, as the specificity of their cultural contexts will help the reader see the specificity of other contexts and reconsider assumptions made about 'all fathers' or 'all fathers of European families'. In addition, it is important to conduct micro-level qualitative studies that contradict prevailing mass-cultural stereotypes. Furthermore, large-scale statistical data about family lives and their economic and socio-political conditions are brought to life by everyday accounts of intimate living. For example, the photograph above is an image of my family taken in 1993 on the grounds of a Romanian Christian-Orthodox church in Bucharest. The social occasion was my younger sister's christening, one of the many cultural and religious rituals that circumscribe the boundaries of Romanian family life. I'm the girl with the Snow-White imprint on her dress, lifted by my father. My father, a 26-year-old man at that time, exhibits, in this image, the typical prerogative of masculine strength expected from

Romanian men of his age and social background. Moreover, the picture is, in many respects, the quintessential image of the nuclear/traditional 'family', depicting adherence to the 'heteronorm', which is a set of customs and practices that maintain the superiority of heterosexual family relations over any alternative family forms (Wilkinson 2013). The 'nuclear' family structure (comprising the mother, the father and their two biological children) belongs to a certain time and place, as modern families are currently undergoing social transformations at a rapid pace, especially in the North-Western part of the globe (Beck and Beck-Gernsheim 2014; Jamieson 1998). So the picture covers the unsaid as well as the obvious (Kuhn 2002) and stands as a testament of time, reflecting the period of quiet and restructuring after the tumultuous social upheaval experienced by my parents just three years before this photograph was taken, during a revolution that brought about the fall of communism, not only in Romania but in the entire, former Eastern-European block (Shapiro and Shapiro 2004). Not only this picture is about a specific social-political landscape, tradition, culture and the representation of gendered bodies, but it is also about love. The love we shared and continue to do as family members. A love complicated by our combined biographies and multiple intersections (of age, gender and generation) and by our everyday lived experiences as members of a connected group, replete with the ideal images we continue to hold about what it means to be a 'family'. This love incorporates power, as it speaks about a form of socialization done according to Romanian cultural and gendered norms and tied into specific cultural family practices.

Contrary to sociologists, psychologists provide significant analyses of familial love, by rather mysteriously refering to love in other terms, such as 'warmth' or 'attachment' (Lamb 2010; Marsiglio and Roy 2012). So why this reluctance to name love by its name in scientific inquiries? One explanation is that because love was considered too amorphous a subject to warrant rational scientific analyses (Jackson 1993), it remained circumscribed to the religious realm (Gucht 1994) or to that of popular entertainment. However, this is no longer the case, and with the simultaneous rise in fatherhood studies, an interest in love studies could also be observed. The present research is unique because it has investigated, from a sociological perspective, the convergences of these two topics.

The data presented in this book was gathered between the winter of 2014 and the summer of 2015. Coincidentally, 2015 also marked the introduction of shared parental leave provisions in the UK, extending for employed fathers the short two weeks' time they could take to look after their children, to a longer three-month period. In Romania, at the moment, fathers can only take 5 days once their baby is born, with the possibility of extending this to 15 days if they attend an infant-care course (Macht and Popescu 2018), while in Scotland, they can take a mere two weeks of paternity leave and the shared leave option, as in the rest of the UK. Nonetheless, this time spent with the baby continues to be far too little compared to the maternal allocation. Mothers in both countries can take a full year or more to take care of the baby since childcare and love continue to be written into social policies as female responsibilities. Even if gender attitudes are changing and there is notable progress in terms of parental leave provisions in both the UK and Romania, it is important to underline that this process continues to happen in 'slow motion' (Segal 2007) and that it is not taking place uniformly across Europe.

Reflections on the experience of love come in this book through the perspective of men rather than the voice of all of their family members because as bell hooks wrote more than a decade ago: 'male domination of women and children stands in the way of love' (p. xxiv, 2004). As such, men's views on how they relate to their children, romantic partners and own parents are the topic of this book because I aimed to empirically address how men as fathers think about love and its meaning in their intimate lives. bell hooks adds that what stands in the way of dismantling patriarchal relations of power and domination towards more positive and nurturing relations is the sociological myopia of not analysing men and masculinities in relation to different forms of love. This book is a rendition of intimate incremental changes, from the viewpoint of a group of European men who are not usually given much attention in fatherhood research. To understand how they adopt a new and (considered by some) 'progressive' form of fathering and how they understand love as part of the social construction of their masculine sense of self, I define below the key terms used throughout this book to help guide the readers.

Conceptual Clarifications

Fatherhood

Any discussion of the role of the father needs to begin with the delineation between the terms father (the biological or social parent), fathering (the everyday practices surrounding caring for a child) and fatherhood (the public meaning of fathering, the social discourse and cultural beliefs regarding fathers)[1] (Featherstone 2009; Lamb 2010; Morgan 2011). In this book, I use the term 'fatherhood' since it describes the cultural dimension of the construction of the father's role and is concerned with the analysis of prevalent discourses, such as that of the love-based family and intimate fatherhood and how Scottish and Romanian men adopt these. Moreover, it has been argued that men's individual narratives of making sense of their lives are created by drawing from pervasive stories and public myths (Jamieson 1998), which means that their views are also influenced by cultural norms.

Involved fatherhood is a socio-psychological concept which refers to the father's participation in their children's lives through three characteristics: accessibility, engagement, responsibility and 'warmth' (Lamb 2010). Previous sociological analyses described fathers as strongly identifying with the act of providing economically for their family members, being emotionally stoic and authoritative or what has been referred to as the traditional model of fathering in the literature (LaRossa 1997). And yet, recent conceptualizations of 'good' fathering advocate for the importance of their emotional involvement. This emotional involvement is dependent on spending 'quality' time and engaging in physical displays of affection with the child through a variety of activities that support the performance of caring masculinity (Elliott 2015). In this book, I consider a conceptualization of fatherhood in relation to masculine emotionality

---

[1] At times, 'fathering' and 'fatherhood' are used interchangeably in the literature since not all researchers make this distinction. As the field of fatherhood is expanding, concerns about the need for commonly shared conceptualizations have been raised (Lamb 2010). The literature also makes references to the 'involved', 'nurturing' or 'new fathering' types.

offered by Esther Dermott (2008), who coined the term 'intimate fathering'. The author conceptualizes the emotional involvement of fathers as 'intimate fathering'.[2] This contemporary form of fathering values close bonding, seeing love as a meeting of minds between family members through repeated personal communication and self-disclosure. Unlike breadwinners or providers, intimate fathers are focused on preserving the quality of the emotional relationship they share with their children and emphasize positive displays of affection, which helps them construct a close and long-lasting bond with their children. Intimate fathering happens in the context of an increased lack of reliance on the durability of other intimate relationships in late modernity. Parent-child relationships are considered more durable than marriage in the age of fluid relating and fluid loving (Baumann 2003). Drawing from the rich literature on the practices of intimacy, as involving verbal 'mutual disclosure' but also non-verbal displays of affection (Jamieson 1998), intimate fathers are emotionally involved fathers who are focused on preserving the quality of the emotional relationship they share with their children; they emphasize positive displays of affection, which help them construct close and long-lasting bonds with their children. It is assumed that intimate fathers reject the dominant discourse of traditional fatherhood, characterized by breadwinning, and construct their new, intimate role in new ways and through trial and error.

Esther Dermott's research was of British fathers who were all resident in England. However, it is important to establish rather than assume the extent to which her finding that involved fathers are doing intimate fathering applies to other cultural groups whether within Britain or in other national contexts. Based on this conceptualization, the present research looked comparatively across two culturally specific contexts, Scotland and Romania, at theoretically selected samples of involved fathers who are engaged and available in their children's lives, even if they

---

[2] In the literature, 'involved fathers' also appear as 'reflexive fathers' (Williams 2008, 2011), 'child-oriented' fathers (Brannen and Nilsen 2006), 'nurturing dads' (Marsiglio and Roy 2012), 'caring' fathers (Johansson and Klinth 2007) and even 'fragile' fathers (Waller and Swisher 2006). If men seem to be able to occupy a variety of roles as fathers, for mothers, there are mostly two polarities available: the good and the bad mother, enhanced by their recent dimensions of a patriarchally compliant 'MILF' or modern 'sexy mother' (Friedman 2014).

are not necessarily their biological fathers and even if they are not always physically present (residency). This was because I was interested in exploring how men's emotions are constructed relationally in their intimate lives.

The literature on fatherhood has consistently addressed issues of fathers' employment, their work-life balance, responsibility, overall involvement, adjustments to fatherhood and fathering practices, but in the quest for gender equality, it has reached a certain impasse, whereby fathers are just being continuously redefined according to the same categories of analysis. The time is ripe to analyse men's emotions in their role as fathers more comprehensively, to capture what might prevent their 'transformation' according to changing gender ideals; if this has been attempted in music (de Boise 2015) and in relation to crime (Goodey 1997), it is necessary to investigate intimate family lives as well. It is for this reason I have referred to fathers as 'involved' rather than 'intimate' throughout the book since intimacy is not a full identity but, to my mind, denotes a dimension of emotional bordering, as a role is a state of continuous becoming rather than a fixed type of identity.

Masculine Emotionality

The analysis of fathers' emotionality implies analysing the 'ways of doing emotions' or of expressing their emotions to others (Holmes 2010). The premise is that the reflexive ways in which men construct their masculine identities are deeply rooted in emotions. For some men, fatherhood continues to be a significant life transition (Eggebeen and Knoester 2001), but rather than seeing fatherhood as a new identity, I argue that masculine definitions continue to be essential to how men build their father's role. Masculinity is a socially constructed gender identity (Holmes 2014). It can be understood as a performance of the self, done according to social expectations of what it means to be 'male', and generally super-imposed on the characteristics of an individual's biological sex (but not always). David Morgan (1992) argues that: 'Gender and masculinities may be understood as part of the Goffmanesque presentation of self, something which is negotiated (implicitly or explicitly) over a whole range of situations' (p. 47). Ralph LaRossa (1997) argued that masculinity is deeply connected to modernity. Masculine sex-role anxieties have also evolved in friction with the advances of modernity, which brought about changes in the collective ideals of masculinity. This has then translated into an account of the social evolution of roles for men from 'the savage man', to 'the respectable man' and finally towards 'the gentleman'. Unlike LaRossa, who sees a linear identity progression, I would, however, surmise that, in practice, there is a comingling of this wide variety of roles. In terms of masculine identity formation, being an involved father is, therefore, not only a social role but also an emotional identity, the boundaries of which are fluid and, in part, negotiated in relationships, as I shall describe in the following chapters.

In addition, male emotionality is presumed to be constructed in opposition to female identity, through emotional repression and self-estrangement, resulting in a gendered model of the 'emotional female' and the 'unemotional male' (Lupton 1998). It has been argued that what has traditionally structured men's private lives is a type of 'limitative' emotionality, built on stoic principles. Jeroen Jansz (2000) expands the discussion by considering that contemporary Western masculinity is focused on four characteristics: autonomy, aggressiveness, achievement and stoicism. Stoicism is described as *control of pain, grief and vulnerable feelings* (pp. 166–167) and is the main attribute in creating a 'restrictive emotionality' in men's daily performances of self. Jansz thinks that cultural models[3] act as masculine motivational forces for young men and argues that in the process of 'doing masculinity', men borrow from the available public resources of masculinity. This is a self-feeding process, whereby through this practice of 'borrowing' cultural models, they also reproduce them and thus help sustain the public and cultural ideals of masculinity:

> the cultural model of masculinity provides the resources for the construction of personal identities: men require other men and themselves to be autonomous, achieving, aggressive and stoic. (p. 169)

---

[3] Defined as a set of public conceptions of what being a man amounts to; a set of shared, conventional ideas about masculinity which are widespread in society and are endorsed by individual men through their practices. However, the extent to which these ideas about masculinity are intimately adopted by all is debatable.

Remarkably, it has been argued that men share a definition of their selves as emotionally stoic even across cultures (Gilmore 1990). The underlying logic this model proposes is that how men express emotions differs from how they feel them, as they are not 'emotionally empty' actors but rather agents who have trouble *expressing* their emotions (Seidler 2006). Rather than immediately expressing a certain feeling, Jansz argues that men would usually resort to a logical and rational deduction. The act of disclosing feelings is risky since men might appear vulnerable or weak in the process; therefore, by resisting, men can maintain emotional distance in their close relationships, which helps them exert control and preserve their autonomy. Through 'diversion tactics' such as concealing their emotions or channelling them into an emotion which is in line with their masculinity (i.e. anger), men can maintain a 'cool and detached' persona, reinforcing, in this way, their dominance. The author concludes that this emotional strategy has the downside that it might make it difficult for men to engage in intimate and meaningful relationships, but it does portray that emotional control is a staple in the construction of men's power and status in the social world.

Moreover, Johansson and Klinth (2007) argue that the development of men's caring attitude towards their family members does not necessarily equate with them being more gender-equal, as there is a difference between being 'child-oriented' and enacting 'gender-equal parenting'. In addition, reflecting on time-diary data from a large Australian survey comprising 4000 people, Craig (2006) shows how mothers are still more involved in child-rearing than their partners. This involvement entailed exerting more physical labour, having a more rigid timetable, spending more time alone with children and having a general responsibility for care arrangements, even when in full-time employment.

Lastly, Rochlen et al. (2008) have shown that for stay-at-home fathers, learning to meet their child's needs is a deeply emotional process. Fathers experienced tension in how they expressed love since they considered it to be a highly feminized emotion, and since men's bodily border-work in physical contact with their children is sometimes socially sanctioned. The research presented above portrays how despite gender-equal discourses, parents are still caught up in feminine/masculine ways of parenting. In this context, fatherhood is a process in the making, replete with contradictions and ongoing negotiations between traditional and new expectations of performing masculinity.

Traditional providing relies on the acquisition of resources for the family through engagement in paid work. This has been conceptualized as clashing with fathers' need to spend more time with their children, as men cut back on social and leisure activities since 'new' fatherhood entails both providing and active parenting (Goldberg et al. 2009). In addition, men do seem to express concerns about ageing and the 'right time' to father (Shirani 2013). Research has shown that spending time forms an important part of the emotional relationship shared with the child (Waller 2002), which becomes even more evident when there are obstacles to a father's capacity to 'be there'. Managing time plays a big role in not only how fathers construct their masculine identity but also in how they are tied in with the capitalist culture of work, which can have consequences on their intimate lives (Smith-Koslowski 2011; Aboim 2010). The 'crisis of fatherhood' debates brought to the foreground the idea that patriarchal power is not permanent and immovable but can also be subject to change and is, in this sense, vulnerable.

However, it is arguable whether becoming a father leads to more caring masculinities (Elliott 2015) rather than falling back on an authoritarian paternal model, which re-asserts masculine dominance. Viktor Seidler (2006) argues that intimacy is seen by many men as threatening their traditional male authority. Opinions are divided, as a growing number of studies have challenged the existence of progressive gender-equal practices in men's transitions into their new roles and identity accommodations (Walzer 2010; Fox 2009; Miller 2010; Åsenhed et al. 2014; Henwood and Procter 2003; Shirani and Henwood 2011) while others such as those studies looking at fathers' involvement with the care of their own children or on men doing emotional labour in nursing professions have found consistent support for them (Coltrane 1997; Deutsch 1999; Hanlon 2012; Cottingham 2015; Cottingham et al. 2015; Ranson 2015; Smith-Koslowski 2011). What needs to be said is that both in the field of men and masculinities and in that of involved fatherhood, it remains a challenge to construct a clear picture regarding men's potential for change if cultural variations and emotions are not considered. In this context, considering Eastern-European perspectives is useful in investigating love's cultural variations and to give voices to 'marginalized' masculinities.

Comparing Romanian and Scottish Fatherhood

Romanian and Scottish families live within different economic systems, even if under the aegis of the European market. The economic system in Scotland is a mixture of social and free-market strategies (Hood et al. 2003) while Romania continues to face a slow transition from a shifting post-communist economy to a free-market one, boosted by the growth initiatives of the European Union (EU) (Raiu 2011; Popescu 2014). The major legislative and political shifts that structured the lives of people in both countries have been: Romania's entry in 2007 into the European Union (Beciu 2009) and the 2012 Welfare Reform Act in Britain[4] which has increased austerity measures across the UK, thus affecting Scotland.[5] In Scotland, the Children and Young People Act (2014) and other local social policies of early intervention and child protection, organize the intrusion of state initiatives into personal lives. While in Romania, the reformation of the social system spurred by EU incentives has attempted some family-based local projects (UNICEF Romania[6]; The Romanian Ministry of Work[7]), but state intervention in family life is generally minimal. This is due to a generalized mistrust in the competencies of the government and a belief in the self-governing abilities of parents considered responsible for protecting the privacy of family life (Popescu 2009).

Romanian society is structured preponderantly around the family and on Christian-Orthodox traditional principles (Voicu 2008; Turcescu and Stan 2005). Religion continues to influence people's customs and habits even in the wake of secularization, and this undoubtedly feeds into their everyday family practices. In Scotland, society is largely secular but continues to be underscored by Presbyterian beliefs (Gordon 2006). The Scottish culture of masculinity is strongly influenced by its history of religion and the historical legacy and ongoing role in British militarism (Streets-Salter 2004), thus Scotland has a specific masculine culture (Howson 1993; McCrone 2001).

---

[4] http://www.legislation.gov.uk/ukpga/2012/5/contents/enacted

[5] At the time of writing this manuscript, Scotland would also be affected by its departure from the European Union due to a political measure termed in the media as 'Brexit'; the social and economic consequences of this change are yet to be ascertained and are not the focus of this research.

[6] https://www.unicef.org/romania/overview.html

[7] http://www.mmuncii.ro/j33/index.php/ro/

Demographically, Scotland's population is smaller than Romania's. In large urban dwellings, such as the ones where I have situated the research, there is a considerable difference in city density between Bucharest (Romania's largest city and political capital), currently at 1,812,290 inhabitants compared to Edinburgh (Scotland's political capital and second-largest city, with a population of 502,536 people). Romania is going through a steady decrease in its inhabitants (National Institute of Statistics 2018) while Scotland's population is projected to increase (National Records of Scotland 2018). However, on the background of these demographic countertrends, in both countries, there are predominant ageing populations (Bodogai and Cutler 2014).

Larger demographic, religious and economic differences affect the daily life of Scottish and Romanian people by influencing the creation or dissolution of their intimate relationships. However, macro-social trends should be complemented by what happens in the lives of family members on a micro-social level, offering a personal perspective to large-scale data. Simply by measuring time, work or family activities, without including emotions, the scope and depth of understanding the processes of change and the dynamics which constrain a social actor's agency continue to remain incomplete.

The omission of Romanian and Scottish families from the literature (or their rendition in a predominantly negative light, as in the case of Scottish masculinity) is to my mind significant, as it points to a form of cultural obtrusiveness. Despite this, there is a general upsurge of interest in fatherhood and fathering. For example, between 2011 and 2016, research on fatherhood proliferated, reaching a peak of interest, which shows little sign of abating (see Goldberg et al. 2009; Dempsey and Hewitt 2012; Meah and Jackson 2016). Initially, a first wave of interest in fatherhood occurred in the mid-1990s, with a concern for expert interventions meant to 'optimize parenting' (intensifying parenting for the well-being of the child) (Hays 1996) and analyses of familial transformations in the foreground of the allegedly collapsing Western breadwinner role (Coltrane 1997). Nowadays, a newly revived interest in fatherhood is fostered by widespread appeals to the gender-equal sharing of childcare and domestic tasks, and by a growing interest in resolving the work-life imbalance (Fox 2009; Ranson 2010) in connection to the intensification of both parenting and work (Brannen and Moss 1998).

Thus, the contemporary social context places expectations on men for emotional closeness in intimate relationships, such as attending antenatal classes, being present at birth, negotiating childcare arrangements with their partner and concerns with how to improve their relationship with their older children (Lupton and Barclay 1997). Being a good father is currently defined along the lines of being nurturing and intimate, not only a good provider, as intimate fathering puts pressure on men to get in touch and reflect upon their emotions and get comfortable *verbalizing* them (Dermott 2008).

Love

Initial attempts at developing a theoretical understanding of love in sociology came from Georg Simmel's account of love as women's cultural vocation in creating a home (1984); Hugo Beigel's (1951) socio-psychological rendition of how modern romantic love evolved from medieval courtly love in Western countries; Talcott Parsons's (1943) discussion of the American open system of personal choice in selecting a marriage partner and how this was influenced by the 'romantic love complex'; and William Goode's (1959) analysis of society's control of passionate love through the involvement of kin in the courtship rituals of the young. For this group of thinkers, love had primarily a moral quality; it upheld tradition and was enmeshed with the institution of marriage, reproducing through this the domestic economy of the home, in the wider context of kin relationships. These classic reflections on love were focused on its moral characteristics and how love existed within relationships to either maintain (parental love, love between friends, philia and agape) or threaten social structures (Eros, romantic and passionate love). However, such accounts were rather disjointed, as there was no 'great theory of love' since love was considered a 'bad word' in Sociology for a while (Jackson 1993). What stands out from these initial accounts of love is that they were anchored in analyses of family relationships.

Furthermore, it has also been argued that conceptions of love transform throughout time. For example, that love grew from the moral and responsible Victorian ideals of the nineteenth century to the desires and pleasure associated with erotic love at the end of the 1970s (Seidman 1991). Reaching that point in time, the moral conceptualizations of marriage, love and intimacy were deconstructed by the critical analysis of second-wave feminist writers, such as Kate Millett, Evelyn Reed and Adrienne Rich among many others, who unearthed romantic love's connection to the abuse of male power, and framed marriage and the traditional 'nuclear' family as the principal site of patriarchal domination of women (see Jaggar 1989, for a review; Hanmer 1990; bell hooks 2004). Men were portrayed in this literature as exerting superior financial, material and institutional control, and as such, they were removed from love and concerned mostly with the acquisition of power. However, the feminist literature acknowledged that men do love but in ways that do not undermine patriarchal power structures.

In what continues to be a patriarchal system of social relationships, it has been argued that alongside with the 'feminization of sex' (Ehrenreich et al. 1987), there has also been a 'feminization of love' (Cancian 1986). A 'feminized love' is focused on the characteristics usually associated with traditional femininity (traits such as warmth, docility and vulnerability) and excludes male identity because it appears as incompatible with such characteristics. Men's power is thus constructed not only by undermining stereotypical feminine values but also by undermining alternative types of masculinity (i.e. homosexuality). Contemporary social 'hegemony' is therefore heterosexual, tied in with the institution of marriage through an ideology of love (i.e. beliefs and narratives about love which are supplied by cultural traditions). In line with this, Anna Jónasdóttir and Ann Ferguson's (2014) try to theoretically rejuvenate the dichotomy by offering the concept of 'love power', which posits that love, instead of being seen as the social actor's private responsibility, can be viewed in a Marxist way, as a human productive force which is 'shaped by' but also 'shaping' social institutions. In this way, love in connection with labour (as one of its expressions) is vulnerable to similar types of disempowering and abusive treatments in a patriarchal capitalist society.[8] It is important then to consider not only *what love is* but also *what love does*.

Furthermore, the current focus on individualism in research on love began when Anthony Giddens published his book *The Transformation of Intimacy* (1992), which built on Niklas Luhmann's (1986 in Turner and Stets 2005) idea of love as validation of individualism. The debates surrounding Giddens' ideas of confluent love and pure relating, which described modern relationships as increasingly influenced by reflexivity and democratic negotiations, led to an increased interest in what Lynn Jamieson (2011) has termed 'love's close conceptual counterpart' (p. 8), the topic of 'intimacy'.[9] However, Anthony Giddens' 'democratization of love' professed widespread gender equality, which Jamieson (1998) has argued is far from being achieved in practice. She proposed that a thorough analysis of intimate relationships actually revealed classed practices, which couldn't be ignored or simply circumscribed to an ideally functioning 'pure relationship', as intimacy could also foster inequalities in social actor's lives; thus, the family and practices of parenting are the main areas where social inequalities take shape.

Following from these sociological debates, love and intimacy appear as momentarily intersected: love can create intimacy and relationships of love involve practices of intimacy (Bawin-Legros 2004). Love also appears to be something that one does and feels with others, rather than what one has (Smart 2007). If intimacy is created through daily intimate practice, then the act of expressing love is one of them. I would, however, argue that love and intimacy are intermingled, to the extent that love exists as an emotion created in social interactions, and intimacy describes a close relationship; therefore, intimacy describes the *relationship* within which love exists and is reproduced.

Nonetheless, such analyses of love focused on American and British populations reveal the ongoing connections of love to values such as

---

[8] A materialist feminist lens should shed light on the life needs of the body (i.e. food, shelter, water and health) in combination with more social needs, such as love, affection, sex and belonging to a group.

[9] Lynn Jamieson conceptualizes intimacy as a 'close connection' which can be '(…) physical, bodily intimacy, although an intimate relationship need not be sexual and both bodily and sexual contact can occur without intimacy' (2011, p. 1).

individualism, democracy and gender equality. In addition, if love has been considered in relation to motherhood (Dewey 2011; Lynch 2007; Paxson 2007) and through a feminist socialist lens (Riley 1987), fathers' love continues to be conspicuously absent. Moreover, parenting also suffers from cross-cultural variations, denoting its socially constructed character (Selin 2013). Bearing this in mind, love would perhaps look different in a more collectively organized culture.

Because paternal love does not have a general definition in sociology, I will employ Ian Burkitt's aesthetic emotional framework (2014) to consider father's love not as an inherent, 'natural' emotion but as a socially created one, which can coexist as a pattern of relationship within which emotions are lived. Therefore, love in this text is used differently from the psychological concept of 'attachment' as an emotion exclusively describing the important role of the mother as the primary caregiver in a child's life (Bowlby 1969). The focus falls on *paternal love* in order to not only include fathers in a comprehensive analysis of love but also to shift the focus away from essentializing and overburdening the mother's role. Sasha Roseneil (2005) remarks on the de-essentialization and the 'de-feminization' of love. She also supports the view that there are cultural aspects of love, gender and identity that delineate practices of intimacy (to which I add here a focus on emotions). As previously mentioned, empirical and comparative research on paternal love in sociology has not been systematically attempted beforehand. Therefore, exploring love in the context of fatherhood is appealing since father's relationship with the child, although embodied (as I argue in Chap. 2), is nonetheless removed from essentialist considerations of the body, which reduce it to its biology.

Emotions constitute a primary means to understand how inequalities are reproduced and sustained in time, though emotional attachments to certain values, identities, ideals and relationships. Seeing the social landscape through the lens of an aesthetic theory of emotion (Burkitt 2014) helps interpret the links between men's emotionality and the father's identity, as deeply processual and relationally bound constructions. Therefore, paternal love is different than romantic love because it is morally enshrouded in the 'incest taboo' and thus non-sexual (Freud 1919), but it is similar in that it is permeated by gendered power. Since previous literature on love has emphasized its socially constructed character, I have used, throughout the book, the terms 'emotion' and 'feeling' interchangeably since I disagree with the idea that emotions are primary 'things' and feelings are complex 'things'. This is because, in a fully sociological conception of love (Jackson 1993), there is no need to label social actors' emotionality as being composed of one set of 'emotions' and another set of 'feelings', as to my mind, emotions do not stagnate at the level of feeling 'within'. Moreover, by drawing from Norbert Elias' theoretical perspective (1939/2000), love can be understood as a relational *process*. In this process, emotions are interiorized and exteriorized, as two people relate, in acts of 'give-and-take', which take places between fathers and their family members. These relational exchanges give meaning to their everyday interactions, in a specific type of emotional process that also contributes to how they understand and performs their masculinity and which I have termed 'emotional bordering'.

Emotional Bordering

Masculinity together with fatherhood and love are dynamic social constructs. What they have in common is the potential of undergoing changes of meaning in time, and across cultures, in terms of how they play out in social actors' everyday lives. In the construction of an individual's identity, researchers who analysed culture and love (whether sociologists or anthropologists) have been concerned with the interpretation of 'borders', 'boundaries', 'thresholds' and 'frontiers' (Horvath et al. 2015) to explain the diffuse spaces where intimate social relationships begin and end and how these influence identity-work. As 'amorphous divisions' which appear between 'intimates who share culture' (Cohen 1994, p. 54), relational boundaries are metaphors that describe social frontiers upon which the formation of culture leaves a long-lasting mark, and which reside in social actor's consciousness, being intimately linked to their identities. Therefore, by intersecting with other categories, such as gender, class and age, relational boundaries reproduce distinct cultural relations. For example, the gendered borders of masculinity have been depicted as 'impenetrable, representing absolute security, defence and control', in contrast to feminine borders perceived to be 'porous and flexible' (p. 72, Skeggs and Moran 2004).

The term 'gender borders' was originally inspired by Barrie Thorne's work (1993) illuminating the 'invisible social lines' which reproduce gender socialization and differentiate boys from girls and vice versa in publicly shared spaces such as the school environment. Furthermore, research on paternal involvement in caregiving (Doucet 2017) examined 'gender borders' in relation to the involved father's emotional responsibility, as men have been shown to care in ways that are perceived to be masculine (encouraging autonomy and risk-taking, participating in play and sports). Where there are borders, there can also be border crossings, as Andrea Doucet's work discussed instances where boundaries relax and where there is space created in everyday interactions for gendered practices to shift flexibly. From this pre-existing empirical content, I devised the concept of emotional bordering to bridge the father's role with the social construction of masculinity from an *emotional* perspective; one that was missing from previous theorizations of men and masculinities (Pini and Pease 2013). Emotional bordering is a term which emerged directly from the analysis of the data I shall present in this book and depicts a form of boundary work that men as fathers reproduce on an emotional level in order to create relational boundaries with the aim of either maintaining *emotional closeness* or *emotional distance* in their intimate relationships.

Within this process, the *boundaries of love* are constantly negotiated through intimate communication, particularly for social actors involved in long-term commitments. The reason behind this is that people in long-term relationships share an awareness that *loving* can help them create their intimate relationships, so they remain careful to emotional interactions (Gabb and Fink 2015). Not only that, but love seems to circumscribe the emotional borders between social actors' understanding of their reality and their ideals (Djikic and Oatley 2004). Implicitly, such findings also speak about intimate power as it is lived in tandem with love, at the intersections between ideals and practices (a point I expand in Chap. 3). Finally, and as a complement to the study of the boundaries of culture in the process of gender socialization, David Morgan (1985) has discussed how *affectual* boundaries can explain how family member's patterns of relating

1 Changing Fathers and Changing Emotional Selves 19

are infused with power. Primarily then, boundaries create power relationships by delimiting who is *inside* or *outside* of the family, thus delimiting between family intimacy and public life (Jamieson 2005).

Following from this, what I propose is that the analytical usefulness of the Thorne's concept of 'gender borders' can be stretched to include emotions, and thereby, it can become emotional bordering. It is an emotional 'bordering' rather than simply a 'border' or a 'boundary' since it has a processual and dynamic character, which implies the gradual lowering or raising of borders around the construction of male emotional expressivity. In this sense, bordering is situationally contingent, and the gerund attached to the noun 'border' is intended to capture this form of 'doing' rather than simply a 'being'. I preferred to use a verb within the conceptualization, as it was better linked to fathers' own definitions of paternal love as a form of 'doing', which emerged from the data I collected in their interviews. In this process, masculinity and emotionality converge and are performed in the father's role (whether that of the stoic breadwinner or of the intimate father depends on the types of emotional bordering adopted). What I am essentially proposing is that relational boundaries are complemented by emotional borders. This affects, for example, how emotional responsibility is embedded in the processes of fathering and loving.

Emotional bordering helps the sociological imagination envision the space of tensions and contradictions which characterizes masculine emotionality, as it (un)comfortably shifts between the perceived 'old' and 'new' male moral identities. It refers to the simultaneous construction and maintenance of everyday close relationships, the creation of gendered selves and gendered ways of feeling in the intimate realm. Based on actions taken in relation to a loved person, fathers try to reconcile the provider's identity with that of the nurturer, in an uneasy role duality which produces tensions. In this sense, fathers' emotionality veers from stoicism to intimacy in a process of establishing relational boundaries (Macht 2018c). Much like previous studies on men and masculinities have argued, masculinity is not an insular and unidimensional identity, a mere role to fit into. It is a continuously practised gendered identity, intrinsically significant to their role as 'good' fathers and dependent on a multitude of social relationships in which power and love are central.

Therefore, in the present work, the term 'intimate' describes those fathers who are leaning more towards the emotionally involved end of the type of bordering, as they incorporate more intimacy in how they create their masculine emotional identity, while stoic fathers, who are also involved, tend to employ slightly more emotional management[10] as they border emotionally between roles.

Furthermore, emotional bordering denotes the combined emotional reflexivity and emotion work necessary to impose or rethink relational boundaries, as these bring into being forms of privacy, of privileged knowledge and feelings of exclusivity (Jamieson 2005). The practice of bordering or of raising boundaries is an emotional process through which fathers experience and sustain love in their intimate relationships; a process filtered through the lens of a masculine and personalized emotionality, as my research reveals. According to them, their emotionality is built in time through interacting with people in their environment, and it leads to the construction of a fathering identity which is emotionally contained and built on 'masculine' prerogatives (ex. involving control, warmth, humour and a give-and-take). As Ian Burkitt's briefly reflects:

> Throughout our lives we may develop habitual ways of acting and responding emotionally in given situations, but these habits are themselves the sedimentation of past patterns of relationships and actions, and they must be open to change and adaptation to the situations we encounter (…) as we enter new situations our emotional habits have to be fluid and open enough for us to be able to interpret our circumstances and to reorientate and adjust ourselves according to our changing feelings and thoughts about such circumstances. (p. 8)

---

[10] Emotional management refers to the rational control of emotions to fit required feeling rules and social norms of conduct (Theodosius 2006). But this is not enough to describe how men combine a construction of their masculine self with more nurturing social expectations. A discussion of emotional bordering, therefore, involves considerations of emotional management, of emotion work—as the work done in relationships to maintain them (Hochschild 1979)—and of emotional reflexivity (defined as a reliance upon emotions to decide how to act in the social world—Holmes 2010). The term encapsulates the dynamic interactions between these three concepts as they are applied to the cultural reproduction of fathers' intimate lives.

Emotional bordering attempts to challenge the emotional unidimensionality of previous models of masculinity. Different to psychological and neuro-physical perspectives, men as fathers do not have emotions hermetically sealed in their bodies and experience them solely as private states, but rather emotions are externalized and internalized in their acts of relating to their children, their partners and their own parents as they maintain closeness; paternal love from this sociological understanding is, therefore, a deeply social emotion, experienced in relation to others (Jackson 1993). In the process of bordering, fathers practice *emotional complexes*, where they create intimate relationships and maintain these with their words (language), actions (practices) and bodies (embodiment), and by relying on memory, imagination and planning. The process of emotional bordering reveals the dynamic, active construction of emotional borders and relational boundaries between themselves and others. Practising bordering can create loose or rigid borders around what it means to be emotional and determine in what contexts one can be emotional; it is not merely a case of deeming whether men are emotional or not.

It is difficult to construct a study looking at men's positive intimate experiences when men continue to be the most perpetrators of violence in the world (Harne 2011, 2013; Hearn and Šmidova 2015). However, one of the reasons for exploring fathers' emotionality, particularly in what is assumed to be a responsible and emotional role, might help to understand how they relate to others and form intimate relationships, experiences which position them as enmeshed within deeply relational contexts rather than isolated from them. Such a piece of research then follows in the footsteps of other works, registering incremental changes in men's intimate practices (Chand 2016; Young 2007; Galasinski 2004; Ranson 2010, 2015). Knowing this, it should be mentioned that fatherhood can also have a problematic side related to abuse, incest and neglect, which has been well documented in the sociological literature and beyond (Inglis 1987; Nelson and McKie 2005; Robertson 2010; Harne 2011). My research, however, takes a different and positive perspective, in that it explores fathers' everyday understandings and practices; it does not expand on traumatic issues because these did enter the scope of the research question. However, a discussion of male power and how it is practised in close relationships is detailed in the second chapter, and feminist analyses remain quintessential in terms of shedding light on the gendered abuse of power in personal lives in this particular area of knowledge.

Researching Love and Fatherhood

The methodological framework used to design the research was a socio-constructionist one, emphasizing the importance of language in producing the social reality of individuals. It is thereby focused on the creation of social actors' emotional experiences through how they communicate and relate to each other (Burkitt 2014). This study relies on data collected through the means of semi-structured qualitative interviews, which lasted, on average, between one hour and an hour and a half. Interviews were supplemented by six spontaneously occurring observations of interactions between fathers and children (three at home and three in the workplace, as fathers brought their children along to our meetings). The process of collecting data and analysing it was designed according to a grounded analysis framework (Charmaz 2013). The grounded analysis was useful because descriptions of the experience of love were anchored directly in the participants' accounts (Macht 2018a). Moreover, fathers supplied me with direct N-Vivo codes (i.e. codes which are directly supplied by the participants) which shaped the analytical framework. The interview guide, constructed together with a couple of fathers during the pilot phase of the research, was focused on the relationships with their children, with their partners and with their own parents and solicited everyday examples of everyday activities, what they thought love was, what interfered with love and what happens when they are separated from their children. Fathers were prompted to give detailed examples and explore their memories as well.

The interviews were digitally recorded, transcribed and the material was anonymized. Case studies for each participant were compiled by incorporating field notes with the most relevant data extracts from the interviews. Because the data collected from Romanian participants was in the Romanian language, to save time, only the relevant themes and quotes were translated into English, although this produced an issue by creating a linguistic hierarchy (Macht 2018b). The analysis was done firstly by hand, using pen and paper, and secondly by uploading the transcripts into the programme N-Vivo, to query the data, conduct word searches and map out associations between themes; my positionality and emotional reflexivity (as I collected data and undertook fieldwork) were embedded parts of the process of constructing meaning together with the participants (Macht 2018a, 2019b).

The findings presented in this book were part of a UK Economic and Social Research Council-funded doctoral research. Recruitment aimed for an equivalent number of participants from each of the two cultures; however, there are slightly more numbers in the Scottish sample due to a pilot phase which comprised seven interviews. The initial sampling strategy was snowball sampling, where participants were selected randomly through personal contacts. The choice to include men of different residencies, ages and occupations was made because I was interested in the accounts of a diversity of involved fathers, not just a specific group. This is because I was apprehensive that men of the same background might describe love in a unidimensional way.

The final sample comprised 47 participants, out of which 40 were married/co-partnered fathers and the rest were single, separated or divorced. Most participants resided in Bucharest and Edinburgh. The exceptions were, one Romanian divorced father commuted for work between Bucharest and Edinburgh and one Scottish separated father lived in Edinburgh and travelled to London for work.[11] Also, 46 of the fathers were biological and only one Romanian resident father was adoptive. The age range of the fathers was between 30 and 57 years in Scotland and between 28 and 50 years in Romania (most fathers were in their 30s). The age range and gender of children were similar: children's age range across the sample was between 3 weeks and 17 years. Out of a total of 77 children, there were 38 girls and 39 boys. There were 41 fathers who had one or two children while only 6 fathers had three or more children.

---

[11] These two fathers due to their special circumstances in terms of being divorced/separated and having to father and love across distances are the subject of a separate and comparative case study on the topic of 'travelling feelings' and changes in fathering—see Macht, A. (2019a, forthcoming).

In terms of their cultural identity, it has been written previously that 'being Scottish' is one side of a dual identity: that of having a local Scottish identity, ensconced within a wider British state-identity (McIvor and Johnston 2004). For Romanians, the two dimensions coincide as being Romanian is both a national/state identity and a personal identity, although these categories were presented as merged in fathers' narratives. Fathers' level of 'involvement' was determined by asking them to take part directly in the study rather than asking their partners, to reduce the 'maternal gatekeeping' bias (Gaunt 2008). Fathers' involvement was also checked according to the usual recruitment categories found in previous literature (Lamb 2010): numbers of hours worked, occupation, and residency status (see Table 1.1).

Outline of the Book

Chapter 1 is focused on fathers' love in relation to their children. It addressed fathers' understandings of love in relation to their own selves, their bodies and how they use emotional reflexivity in maintaining close relationships with their children. The first chapter also contextualizes the concept of emotional bordering, which is then utilized throughout the following chapters. Chapter 2 is focused on fathers' love as it emerges in relation to their own mothers and fathers. This section establishes a processual and relational account of power and love as intergenerationally shaped emotions. It posits that fathers' emotional bordering and identity as fathers is constructed in relation to that of their family members and their 'memories of love'. Chapter 3 explores fathers' love for their children in comparison to their romantic love for their partners; this section is focused on how negative feelings and power games feed into fathers' love without destroying it as Theodore Kemper's theory on love discussed. Rather, I argue that fathers are relationally determined to border emotionally as they enact interdependent power and, as such, maintain positive close relationships with their children and their partners. Lastly, the discussion presents a summary of the main findings by reflecting on the intersections of culture, emotions and masculinity and provides some new directions for future research.

Table 1.1 Table of participant demographics

Nr.	Name (anon.)	Age	Profession	Work hs./ week	Relationship status	Gender and age (y) of child/children
1	Ben	57	Support worker	35	Married	a girl (17y), a girl (16y), a girl (5), a girl (1y), a boy (6mth)
2	Rod	37	Investment professional	60	Married	a boy (5y), a girl (3y), a boy (3 weeks)
3	Malcolm	42	Investment professional	35	Married	a boy (11y), a girl (9y)
4	Logan	34	Solicitor	35	Partnered	a girl (1y, 5mth)
5	Patrick	42	Computer specialist	35	Married	a girl (8y), a girl (5y)
6	Nicholas	38	Engineer	45	Married	a girl (6mth)
7	Martin	37	Computer specialist	28	Married	a boy (1y, 2mth)
8	Adam	38	Lecturer	40	Partnered	a boy (2y)
9	Mark	36	Team leader	45	Partnered	a boy (3y)
10	Charlie	41	Doctor	60	Married	a girl (7y), a girl (5y)
11	David	38	Researcher	38	Married	a boy (4y), a boy (expecting)
12	Ewan	36	Accountant	45	Partnered	a girl (3y), a boy (expected)
13	Fergus	38	Manager	48	Married	a girl (3y, 6mth), a boy (6mth)
14	Gavin	53	Full-time dad[a]	Full-time	Married	a girl (9y), twins (4y) boy and girl
15	Gordon	36	Lecturer	35	Married	a boy (3y, 6mth), a boy (6mth)
16	Hamish	52	Engineer/unemployed	–	Partnered	a girl (2y)
17	Hugh	36	Manager	35	Married	a boy (3y), a boy (5y)
18	Ian	36	Investment professional	50	Married	a girl (7y), a boy (4y)
19	John	36	Accountant	40	Married	a boy (6y), a girl (7y), a girl (1y)
20	James	39	Manager	35	Married	a boy (3y), a girl (1y)
21	Keith	51	Consultant	35	Separated	a boy (9y), a girl (7y)
22	Lewis	39	Computer specialist	38	Married	a girl (8y)
23	Ray	51	Full-time carer	Full-time	Single	a boy (9y)
24	Stewart	53	Full-time carer	Full-time	Single	a girl (33y), a boy (3y)
25	Stephen	35	Part-time dad	30	Single	a girl (5y)
26	Tim	30	Supermarket assistant	25	Single	a boy (6y)

(continued)

Table 1.1 (continued)

Nr.	Name (anon.)	Age	Profession	Work hs./week	Relationship status	Gender and age (y) of child/children
27	Will	36	Sports instructor/on sick leave	–	Single	a girl (17y), a boy (6y)
28	Alexandru	42	Computer specialist	40	Married	a girl (7y)
29	Emil	37	Executive director	60	Married	a girl (3 months), a girl (4y)
30	Florin	35	Engineer	40	Married	a girl (2y, 4mth)
31	George	46	Computer specialist	48	Married	a girl (15), a boy (17)
32	Horia	32	Actor	20	Married	a boy (5y), a girl (4y), a boy (1y)
33	Ion	40	Executive director	60	Married	a boy (4y)
34	Iustin	32	Engineer	40	Married	a girl (2y)
35	Lucian	38	Engineer	40	Partnered	a boy (3y, 1mth)
36	Mihai	43	Computer specialist	60	Married	a boy (14y)
37	Liviu	36	Car mechanic	50	Married	Twins (6 y) boy & girl
38	Ciprian	35	Computer specialist	40	Married	Twins (6 y) boys
39	Sergiu	39	Supply worker	50	Divorced	a girl (11y), a boy (15y)
40	Vasile	30	Bus driver	60	Married	a boy (2y, 4mth)
41	Nelu	34	Animal trainer	50	Married	a boy (3y)
42	Bogdan	50	Factory worker	40	Married	a boy (8y, 6mth)
43	Ovidiu	34	Economist	50	Married	a boy (2y, 10mth)
44	Petre	28	Pilot	25	Married	a boy (2y)
45	Remus	35	Manager	40	Married	a girl (7y), a girl (5y)
46	Daniel	38	Engineer	40	Married	a boy (4y)
47	Vlad	41	Painter	Full-time	Partnered	a girl (11y)

[a]The participant specifically filled in the form in this way—this is not my classification; this explanation applies to all instances of 'full-time/part-time dad' present above

References

Aboim, S. (2010). *Plural Masculinities : The Remaking of the Self in Private Life*. Farnham: Ashgate.

Åsenhed, L., Kilstam, J., Alehagen, S., & Baggens, C. (2014). Becoming a Father Is an Emotional Roller Coaster: An Analysis of First-Time Fathers' Blogs. *Journal of Clinical Nursing, 23*(9–10), 1309–1317.

Baumann, Z. (2003). *Liquid Love: On the Frailty of Human Bonds*. Cambridge: Polity Press.

Bawin-Legros, B. (2004). Intimacy and the New Sentimental Order. *Current Sociology, 52*(2), 241–250.

Beciu, C. (2009). The Perception of Europeanization in Public Institutions: The Imagery of the 'Adaptation' to a New System. *Revista Română de Sociologie (The Romanian Journal of Sociologie), XX*(3–4), 193–214.

Beck, U., & Beck-Gernsheim, E. (2014). *Distant Love: Personal Life in the Global Age*. Cambridge: Polity Press.

Beigel, H. G. (1951). Romantic Love. *American Sociological Review, 16*(3), 326–334.

Bodogai, S. I., & Cutler, S. J. (2014). Aging in Romania: Research and Public Policy. *The Gerontologist, 54*(2), 147–152.

Bowlby, J. (1969). *Attachment and Loss – Vol. 1: Attachment*. New York: Basic Books.

Brannen, J., & Moss, P. (1998). The Polarisation and Intensification of Parental Employment in Britain: Consequences for Children, Families and the Community. *Community, Work & Family, 1*(3), 229–247.

Brannen, J., & Nilsen, A. (2006). From Fatherhood to Fathering: Transmission and Change among British Fathers in Four-Generation Families. *Sociology, 40*(2), 335–352.

Burkitt, I. (2014). *Emotions and Social Relations*. London: Sage.

Cancian, F. M. (1986). The Feminization of Love. *Signs: Journal of Women in Culture and Society, 11*(4), 692–709.

Chand, A. (2016). *Masculinities on Clydeside: Men in Reserved Occupations During the Second World War*. Edinburgh: Edinburgh University Press.

Charmaz, K. (2013). *Constructing Grounded Theory*. London: SAGE.

Children and Young People Scotland Act. (2014). Available from http://www.legislation.gov.uk/asp/2014/8/pdfs/asp_20140008_en.pdf. Accessed 12 Mar 2019.

Cohen, A. (1994). Culture, Identity and the Concept of Boundary. *Revista de Antropología Social, 3*, 49–62.

Coltrane, S. (1997). *Family Man: Fatherhood, Housework, and Gender Equity*. Oxford: Oxford University Press.

Cottingham, M. D. (2015). Learning to "Deal" and "De-Escalate": How Men in Nursing Manage Self and Patient Emotions. *Sociological Inquiry, 85*(1), 75–99.

Cottingham, M. D., Eriksson, R. J., & Diefendorff, J. M. (2015). Examining Men's Status Shield and Status Bonus: How Gender Frames the Emotional Labor and Job Satisfaction of Nurses. *Sex Roles, 72*, 377–389.

Craig, L. (2006). Parental Education, Time in Paid Work and Time with Children: An Australian Time-Diary Analysis. *The British Journal of Sociology, 57*, 553–575.

de Boise, S. (2015). *Men, Masculinities, Music and Emotions*. Basingstoke: Palgrave Macmillan.

Dempsey, D., & Hewitt, B. (2012). Fatherhood in the 21st Century. *Journal of Family Studies, 18*(2–3), 98–102.

Dermott, E. (2008). *Intimate Fatherhood: A Sociological Analysis*. London/New York: Routledge.

Deutsch, F. (1999). *Halving It All: How Equal Shared Parenting Works*. Cambridge: Harvard University Press.

Dewey, S. (2011). *Neon Wasteland: On Love, Motherhood, and Sex Work in a Rust Belt Town*. Berkeley: University of California Press.

Djikic, M., & Oatley, K. (2004). Love and Personal Relationships: Navigating on the Border Between the Ideal and the Real. *Journal for the Theory of Social Behaviour, 34*(2), 199–209.

Doucet, A. (2017). *Do Men Mother? Fathering, Care, and Domestic Responsibility* (2nd ed.). Toronto: University of Toronto Press.

Eggebeen, D. J., & Knoester, C. (2001). Does Fatherhood Matter for Men? *Journal of Marriage and Family, 63*(2), 381–393.

Ehrenreich, B., Hess, E., & Jacobs, G. (1987). *Re-Making Love: The Feminization of Sex*. New York: Doubleday.

Elias, N. (1939/2000). *The Civilizing Process: Sociogenetic and Psychogenetic Investigations* (Trans. E. Jephcott). Oxford: Blackwell Publishers.

Elliott, K. (2015). Caring Masculinities: Theorizing an Emerging Concept. *Men and Masculinities, 12*, 240–259.

Engdahl, E. (2018). *Depressive Love: A Social Pathology*. London: Routledge.

Featherstone, B. (2009). *Contemporary Fatherhood: Theory, Policy and Practice*. Bristol: Policy Press.

Fergusson, A., & Jónasdóttir, A. G. (2014). *Love: A Question for Feminism in the 21st Century*. New York: Routledge/Taylor and Francis.

Fox, B. (2009). *When Couples Become Parents: The Creation of Gender in the Transition to Parenthood*. Toronto: University of Toronto Press.

Freud, S. (1919). *Totem and Taboo: Resemblances Between the Psychic Lives of Savages and Neurotics*. London: Routledge & Sons.

Friedman, M. (2014). Unpacking MILF: Exploring Motherhood, Sexuality and Feminism. *Atlantis: Critical Studies in Gender, Culture & Social Justice, 36*(2), 49–60.

Gabb, J., & Fink, J. (2015). *Couple Relationships in the 21st Century*. Basingstoke: Palgrave Pivot.

Galasinski, D. (2004). *Men and the Language of Emotions*. Basingstoke: Palgrave Macmillan.

Gaunt, R. (2008). Maternal Gatekeeping. *Journal of Family Issues, 29*(3), 373–395.

Giddens, A. (1992). *The Transformation of Intimacy: Sexuality, Love, and Eroticism in Modern Societies*. Stanford: Stanford University Press.

Gilmore, D. D. (1990). *Manhood in the Making: Cultural Concepts of Masculinity*. New Haven: Yale University Press.

Goldberg, W. A., Tan, E. T., & Thorsen, K. L. (2009). Trends in Academic Attention to Fathers, 1930–2006. *Fathering, 7*(2), 159–179.

Goode, W. (1959). The Theoretical Importance of Love. *American Sociological Review, 24*(6), 38–47.

Goodey, J. (1997). Boys Don't Cry: Masculinities, Fear of Crime and Fearlessness. *British Journal of Criminology, 37*, 401–418.

Gordon, E. (2006). The Family. In L. Abrams, E. Gordon, D. Simonton, & E. Yeo (Eds.), *Gender in Scottish History Since 1700* (pp. 235–267). Edinburgh: Edinburgh University Press.

Gucht, D. V. (1994). The Religion of Love and the Culture of Marriage (La religion de l'amour et la culture conjugale). *Cahiers Internationaux de Sociologie (International Journals of Sociology), 97*, 329–353.

Hanlon, N. (2012). *Masculinities, Care and Equality: Identity and Nurture in Men's Lives*. Basingstoke: Palgrave Macmillan.

Hanmer, J. (1990). Men, Power, and the Exploitation of Women. *Women's Studies International Forum, 13*(5), 443–456.

Harne, L. (2011). *Violent Fathering and the Risks to Children: The Need for Change*. Bristol: Policy.

Hays, S. (1996). *The Cultural Contradictions of Motherhood*. Yale: University Press.

Hearn, J. (2013). The Sociological Significance of Domestic Violence: Tensions, Paradoxes and Implications. *Current Sociology, 61*(2), 152–170.

Hearn, J., & Šmidova, I. (2015). The Multiple Empires of Men. *Gender, Equal Opportunities Research, 16*(1), 74–82.

Henwood, K., & Procter, J. (2003). The 'Good Father': Reading Men's Accounts of Paternal Involvement During the Transition to First-Time Fatherhood. *British Journal of Social Psychology, 42*(3), 337–355.

Hochschild, A. R. (1979). Emotion Work, Feeling Rules, and Social Structure. *American Journal of Sociology, 85*(3), 551–575.

Holmes, M. (2010). The Emotionalization of Reflexivity. *Sociology, 44*(1), 139–154.

Holmes, M. (2014). Men's Emotions: Heteromasculinity, Emotional Reflexivity and Intimate Relationships. *Men and Masculinities, 18*(2), 176–192.

Hood, N., Peat, J., Peters, E., & Young, S. (Eds.). (2003). *Scotland in a Global Economy: The 2020 Vision.* Basingstoke: Palgrave Macmillan.

hooks, b. (2004). *The Will to Change: Men, Masculinity, and Love.* Washington: Washington Square Press.

Horvath, A., Thomassen, B., & Wydra, H. (Eds.). (2015). *Breaking Boundaries: Varieties of Liminality.* New York/Oxford: Berghahn.

Howson, A. (1993). No Gods and Precious Few Women: Gender and Cultural Identity in Scotland. *Scottish Affairs, 2*(1), 37–49.

Illouz, E. (2012). *Why Love Hurts: A Sociological Explanation.* Cambridge: Polity Press.

Inglis, R. (1987). *Sins of the Fathers: A Study of the Physical and Emotional Abuse of Children.* London: Owen.

Jackson, S. (1993). Even Sociologists Fall in Love: An Exploration in the Sociology of Emotions. *Sociology, 27*(2), 201–220.

Jaggar, A. M. (1989). Love and Knowledge: Emotion in Feminist Epistemology. *Inquiry, 32*(2), 151–176.

Jamieson, L. (1998). *Intimacy: Personal Relationships in Modern Societies.* Cambridge: Polity Press.

Jamieson, L. (2005). Boundaries of Intimacy. In J. Campling, S. Cunningham-Burley, & L. McKie (Eds.), *Families in Society Boundaries and Relationships* (pp. 189–207). Bristol: Policy.

Jamieson, L. (2011). Intimacy as a Concept: Explaining Social Change in the Context of Globalisation or Another Form of Ethnocentricism? *Sociological Research Online, 16*(4), 1–13.

Jansz, J. (2000). Masculine Identity and Restrictive Emotionality. In A. H. Fischer (Ed.), *Gender and Emotion: Social Psychological Perspectives* (pp. 166–186). Cambridge: Cambridge University Press.

Johansson, T., & Klinth, R. (2007). Caring Fathers: The Ideology of Gender Equality and Masculine Positions. *Men and Masculinities, 11*(1), 42–62.

Kuhn, A. (2002). *Family Secrets: Acts of Memory and Imagination* (2nd ed.). London: Verso.

Lamb, M. E. (Ed.). (2010). *The Role of the Father in Child Development* (5th ed.). London: Wiley.

LaRossa, R. (1997). *The Modernization of Fatherhood: A Social and Political History*. Chicago: University of Chicago Press.

Lupton, D. (1998). *The Emotional Self: A Sociocultural Exploration*. London: SAGE.

Lupton, D., & Barclay, L. (1997). *Constructing Fatherhood: Discourses and Experiences*. London: Sage.

Lynch, K. (2007). Love Labour as a Distinct and Non-Commodifiable Form of Care Labour. *The Sociological Review, 55*(3), 550–570.

Macht, A. (2018a). Grounding Reflexivity in a Qualitative Study on Love with Fathers. *SAGE Research Methods Cases* Part 2, Sage. Available at http://methods.sagepub.com/case/grounding-reflexivity-in-qualitative-study-on-love-with-involved-fathers

Macht, A. (2018b). From Romanian "Soul" to English "Heart": Dilemmas of Cultural and Gender Representation in Translating Qualitative Data. *Forum: Qualitative Social Research/Forum Qualitative Sozialforschung, 19*(2), ISSN: 1438-5627/eISSN: 1438-5627.

Macht, A. (2018c). Resisting the Commodification of Intimate Life? Paternal Love, Emotional Bordering and Narratives of Ambivalent Family Consumerism from Scottish and Romanian Fathers. *Families, Relationships and Societies, 8*, 21. https://doi.org/10.1332/204674318X15384702551202.

Macht, A. (2019a, Forthcoming). Travelling Feelings: Narratives of Sustaining Love in Two Case Studies with Fathers in Family Separations. In L. Murray et al. (Eds.), *Families in Motion: Ebbing and Flowing Through Space and Time* (pp. 19–37). Bingley: Emerald Publishing.

Macht, A. (2019b). Shifting Perspectives: Becoming a Feminist Researcher While Studying Fatherhood and Love. *Vitae Scholasticae: The Journal of Educational Biography, 35*(2), ISSN: 0735-1909/eISSN: 0735-1909.

Macht, A., & Popescu, R. (2018). Romania Country Note. In S. Blum, A. Koslowski, A. Macht, & P. Moss (Eds.), *International Review of Leave Policies and Research 2018*. Available at http://www.leavenetwork.org/lp_and_r_reports/

Marsiglio, W., & Roy, K. (2012). *Nurturing Dads: Social Initiatives for Contemporary Fatherhood*. New York: Russell Sage Foundation.

McCrone, D. (2001). *Understanding Scotland: The Sociology of a Nation* (2nd ed.). New York: Routledge.

McIvor, A., & Johnston, R. (2004). Dangerous Work, Hard Men and Broken Bodies: Masculinity in the Clydeside Heavy Industries. *Labour History Review, 69*(2), 135–152.

Meah, A., & Jackson, P. (2016). The Complex Landscape of Contemporary Fathering in the UK. *Social and Cultural Geography, 17*(4), 491–510.

Miller, T. (2010). *Making Sense of Fatherhood: Gender, Caring and Work.* Cambridge: Cambridge University Press.

Morgan, D. H. J. (1985). *The Family, Politics and Social Theory.* London: Routledge.

Morgan, D. H. J. (1992). *Discovering Men.* London: Routledge.

Morgan, D. H. J. (2011). *Rethinking Family Practices.* Basingstoke: Palgrave Macmillan.

National Institute of Statistics. (2018). *Social Trends for 2017.* Bucharest: INS – National Institute of Statistics Publishing Press.

National Records of Scotland. (2018). *Mid-2016 Population Estimates for Settlements and Localities in Scotland.* Available from https://www.nrscotland.gov.uk/files//statistics/settlements-localities/set-loc-16/set-loc-2016-publication-updated.pdf. Accessed 12 Mar 2019.

Nelson, S., & Mckie, L. (2005). *Child Sexual Abuse: Fracturing Family Life; Families, Violence and Social Change.* Maidenhead: Open University Press.

Parsons, T. (1943). The Kinship System of the Contemporary United States. *American Anthropologist, 45*, 22–38.

Paxson, H. (2007). A Fluid Mechanics of Erotas and Aghape: Family Planning and Maternal Consumption in Contemporary Greece. In M. B. Padilla, J. S. Hirsch, M. Munoz-Laboy, R. E. Sember, & R. G. Parker (Eds.), *Love and Globalization: Transformations of Intimacy in the Contemporary World* (pp. 120–139). Nashville: Vanderbilt University Press.

Pini, B., & Pease, B. (Eds.). (2013). *Men Masculinities and Methodologies.* Basingstoke: Palgrave Macmillan.

Popescu, R. (2009). *Introducere in Sociologia Familiei: Familia Romaneasca in Societate Contemporana (Introduction to the Sociology of Family Life: The Romanian Family in Contemporary Society).* Bucharest: Polirom.

Popescu, R. (2014). Family Policies in Romania Within the European Framework. *Journal of Community Positive Practices, XIV*(3), 99–113.

Raiu, S. L. (2011). The Process of Globalization in Romania. *Revista Română de Sociologie (The Romanian Journal of Sociology), XXII*(3–4), 373–380.

Ranson, G. (2010). *Against the Grain: Couples, Gender, and the Reframing of Parenting.* Toronto: University of Toronto Press.

Ranson, G. (2015). *Fathering, Masculinity and the Embodiment of Care.* Basingstoke: Palgrave Macmillan.

Riley, D. (1987). The Serious Burdens of Love? Some Questions on Child-Care. In A. Phillips (Ed.), *Feminism and Socialism* (pp. 176–199). Oxford: Basil Blackwell.

Robertson, R. P. (2010). Child Sexual Abuse, Masculinity and Fatherhood. *Journal of Family Studies, 18*(2–3), 130–142.

Rochlen, A. B., Suizzo, M., McKelley, R. A., & Scaringi, V. (2008). "I'm Just Providing for My Family:" a Qualitative Study of Stay-at-Home Fathers. *Psychology of Men and Masculinity, 9*(4), 193–206.

Roseneil, S. (2005). Living and Loving Beyond the Boundaries of the Heteronorm: Personal Relationships in the 21st Century. In L. Mackie, S. Cunningham-Burley, & J. McKendrick (Eds.), *Families in Society: Boundaries and Relationships* (pp. 241–258). Bristol: Policy Press.

Seebach, S. (2017). *Love and Society: Special Social Forms and the Master Emotion.* London: Routledge.

Segal, L. (2007). *Slow Motion: Changing Masculinities, Changing Men.* Basingstoke: Palgrave Macmillan.

Seidler, V. J. (2006). Gender, Power, Ethics and Love. In V. J. Seidler (Ed.), *Transforming Masculinities: Men, Cultures, Bodies, Power, Sex and Love* (pp. 128–142). London: Taylor and Francis.

Seidman, S. (1991). *Romantic Longings: Love in America, 1830–1980.* Charlottesville/New York: University of Virginia/Routledge.

Selin, H. (2013). *Parenting Across Cultures: Childrearing, Motherhood and Fatherhood in Non-Western Cultures.* New York/London: Springer.

Shapiro, S. G., & Shapiro, R. (2004). *The Curtain Rises: Oral Histories of the Fall of Communism in Eastern Europe.* London: McFarland & Company.

Shirani, F. (2013). The Spectre of the Wheezy Dad: Masculinity, Fatherhood and Ageing. *Sociology, 47*(6), 1104–1119.

Shirani, F., & Henwood, K. (2011). Continuity and Change in a Qualitative Longitudinal Study of Fatherhood: Relevance Without Responsibility. *International Journal of Social Research Methodology, 14*(1), 17–29.

Simmel, G. (1984). *On Women, Sexuality and Love.* New Haven: Yale University Press.

Skeggs, B., & Moran, L. J. (2004). *Sexuality and the Politics of Violence and Safety.* London: Routledge.

Smart, C. (2007). *Personal Life: New Directions in Sociological Thinking.* Cambridge: Polity.

Smith-Koslowski, A. (2011). Working Fathers in Europe: Earning and Caring. *European Sociological Review, 27*(2), 230–245.

Streets-Salter, H. (2004). *Martial Races: The Military, Race, and Masculinity in British Imperial Culture, 1857–1914*. Manchester: Manchester University Press.

Theodosius, C. (2006). Recovering Emotion from Emotion Management. *Sociology, 40*(5), 893–911.

Thorne, B. (1993). *Gender Play: Girls and Boys in School*. New Brunswick: Rutgers University Press.

Turcescu, L., & Stan, L. (2005). Religion, Politics and Sexuality in Romania. *Europe-Asia Studies, 57*(2), 291–310.

Turner, B., & Stets, J. (2005). *The Sociology of Emotions*. Cambridge: Cambridge University Press.

Voicu, M. (2008). Religiosity and Religious Revival During the Transition Period in Romania. In B. Voicu & M. Voicu (Eds.), *The Values of Romanians 1993–2006: A Sociological Perspective* (pp. 144–170). Iasi: The European Institute.

Waller, M. R. (2002). *My Baby's Father: Unmarried Parents and Paternal Responsibility*. Ithaca: Cornell University Press.

Waller, M., & Swisher, R. (2006). Fathers' Risk Factors in Fragile Families: Implications for "Healthy" Relationships and Father Involvement. *Social Problems, 53*(3), 392–420.

Walzer, S. (2010). *Thinking about the Baby: Gender and Transitions into Parenthood*. Philadelphia: Temple University Press.

Williams, S. (2008). What Is Fatherhood?: Searching for the Reflexive Father. *Sociology, 42*(3), 487–502.

Williams, S. (2011). Chaotic Identities, Love and Fathering. *Folklore: Electronic Journal of Folklore, 48*, 31–54.

Wilkinson, E. (2013). Learning to Love Again: 'Broken Families', Citizenship and the State Promotion of Coupledom. *Geoforum, 49*, 206–214.

Young, H. (2007). Hard Man, New Man: Re/Composing Masculinities in Glasgow, c. 1950–2000. *Oral History, 35*(1), 71–81.

2

Doing Love: Fathers' Emotions in Relation to Their Children

Adopting the Intimate Father's Role: Emotional Vocabularies

In order to overcome the Cartesian divide between reason and emotion upon which the construction of traditional masculine identity is presumably built, it is important to explore how emotions are put into language by men (Lupton and Barclay 1997; Seidler 2006; de Boise 2015). Research has shown that for involved fathers, the process of learning to meet a child's needs is a deeply emotional one and that there are tensions in how men choose to express love (Rochlen et al. 2008), since this continues to be understood as a 'feminized' emotion (Cancian 1986). The evidence below aims to complement this knowledge by referring to Scottish and Romanian fathers' *emotional vocabularies*, which are a set of verbal labels attributed to emotions (Turner and Stets 2005). This view holds that an emotion can carry various meanings. Therefore, analysing how language is used provides clues as to how social actors experience and interpret their emotions. Social actors can rectify the meanings attributed to their emotions and their emotional experiences through ongoing reflections. By reflecting on their emotions, social actors give us

© The Author(s) 2020
A. Macht, *Fatherhood and Love*, Palgrave Macmillan Studies in Family and Intimate Life, https://doi.org/10.1007/978-3-030-20358-0_2

35

36   A. Macht

clues as to how reason and emotions dynamically support each other, matching what the literature describes:

> My view of emotion is not of a static state or a thing in itself – such as a psychological phenomenon – which then moves us to act, but as movement itself within relations and interaction. In these interactions we are constantly being affected by others, being moved by them to other actions, in the process constantly feeling and thinking – being moved from one feeling or emotion to another. (Burkitt 2014, p. 9)

Speaking about love thus reveals the extent to which involved fathers are *emotionally reflexive*[1] (Holmes 2010) and the extent to which they are *moved* to put love into words.

Describing Paternal Love

A previous study argued that men do not seem to have for emotions a 'masculine vocabulary' and, therefore, tend to dissociate themselves from thinking that they are 'talking subjectivities' (Lupton 1998). However, in this research, the main pattern that emerged across all 47 interviews with involved fathers was that they understood love as a *'doing'*, a form of activity. Because fathers across cultures thought of paternal love as a 'verb', it had to be demonstrated through daily acts for them to feel that their love for their children actually existed.

Most Scottish and Romanian participants described love for their children in a rich language, peppered with superlative adjectives to indicate various instances of emotional intensity. In this sense, for involved fathers, love was 'a feeling of bursting, popping', 'intense', 'powerful', 'strange to describe' and 'hard to control' or 'an over-arching and over-riding', 'overwhelming', 'disorienting', 'all-consuming' and 'mysterious' emotion. Despite initial struggles at defining love across both cultures, a sense of bewilderment, awe and joy emanated from fathers' verbal constructions of love. For John (Scottish, resident, 36), the love he had for his three

---

[1] According to Mary Holmes, emotional reflexivity is '(…) an emotional, embodied, and cognitive process in which social actors have feelings about and try to understand and alter their lives in relation to their social and natural environment to others' (p. 140, 2010).

2 Doing Love: Fathers' Emotions in Relation to Their Children

children made him experience not only physical sensations but also a certain kind of power:

> I'm going to burst! [laughter]. I'm just going to pop! And it's a bizarre feeling. I remember when we had Emma first, just being overwhelmed and thinking 'Wow, I love this little baby' and all the importance of (…) she relies on me for everything and that kinda brings it another level of love I suppose. Thinking you're going to shape that person's life in many ways.

It was not only love which was described in absolute and romantic terms, but also the child who was often referred to as 'my life', 'everything to me', 'the best', and so on. Compared to other feelings, paternal love was *new* because it was connected to the physical appearance of the child in the couple's life and expanded men's range of emotions. In connection to the concept of emotional bordering, this could be otherwise interpreted as a temporary lowering of their stoic emotional bordering into enhanced intimacy, as relational boundaries could be crossed or even merged when emotions were expressed. What was new about this experience for fathers was its *unconditional* character, which distinguished it from other types of love. Ewan (Scottish, resident, 36),[2] the father of three-year-old Anni, recounts how having a baby changed him emotionally:

> It was a new sort of emotion. I think that was something that was really exciting (…) it was sometimes really scary because I was trying to understand what you're feeling which is different to anything you felt before. And also it was slightly odd to feel yourself falling in love with a child and matching that up with, you know, it's been produced from these two people and we're loving it. It was all simultaneously slightly scary [and] completely wonderful. Yeah (…) I can't remember consciously ever having experienced emotion in the same way (…) Having this kind of very strong emotion, very intense, developing in such a calm[3] situation it meant (…) it was almost highlighted even more.

---

[2] To help situate fathers' quotes in the analysis, I have recorded for each father the following descriptors: culture (Scottish or Romanian), age and residency (resident or non-resident); these identifiers appear within the text after each name, in round brackets.

[3] The 'calm situation' he refers to was represented by the two weeks of paternity leave, which he took after her birth.

At the time of the interview, Ewan and his partner were expecting another baby, and the context of preparing for the new birth made him vividly reminisce the moment his first-born came into the world. He described love as being enhanced by other feelings such as fright and wonder. Love was directed to their children, but it also can be influenced and nuanced by other people in their social environment. Therefore, and slightly different to Ian Burkitt, who distinguishes between feelings and emotion, I would ascertain that it is difficult to draw clear lines between the two; fathers described how 'enmeshments' are taking place, whereby an instinctive feeling becomes an emotion in time by relating to the child and getting to know him/her. Ian Burkitt himself hints at this processual unfolding when he writes:

> What I want to develop here is that there is a range of experiencing feeling and emotion, and that our control of these experiences will vary across a range, from being helplessly affected at one end to being very much in control and affecting the required response at the other end. (2014, p. 17)

As such, feelings and emotions are not distinct experiences; rather, they form an emotional continuum and are integrative parts of the process of relating between social actors. Within this process, the actions of imposing relational boundaries and dissolving them can be illustrated on an emotional level through emotional bordering. Furthermore, paternal love had a *spontaneous* character—one that made it different from anything else fathers have felt before in their 'emotional repertoire' (Sampson and Atkinson 2013) because it appeared to escape verbal rationalizations. To illustrate, I present George's (Romanian, resident, 46) explanation:

> It's something really difficult to describe, it's something that you feel, or not. I have never thought too much about it. I don't think I know how to describe it. I'm sorry. Because it's something that appears spontaneously, so you don't have time to think 'Well now I am supposed to do this thing because so and so'.

This quote reminds of Ian Burkitt's idea that emotions are unpredictable, and that they can be contradictory, rather than irrational (2014), and it means that masculine emotionality can include reflexive thinking

2 Doing Love: Fathers' Emotions in Relation to Their Children 39

and sometimes clashes with the limits of reason. Paternal love also had a *unique* character, in that the circumstances of becoming a father allowed one to feel close to the child in a way he couldn't be with other people. This had an impact on how the father would then emotionally conceive of the child and discursively reconstruct the relationship (Nielsen 2017). Since loving the child couldn't be compared to any other emotion, love had a specific power. For example, Vasile (Romanian, resident, 30) described his love for his son as:

> Something supreme, it's everything that matters to me since he was born. It's constantly there. Wherever I go, he's in my mind and my heart.

The phrase '*you can't know how it feels until you have children yourself*' appeared often in relation to this aspect, implying that having children enriches one's emotional life and can be pursued for this goal only, reminding of Anthony Giddens' (1992) 'pure relationship'.[4] It also implied that fathers were part of a select group, which was exposed to a new range of emotional experiences and were different from other childless men. However, paternal descriptions of awe and uniqueness are not new and have been considered in previous works (Jamieson 1998).

Love Grows in Time

Perhaps the most interesting finding is that many fathers (30 participants) described love as a process that *grows in time*, as a relational give-and-take within which different emotions are experienced, thereby only partially confirming Ian Burkitt's idea that:

> Emotional responses are unpredictable because emotions are ambivalent and are constantly shifting: we can feel both love and hate for the same person or thing; can be moved by affection and anger at the same time; or emotions like sympathy, anger and grief can quickly follow on from one another and alternate. (p. 150)

---

[4] The focus on individualism in connection to love was emphasized when Anthony Giddens published his book *The Transformation of Intimacy* (1992), which built on Niklas Luhmann's idea of love as validation for individualism; romantic love is understood as sustaining 'the project of the self' in post-modernity.

Rather than experiencing emotions as constantly shifting, from fathers' accounts, a sense of the durability of love for their children emerged. What was 'shifting', however, was how fathers view themselves and their role and worked at changing their self-image as men and as fathers. If initially, paternal love felt like a spontaneous emotion, it became meaningful and gathered 'strength' as the father got to know the child's personality and spent time together with him/her. For example, Florin (Romanian, resident, 35) described love in terms of a 'solid cable that should never break'.

In addition, David (Scottish, resident, 38), the father of a three-year-old boy, describes that bonding was 'a slower burn' for him as a father:

> Yes, you do love them. It's an instinct without question *but*[5] especially more for the fathers it's a bit of a slower burn. For the mother the baby has been inside them and it's a bond that I don't know that you could replicate it. With the fathers, it's slightly (...) a longer burn because you begin to see them as a person after a while (...) I just remembered this point when Michel was about ten months and I was changing his nappy and he was lying on the thing for nappy change. I was sort of talking to him you know in baby-speak and I said 'Hiya!' and he said 'Hi!' back and I was like 'WOW'. And honestly just in my mind something changed. It's like (...) I'm actually going to be able to exchange communication, you know properly. Now, Michael as soon as he gets up, he talks all day to you. He doesn't stop talking. It's a constant exchange of information and ideas. But until that point it can be a bit of a one way street, you know?

Previous studies on the range of emotions men experience at childbirth included descriptions of falling in love 'at first sight' with the baby (Hall 1995). But David, despite acknowledging earlier in the interview that he experienced an initial powerful feeling (the activation of an instinct), also described how love for him took time to develop. This points towards previous research literature on involved fatherhood which situates the father's role as increasingly important as the child grows older (Lamb 2010), and supports the view that love is something that we *do* as we get to know someone.

---

[5] Emphasis his own.

Practices of Love

Even if fathers employed emotional vocabularies, what seemed to matter most to most of the involved fathers I interviewed was expressing love in practical and embodied ways: through playing, through hands-on care, holding, kissing or cuddling their children. In the father-child dyad, practices of love[6] are defined as non-sexual interactions enacted to elicit positivity and closeness (i.e. warmth, tenderness, fun) and form part of a larger set of family practices inclusive of other forms of intimacy (e.g. sexual intimacy between partners) (Gabb and Fink 2015). These also involve routine activities, fun games and disciplining practices. There was a concern with the 'visibility' of their love rather than their capacity to verbalize feelings to their loved ones. I highlight in this part how fathers of both cultures mentioned how they 'performed' love since these are significant in explaining how paternal love is maintained in an intimate relationship, particularly in how fathers employ emotional reflexivity. For example, Ciprian (Romanian, resident, 35) who is the father of twin boys, explains how, for him, actions matter more than words in how he expresses his love:

> I don't think that there are certain words which need to exist. I mean aside from the fact that: you communicate with them, you try to get along with them [deep intake of breath] you relate to them, you listen. Words without weight have no value. It's useless to say 'I love you' if that was everything (…) Yes, you do interact with them differently than how you speak to them. It's more of a mixture of gestures, actions, touches. I think that is the only way in which you can express it. But simply just by talking or just by touching, that is a bit hard to do.

Ciprian describes how in practising love, he experiences a combination of words and actions, but he also reflects on how he attributes

---

[6] Practices of intimacy are assumed to be innovative, relationship-specific or habituated (Jamieson 2011); they are part of family practices but can also be commodified and non-familial (see Padilla et al. 2007). The practices presented in this chapter stemmed from fathers' own descriptions during the interviews. Personally, my access to observing family practices was restricted to only six spontaneous observations.

more emotional weight to actions over words; he is balancing an adherence to a form of masculinity legitimated through action with a belief in the importance of intimate communication with his children in order to teach them how to be 'good'. Not only that, but he also recounts how he borders in public places to avoid appearing too physically loving:

> At home it's a different story. At home I hug my little ones (…) but even at home this censorship keeps appearing, when you can't just (…) OK, something usually happens, and you can't go to extremes. You just can't. It's abnormal and then you must control yourself.

Continuing from this, Emil (Romanian, resident, 37) describes how after being confined to the home for one week because all family members got sick, they had some emotionally fraught interactions. But going outside and playing together helped strengthen the emotional bonds between his family members, especially the one with his older daughter:

> After a week of being sick, we came out with her in the sun, and we went many times to the park. We would let her play by herself most of the time, but this time we all played together. We played 'tag', I thought her how to play 'tag' by climbing and then with animal names. She was fascinated, she was glowing with happiness while both I and her mum were running around the park. It was just the four of us in the park – my youngest was in her mobile crib – and we were running around and chasing each other. It was so interactive. I wasn't sitting around with my phone plugged to my ear, we were there with her and there was a marked difference in how she saw everything. I mean it relaxed her. She really enjoyed it, she was present.

Emil not only describes his daughter's joy at playing together with her family members, but also describes how by 'being there' emotionally and not only physically, he managed to let go and enjoy the time spent with his daughter. The stoic emotional bordering he usually employed was evidenced not only by his conscious unplugging from work-related activities but also by remarking with surprise that his daughter's joy was dependent in that moment on his enjoyment of their shared togetherness as well.

2 Doing Love: Fathers' Emotions in Relation to Their Children   43

Furthermore, Ion (Romanian, resident, 40) who works, on average, 60 hours per week, describes how he manages to fit into his busy schedule some daily moments of father-son intimacy through the intimate ritual of secret sharing:

> For example, I used to read to him. Now he won't let me do that anymore, he prefers his mother to read to him before bedtime. So we have a ritual, that before bedtime we tell each other a secret. I tell him one and he tells me one. So yeah this is a kind of [makes a puffing noise with his mouth to signal awe]. Now, he did get into the habit of falling asleep only with his mother, but we are trying to get him to give this up, as we want to raise him to be independent. He still seems to be afraid of the dark. So in the morning, when he wakes up, he comes to me with heavy eyelids and I ask him 'What did you dream about? How did you sleep?'

Noticing that his absence from home due to work was increasingly excluding him emotionally from maintaining closeness to his son and partner, Ion addressed this by getting emotionally involved in his son's life through self-created rituals. At the same time, he is also emotionally bordering the situation, as he rationalizes the intimacy with his son by arguing that it is an attempt to separate the son from the mother in order to teach him autonomy. This type of practice seems to be a counterpoint to the process of enculturating boys into the 'guy code' of stoic masculinity (Kimmel 2008) and done according to Romanian cultural norms of collective warmth and familialism. What these accounts remind is that boundaries in relationships are created and dissolved by paying attention to emotions; it is in this manner that emotional reflexivity is important to the process of constructing emotional borders.

Furthermore, another practice of love that shows how some fathers were bordering towards the intimate father's role was co-sleeping. Bogdan (Romanian, resident, 50) describes here how he is conveying to his son that he is loved and protected through the embodiment of another practice of love meant to transmit warmth and closeness to the child, co-sleeping:

> A lot of people put their children to sleep in separate beds, but then he won't feel a mother's love or a father's love: to be caressed, to have him

caress you, to feel you close. And this counts a lot for him, being a child. If he turns around in bed with his mom and dad being next to him, he can touch us and he knows that we are there. So he is calm emotionally and psychologically.

It has been argued that for mothers 'skinship'[7] (Lupton 2013) can be experienced through the practice of co-sleeping, which leads to the development of a strong sense of emotional and embodied intimacy. Bogdan's example above demonstrates that co-sleeping, as it exists in the context of shared family practices, can also be meaningful to a father in building closeness with the child. The replacement of separate sleeping with co-sleeping alludes to a social change in parenting practices, which Bogdan is participating in, namely, that of increasing father-child intimacy (Ranson 2015). Observed from a contextual viewpoint, Bogdan did allude to the fact that his son has just turned eight and is therefore old enough to sleep by himself, but also that his family is struggling financially. Therefore, from a more pragmatic perspective, the act of engaging in co-sleeping might hint to a lack of additional sleeping spaces or of good heating in the house, constricting members of the family to sleep together in order to keep warm and reduce energy costs.

With daughters, the situation was slightly different. Florin (Romanian, resident, 35) describes how his stoic resistance and, consequently, his emotional bordering is usually undermined by his two-year-old daughter's persistent attempts at interacting with him to establish closeness:

First of all every time she contacts me with a certain problem I answer her, and I am paying attention to what she wants (...) I also have to get her feedback in what we do, so that everything is ok with her too, because things might not be what she believes them to be. I have tried to be more detached but I've noticed it's not working. She always comes and does something around me, and then I see her sighing, and afterwards she comes

---

[7] According to Lupton, skinship is '(...) the relational state created by close physical proximity, touch and intimacy. This concept is useful as a way of describing the intercorporeal interactions and development of intimate relationships between infants and their careers' (p. 40).

towards me. I realize it then and I'm not insisting with my detachment and I immediately join in and help her with whatever it is she's doing. I mean I won't let her be alone. If she goes and tries some activities and I see that she's struggling, I call for her and tell her 'Let's do this thing' and she quickly comes toward me 'pac-pac-pac' [laughter].

Florin describes how his apparent indifferent demeanour and attempts at 'ignoring' his daughter, are dissolved by his daughter's presence and proximity to him. In this process of relating, 'helping her out' is a practice of love, a daily emotional performance in which the rigidity of Florin's emotional bordering is shaped by his daughter's requests for closeness; it is mutual, however, since Florin also 'checks-in' emotionally with her, on the activities they plan to do. Asking for help and receiving it would be a situation involving exchanges of power, but in this case, it also brings to light that such an interaction can develop closeness. Florin positions his daughter as also taking initiative in their interactions, and himself as being responsive to her needs. Their interactions are, to a certain extent, indicative of democratic organizations of intimate relationship in which child's agency is encouraged and which have been echoed in other studies on involved father-child intimacy (Ranson 2015).

Practices of Care

To emphasize the connection between the practices of love and the practices of care, I draw from Gavin's narrative (Scottish, resident, 53) the father of three children who had lost his job a mere three months before our interview. He used to run a prestigious firm but due to the recession, he found himself 'involuntarily involved' in the daily care of his children, as his wife had to take on extra work to continue to support the family. At the time of the interview, the family was also without help from paid childminders. Despite having to deal with what was, according to him, 'an emotionally painful job dismissal' and experiencing unease at being given most of the responsibility for childcare, Gavin quickly adapted to the daily task of caring for his children. He described childcare as a chaotic process of 'being pulled in all directions':

> Suddenly everyone's awake at six o'clock (…) and they're full of wanting this and that. It's like you know 'One at a time!' when they're all asking for stuff. It's quite hard. So last night (…) [my partner] had to get into work at about five.[8] So you know: you're getting the tea on, the washing machine needs emptying, the dishwasher needs emptying, you need to hang up the coats and shoes 'cause they've just dropped it on the floor and [are] running again and one of them wants you to play with them. You know that you need to get them fed and bathed and Lucy needs to do her homework, but she's on the iPad and you're saying 'Lucy do your homework!'. And you know you want to make the packed lunches, you know you've all these chores and fitting them in. Suddenly Eva still needs to go to the toilet and she still needs help to wipe her bottom or wash her hands and you just need to stay on the case. It's like, you just get pulled in all directions.

This falls in line with Gillian Ranson's research (2015) wherein she also uncovered how practices of care that were generated through engagement became in time practices of love. However, if relating is included into this discussion, then we can begin to reflect on how practices of love form part of the process of relating but they might not lead to practices of care; in this manner, in spite of *acting* and *being loving*, fathers might not need to sustain practices of care.

One point to consider here is that many times, in fathers' accounts, involvement appears as *things accomplished together with* their children and not as *things done for* their children, which is assumed to be the mother's role. Through this discursive device, fathers maintain the image of the 'good' and 'involved'/'intimate' father without necessarily having to assume full caregiving and domestic responsibilities, unless other circumstances might pressure them to, such as in Gavin's example below. Nonetheless, after a period of initial adaptation, of fathering through 'trial and error', Gavin got pragmatically *and* emotionally involved in all aspects of caregiving:

---

[8] His wife worked in a hospital.

at the end of the day you have to deal with your own children and the problems that confront you on a day to day basis you can't go 'oh hang on a minute, you're not eating this cereal, I'll just check the manual!' You can't [laughter] it isn't like that you have to, you don't have that time and luxury. You need to suck it in and see.

In relation to this form of fathering 'through trial and error', a contradiction which appeared regarding fathers' overall understanding of love as something they *do*, was expressed by a few Scottish fathers in the phrase 'spending quality time'. Among the dicta of capitalist consumption, one that has become so all-pervasive that it reached the status of cliché, is the idea that 'time is money'. In such a context, time can be considered a commodified resource. The use of time also has an emotional component to it, which sees men doubly emotionally invested in the work and their family, and, in this sense, it can become an intangible emotional resource, offered as a 'gift'. Some fathers who struggle financially seem to see the offer of their time and love to their children as their most important contribution (Edin and Nelson 2013). In this research, fathers described quality time as shared through 'inaction' rather than action or doing things together. For Charlie (Scottish, resident, 41), sometimes just sitting about doing nothing and being close to each other was enough to create a sense of meaningful togetherness, as he began making changes at work and cutting back on his demanding work schedule as a doctor. He described that he enjoyed being active with his two daughters and liked to take them climbing and scuba-diving. However, based on his memories of growing up with a stay-at-home mother, he had started recently to focus more on allowing his children just to be in their domestic space, and father 'without an agenda' as he put it:

I had a lot of freedom to explore or to, to do stuff (…) so hopefully, I can reflect that because I think perhaps initially I was in that modern parenting way of trying to do much with the kids all the time (…) so I just let them be and let them get on with it (…) time to dream and mess about, get things wrong, make a mess, you come in their room and go 'Wow [laughs] mmm, OK?!', so (…) yeah I think time and just being available without an agenda, I think is important.

It could be that Charlie might be encouraging passivity in his daughters as an ideal in line with 'traditional femininity' (Cancian 1986), but this is counteracted by the mess he mentions he finds in their room, indicating that the home is a hub of playful activity. In addition, this might not be a gender-socialization concern, as accounts of just 'being together' as a definition of love were also expressed in relation to sons as well and across residential variations, as Tim (Scottish, non-resident, 30) shares:

> I just want to be with him. I just want to see him, that's what it is (…) it's just like a warmth or something I don't know what it is. Just being with him that's it. As well as having a good time. And he's hilarious he makes me laugh so much.

The quotes above points to what Julie Brownlie (2014) has identified in her research, as the practice of emotional reflexivity through 'stillness', and can be loosely applied here to mark practices of love which also can be 'still', where intimate individuals establish closeness simply through being next to each other; this would perhaps add another layer of meaning to the state of 'being there' reported in a variety of studies on fathers' involvement (Lamb 2010). In this light, just 'being there' at home might be a way to increase intimacy, on the foreground of precarious economic situations, and complements how fathers are mostly 'doing' love.

Resisting 'Love'

Some fathers struggled with love and their role as fathers.[9] Three Romanian fathers were not as comfortable with love or with expressing it through 'love-like' actions. They were demonstrating love to their children by 'doing the right thing', 'keeping in regular contact', 'enjoying their company' and 'trying to see each other'. They espoused a 'sceptic view of love' and found it hard to live up to the social expectations

---

[9] Love and its social enmeshment might not necessarily be a pleasant and enjoyable emotional experience, as Donna Haraway (2003) wrote about 'significant otherness': 'we signify in the flesh a nasty developmental infection called love' (p. 3).

attached to their role as a father. What they had in common was a background of intense emotional experiences, commonly expressed in physical violence in the family and intergenerationally transmitted through their fathers and grandfathers (described in all three interviews as 'emotionally distant' men). This made them cautious with adopting the role of the 'father'. In this way, they attached to it connotations modelled from their own fathers, who were perceived as authoritarian figures. To incorporate into their self-identity the image of the intimate father, they distanced themselves from the traditional role of 'the father' and preferred to position themselves on equalitarian roles, as first and foremost the 'friends' of their children.

Too much intimacy with their child was perceived as 'unhealthy', and they justified the emotional distance they created between themselves and their children by focusing on building intimacy with their wife/partner. Love for their child was not considered more special than the love they showed to their partner or their colleagues; the reasoning behind this was described that their behaviour with their children needed to be consistent to how they behaved in all social relationships. Framing love in this way denotes that the child does not receive a special status, and their role as a father is not fully inhabited. Ion (Romanian, resident, 36) succinctly explains the dissociation from the fathering role he experiences:

> I don't think it's necessarily love. I don't know. It's a relationship with a tiny human. And here there are two things: it's an ego thing, your legacy, saying to yourself 'he's mine' and I try not to have this ego [clears throat] because when you have this ego, you are very subjective and you say that your kid is the best and the coolest and the smartest and I try not to fall into this sin. But this ego thing will always make you talk a lot about your child (…) And I think that in the moment when you give him a lot of your time, and you prioritize this time and your resources and your attention, this is also a form a love, right?

In this context, Ion explains how emotions matter less than time and resources in building a connection with his son. For him, valuing emotions is risky, as these could interfere with the stoic model of emotionality that he confessed has shaped his identity as a man. The 'struggle' I mentioned before refers to a sense of uncertainty in how to define love. This is underscored by a feeling of mistrusting that what fathers are feeling towards their children is indeed love. The men in this group were actively trying not to be too proud of their children and worked emotionally to stomp their 'ego-pride' while describing not always feeling love towards their children. Whether they were committed to the idea of love or struggling with it, love was still considered, to a certain extent, important, particularly for their child's emotional well-being. In their eyes, the value of feeling love was diminished, proportionally with an increase in the value of 'seeing the love' reflected in material and practical exchanges. If this is not the first time when social actors prove to 'resist the romantic discourse' (Duncombe and Marsden 1995), it is surprising, however, that paternal love can also be resisted. However, it's important to underline here that simply resisting the discourse does not replace its complete existence: resisting love is not the same as an absence of love.

These three fathers reasoned that 'conditionally' loving their children contributed to their child's social development. The assumption was based on a belief that it was the mother's nature to accept everything and love the child for who he/she is, and it was left to the father to be more critical and push the child to 'do more'. Unconditional love was delegated to their partner who, it was believed, could love unrestrained and, through this, build the child's confidence while father's love set limits which helped the child fit into society; they understood their love as having an influence on how their children respected social norms.

This section dealt with the important role that language plays in constructing the intimate father's role and describing specific forms of masculine emotionality. However, language is limited, as Burkitt asserts:

> Language is the main mode of adult emotional circulation, but this is supported (and at times contradicted) by the repertoire of the bodily soundingboard which includes vocal intonation, gestures, looms and body posture. (p. 171, 2014)

The body is as important as verbal communication in understanding how fathers express and interpret love, especially since for all of them paternal love was a 'verb'. Therefore, in the next section, I explore in-depth how fathers experience love as *a relational complex* enacted primarily through their bodies.

Embodied Love

It's important to expand on the role of embodiment in the practices of love of involved fathers', particularly since these have an influence on their emotional bordering. Contradicting the Cartesian divide between reason (associated with masculinity and seen in connection to the mind), and emotions (which are assumed to be feminine and embodied), it has been discussed that physical contact—whether as a sign of strength, connection and vulnerability—is important in the construction of masculine identity (Seidler 2006; Waitt and Stanes 2015; Robinson and Hockey 2011). New links are currently established between the male body and the visceral and physiological expression of emotions or what has been called the 'turn to affect' (Wetherell 2012; Reeser and Goetzén 2018). In this literature, the embodiment of fathers' caregiving is defined as 'a series of activities to which they bring particular body capital to their relationships, through an assemblage of learned "body techniques" or new ways of using the body to accomplish a goal' (Ranson 2015, p. 39). It has been argued that the functions of involved fathers' embodiment are to maintain positive emotions, to build intimacy and to provide care to their children.

In addition, embodiment is relational, especially in showing how the bodies of young babies are central to their parent's lives, as they invite care alongside with intimacy and love (Jamieson 1999; Lupton 2013). Furthermore, as each body's being in the world is shaped through social interactions, the child influences the parent's body and vice versa. The findings of this research confirm previous arguments. To illustrate how this functions, I make use of an excerpt from Stewart's interview (Scottish, resident, 53), the father of three-year-old Matthew, in which

52 A. Macht

he reconstructs 'good fathering' (Henwood and Procter 2003) through his embodied interactions with his son[10]:

> I know I'm a good parent and it gives me a chance to actually (...) [Matthew interrupts him; he wants his dad to interact with his game, which his dad does and tells him after 'Well done Matt'] So yeah, it just gave me an opportunity again to actually pull all the ethos and everything else that my (...) [Matthew says something and his dad adds 'Are you going to play quietly?'. His son nods. He says 'Good boy, top man' then he gives him his mobile phone to play a game on it] (...) I'm actually learning just now. I'm even going back to my studies again. It not only benefits him because I'm learning, but it also makes me more aware of the changes that have actually happened [A noise is heard. Matthew tells us that something dropped. Stewart says 'Well go and pick it up, please' his son says 'You, you!'. Stewart looks at him and asks 'Did I drop it? Who dropped it?' Matthew gestures away. Stewart says 'Well you go and pick it up then'. He does so. Then they quickly settle on what to play after we're done with the interview] but this is the reason why, because he gets 100% of my attention and when I don't give it to him [Matthew talks over him. Spontaneously Stewart gets up and picks him up and cuddles him. They laugh and make funny voices. Stewart asks Matthew 'How much do you love daddy?' and Matthew says 'Two weeks'. We all laugh. Stewart adds 'It was a hundred weeks yesterday!'. They cuddle again.]

Interacting with the child in not only an embodied but also a communicative way influenced Stewart himself, who briefly broke the seriousness he has portrayed throughout our interview by smiling, changing the tone of his voice to sound playful and by pulling faces in order to entertain Matthew. Of course, my presence as a researcher influenced these displays, so I was bound to see mostly polite and positive interactions. Although there were situations such as the one above, when children tested their fathers and, overall, reacted with patience even if they were momentarily frustrated. The interactions might have been socially

---

[10] This data excerpt includes notes from the observations of father-son interactions on the day of our interview, which were spontaneously recorded on a notepad whenever the interview was interrupted by Stewart's son; combining transcripts with field notes can be a useful technique to capture father's embodiment in research.

kept in check by my presence, but they did show a certain degree of habituation and the reproduction of fathers' intimate knowledge of their children's needs and behaviours. This was evident when I was frequently instructed on their children's personality through commentaries such as: 'gets grumpy in the afternoon', 'can draw silently for hours', 'wants a cuddle', 'loves loud toys', and so on.

For example, when asked to explain in his own words what his love for his three-year-old son is, Daniel replied in both verbal and physical ways, revealing a relational account of love supported through the body:

> Let's start from the beginning. Magda knows [gestures towards his wife and touches his partner's arms, who was silently cleaning the dishes behind him in the kitchen]. The first time, when he came into the world, I honestly can say I didn't understand much. I don't know how others say that 'The first time I saw him and wow it was such great love!' In those moments, there was someone new who appeared, I knew that he was mine and good job. But after all of this, and the events that took place, like waking up at night, his first smile, all of these things, led me to care for him, as he reacted to me, that he resonates with me. You know, all of these things that followed afterwards, which led me to think I can not imagine my life without him anymore (…) if you do things together, I think this is where things connect. If you spend time, if you do things, if you love them, if you remember, that's when I think that the relationship ties in—not just for father and son, but in general as well.

The observations have further revealed that Scottish and Romanians alike resolved moments of conflicting interests[11] with their children in verbal and embodied ways. This took the form of (a) resorting to physical touch (i.e. fathers picked them up, held them, placed their children on their legs and sometimes rocked them) and (b) amusing the children (fathers pulled faces, spoke in a funny voice, tickled them and made them laugh), all the while keeping negotiations with them in order to reach a compromise together (or to 'strike a deal'). These behaviours occurred both in public spaces (at work and in a park) and in their homes. Caring or intimate fatherhood was expressed both in language and through the body.

---

[11] Such as the child wanting the father to do something, and the father was unwilling or vice versa.

Furthermore, embodiment also engaged their senses. Romanian and Scottish fathers referred to how they created a connection with the child through seeing them, smelling them, hearing them and touching them. For example, Daniel (Romanian, resident, 38), Gordon (Scottish, resident, 36) and John (Scottish, resident, 36) recalled moments of their children's dancing with them and singing to them. Charlie (Scottish, resident, 41) described his family as 'a huggy family' while Ovidiu (Romanian, resident, 34) was particularly fond of his young son's familiar smell. Moreover, for Horia (Romanian, resident, 32), the father of three children, experiencing strong emotions goes hand in hand with wanting to act on them, in deeply embodied ways. When I asked him, what is the first thing that comes to mind when he thinks of the love that he feels for his children, he said:

> Just a big child-like smile. Which is sometimes a bit like a trickster[12] [laughter]. I mean it's then when you feel the need to pick them up, to hold them tightly, to caress and kiss and love them so much. When you see that they have that smile. And then I think it's important as a parent, to keep in mind when you are raising the children that it's important to smile, to enjoy things and make some jokes.

Emil (Romanian, resident, 37), the father of two girls, pictured a halo around his infant girl's head as he described her looking 'like a little Buddha—tranquil and content'. The 'halo effect' appears in the literature as a picture of the accumulation of the loved person's physical characteristics which are given special status (Kemper 1978). Emil's mention of his youngest daughter's face is significant since he also revealed how frustrated he felt in the past that he couldn't visualize his eldest daughter's face when she was little. By engaging in emotional reflexivity, he made a conscious effort to think of the particularities of his daughter's physical features:

> When Maria was little, I tried one night when I was away to picture her and I couldn't represent her visually. This really frustrated me 'I mean how

---

[12] The word in Romanian is 'smecheraş', and it is difficult to find a perfectly corresponding translation. It implies a sort of clever way of deceiving someone, and getting one's way, but it has jovial and pleasant undertones—especially in the context in which Horia used it.

come I can't picture her? What if I lose my child in a crowd, I won't be able to recognize her?!' Yes, I really didn't have a clear image. I was unable to say well 'How are her eyes? What about her mouth? Or her nose? How does every trait look like?' So, now I have worked at remembering her image, and it is very powerful.

This example underlines how love grows in time, as remembering the loved person enhances emotional reflexivity. Having a clear mental picture of his daughters' embodiment is also a marker of 'the good father' identity (Shirani and Henwood 2011), as it reinforces paternal legitimacy in situations in which it might need to be explained to others (such as during the interview encounter). But it also denotes how visualizing the loved person is aiding in the construction of love. The 'strategy' links of remembering the loved person's body links love as a relationally shaped emotion to a material, embodied anchor, portraying how the 'generalized other'[13] (Mead 1934) is retained on an emotional as well as a physical level. Thus, to embody the intimate father's role, fathers have to sustain a dialogue between their reason and their emotions and take into account their children's embodiment.

Embodied Intuition

In situations where the father's role was that of a primary caregiver to the child, something akin to intuition developed through embodied interactions (Vandenberghe 2008). To illustrate this, Ray (Scottish, resident, 51) describes that when he communicates with his disabled son, he relies on a quick reading of his son's bodily cues:

> Language is very important but also body language is very important as how you think. With me he can just (…) he knows he can get a cuddle. You know, we don't have to really speak (…) It's body language and other things, that you can (…) you just have that sense. It's hard to say. You just

---

[13] Defined by G. H. Mead as 'The organized community or social group which gives to the individual his unity of self may be called "the generalized" other. The attitude of the generalized other is the attitude of the whole community. Thus, for example, in the case of such a social group as a ball team, the team is the generalized other insofar as it enters—as an organized process or social activity—into the experience of any one of the individual members of it' (p. 154).

have that sense that when things are right or when things are wrong, you know. I can tell the way Scott is: if something's on his mind, if he goes quiet. So I can just tell by his body language and things, and I think he can tell too.

Sociologically speaking, in his role as a primary caregiver to his son, Ray experiences what has been called 'an intra-active becoming' (i.e. physically growing together with his son as their relationship develops) (Doucet 2013). He gained knowledge of his son's habits through caring for him and interacting with him daily. Based on his engagement in caregiving, Ray acquired intimate knowledge of his son's bodily cues and can attribute specific meanings to them, such as using this knowledge to change a specific emotional situation (distress) and alleviate his son's anxiety. Furthermore, such aspects were not only limited to full-time fathers. For example, Adam adds being aware of shared visual cues:

Sometimes when say you are on the playground and there are bigger kids and they all go down the chute and he feels it's his turn and then sometimes you feel, you know that he checks with you whether to step in. You don't often need to step in you know, it's just like checking to see if it's ok. And then you give him maybe some reassurance and then you either let the other person in front of him or he does what he's supposed to do. So it's just like this checking in sometimes, 'What's going on? Is it ok?'

In a similar vein, Hugh defines love as this shared understanding that he shares with his son. For Hugh (Scottish, resident, 36), love is something he feels in the stomach or is expressed even in little gestures such as the reciprocal glimpses he exchanges with his son:

Oh God! What is love? I don't know. I think it's a connection where you understand how the other person is feeling, just by the way that they behave and the way that they respond. (…) So I think it's a connection that I don't think you can put down on paper, it's a (…) I suppose it comes in many forms. I just think about the times when Emmett's looked at me and I looked at him and we pulled a face at the same time, we kind of, straight away you know that it's a team and a family, so it's that. And I think it's probably a bit of worry and concern around if I see them fall off a bike or something. Your heart sinks. It's hitting you right in your stomach, but then you balance that with not over-reacting when they fall down, because otherwise they'd be crying at everything.

Andrea Doucet (2013) has argued that fathers usually choose to display four topics in their narratives: gendered domestic work, happiness, masculinity and heroism. However, Hugh was also talking about how he processes worry and concern through his body, a visceral feeling linked to love. This example matches previous literature, which explains how the act of caregiving can create a visceral attachment in the caregiver's body[14] (Ranson 2015). Although this level of subtle communication, which Hugh describes, might foreshadow the father's lack of actual involvement in domestic and childcare work,[15] as he confessed to relying on childminders and au-pairs.

Culturally, there were mostly similarities, as an awareness of empathic checking in with each other could be noticed for both Scottish and Romanian fathers, as Liviu details:

I think it gives them confidence, if they feel loved. What they see in the home, when they are protected (…) it's true that often they search our gaze for encouragement, they look to see if you approve from a glance 'Yes, should I go on?' There is an impetus, to know that we are all there in the background as parents [supporting them].

These examples allude to the social experience of what Ruth Feldman (2012) has termed 'parent-infant visual affective synchrony' that describes the visual signals exchanged between fathers and their children in the act of embodied relating. They also link back to the 'give-and-take' of involved fathers' emotional vocabularies from the first part

---

[14] Even if fathers experience visceral attachments to their children, as a marker of the masculine embodiment of the experience of transitioning to fatherhood and love, these are, nonetheless, a different phenomenon than the most commonly known 'couvade' or 'sympathy pains' that fathers experience when their partners are giving birth (Brennan et al. 2007).

[15] Both Hugh and his partner worked in high-ranking jobs in the financial sector, which saw them enlist their children in after-school clubs and rely on the help of a nanny. He was also spending a day a week engaging in leisure, and after our interview ended—which took place at the end of his working day—he went golfing.

of this chapter, demonstrating how discourses function together with embodiment in how fathers construct love. In this way, love is sustained through everyday engagement, shared exchanges and mutual attention. Intuitive knowledge of the loved 'other' developed for fathers of both cultures a mutual sense of a bodily being in the world, confirming Burkitt's theoretical arguments. Paternal love is, therefore, much like romantic love, felt through the body, and the body is central in the process of relating through love (although it is morally and legally sanctioned in terms of sexuality).

Embodied Emotional Bordering

Involved fathers' use of emotional reflexivity can be applied to knowing what they should feel, in order to decide what to do in establishing closeness with their children. It underlines the extent to which men *allow* themselves to rely on their emotions; this process is, however, 'bordered' in relationships with others through the imperative to perform a certain type of normative masculine identity, which can occur simultaneously with performing involved fatherhood (and, many times, also clashes with it). More generally, the concept can be used to explain how a parenting role and a gendered identity interact with each other and mutually construct one another. It has been argued that men tend to limit their emotionality (especially their positive feelings) by setting relational boundaries in the everyday management of complex emotions (such as love). In this capacity, they are usually bordering on stoicism, as they exert emotional control. However, fathers can also border on intimacy within the same identity (whether intimate or breadwinning fathering). As they do so, they have to work through a variety of contradicting emotions in the reshaping of their selves. For example, Ewan's (Scottish, resident, 36) excitement at discovering this intense and new feeling of unconditional love for his daughter was, however, curtailed by doubts whether it was normal for him to feel love so intensely. Ewan was worried that his love might turn into something sinister:

Yeah, but because it was so strong, because it felt slightly weird in the context of you know (…) Love for your child isn't something that people talk about very much and in the media all that's talked about is abused children. So I felt slightly that there was this danger of it crossing over or something. Of it becoming 'Is this right? Is this feeling ok?' (…) It was a genuinely new emotional experience.

The significant part of his quote is 'the danger of it crossing over', signifying there is a certain delimited emotional space (marked by an emotional border) within which Ewan can experience love. Love is powerful enough to make him feel like he is about to cross over the gendered border imposed by his masculine identity and transform its usual demands for emotional stoicism. What Ewan also alludes to here is that, despite feeling a positive emotion in relation to his daughter, he is aware of the 'risk' of *being* seen as a loving father. Jacqui Gabb (2013) draws attention to the repressive influence of social norms in coordinating men's public conduct around children. Since masculinity continues to be associated with a predatory sexuality, its proximity to children is judged as potentially dangerous. Being physically loving can thus be negatively interpreted. Fathers are made aware through public discourses and social interactions with others, as to what they *can* and *cannot* display, in relation to not only their children but also other people's children. Therefore, Ewan remarks on the example of 'abused children'. He uses a social norm to constrict love, draw a relational boundary and thereby raise a stoic border around his emotions. The scrutiny of the 'social gaze' was discussed as well by Norbert Elias who explained how the civilizing forces of society, through processes of socialization, affect individual agency:

The controlling agency forming itself as part of the individual's personality structure corresponds to the controlling agency forming itself in society at large. The one like the other tends to impose a highly differentiated regulation upon all passionate impulses, upon people's conduct all around. Both – each to a large extent mediated by the other – exert *a constant, even pressure to inhibit affective outbursts*. They damp down extreme fluctuations in behaviour and emotions. (Elias 1939/2000, p. 373)

This strategy of restricting emotions is at the core of a processual account of how emotional bordering emerges. The act of managing emotions is followed by the act of releasing them. Love never fully disappears even when fathers exert emotional control, and it begins for fathers as an 'intense' and powerful emotion that occasionally needs to be damped down to be experienced according to contextually relevant feeling rules (those social and gendered norms that demarcate the accomplishment of successful masculinity). However, it might show up in other unexpected ways, as Ben describes that, at times, emotional bordering needs to be readjusted when relational boundaries appear:

> I think it's an emotional prison that a lot of men find themselves in, without really understanding why. I think that explains a lot of (…) well it seeps out in other ways, it doesn't evaporate. Your emotions and feelings don't evaporate. They're still there.
>
> Me: Where do they go?
>
> Int: Well, they can (…) they either stay inside and kind of boil and cook and swirl about and then blow up into something else. They can blow into a sort of anger, addiction, suicidal thoughts kind of losing your centre of moral gravity. Or I think it can more often seep out in other ways, so it releases itself but you're never really dealing with it.

From Ewan's and Ben's accounts, it can be discerned that some involved fathers might see their emotions as 'risky' in relation to their own children even if they persevere in embodying the role of the intimate father. The image of the family provider continues to hold a more respectable, moral status than that of a childless man (Aboim 2010), so fathers are increasingly mindful of their actions because gendered expectations 'of acting masculine' are in tensions with displaying 'good fathering'; it might, therefore, be safer to remain stoically detached even if one is outwardly seen as an involved father. Having children and actively caring for them allows men to express sides of themselves, which are usually emotionally stagnant or controlled. In this way, paternal love dynamizes men's sense of self. Although, love and being loving can also enhance a father's respectable character and social status more than mothers' (Sharpe 1987) since it is not usually expected.

Emotional Border Crossings

Border crossings between gendered identities were defined in the literature as instances where boundaries relax and gendered practices can be flexibly swapped between each other (Doucet 2017; Thorne 1993). Complementing this, Gillian Ranson's research (2010) found that mothers and fathers exhibited a 'functional interchangeability' when both were similarly engaged in direct caregiving. I find this concept to be analytically useful in how gendered differences are described. Therefore, I'm proposing the addition of the emotional dimension to it, in order to explain the tensions which form masculine emotionality, as it shifts between stoicism and intimacy. If emotional bordering is understood as a *process,* then such gendered border crossings become harder to clearly identify and describe, as they would fluidize in the act of relating to someone. This happens as border crossings are blurred by ongoing verbal and embodied adaptations to the other person's spontaneous emotional reactions.

Male embodiment in the context of fatherhood can be a useful illustration. Even if physical non-sexual intimacy between parents and children is pleasurable (Gabb 2013), it is problematic in the cultural context which holds up an image of the ideal male body as a tightly controlled one, with clearly defined boundaries. For example, emotional reflexivity could be ignited from the outside, as it did not always require fathers' initiative, and it wasn't necessarily a pleasant experience. Stewart (Scottish, non-resident, 53), a father who retained full custody of his biological son, Matthew, but lost custody of his two other adopted sons, describes how a spontaneous and public display of emotion ended up being socially sanctioned:

> I'm not a male that's not actually able to show my emotions (…) As an example when I went to school with the whole carry-on, when all of my kids were taken off me, if I was a woman and if I went to the headmistress and all of that, she would have put her arms around about me. But I broke down in tears just because my kids have been taken off me, in such horrendous circumstances. And she thought that it's actually not very becoming of a male to show his emotions, which I think it's utterly disgraceful.

This moment describes the influence of gender norms and power relations in the exercise of fathers' emotional bordering. If Stewart resisted bordering into stoicism and loosened momentarily into emotional vulnerability, he also simultaneously lost a measure of social respect because he contravened a traditional masculine rule: that crying is weakness. In this situation, Stewart's role as a single father left an imprint on how his public display of sadness at losing his child was seen by those in positions of authority. His crying, rather than being considered a legitimate response to loss, was interpreted as un-masculine.[16]

Previous arguments described embodied practices of love as having to be managed because interconnectedness can also pose a threat to autonomy (Lupton 2013). I would ascertain that even if it might be an issue about autonomy, the underlying emotional undercurrent is reconciling the tensions between a certain pride inherent in the masculine construction of the self, built on 'sexual prowess', which runs contrary to the experience of a warm, loving relationship with a child, as an intimate father. This is the underlying contradiction between love and traditional forms of masculinity. It is as if the male body through socialization is 'built' for one type of identity which is incompatible with another (norms of masculinity versus caring fathering). However, contemporary media images and data from research such as this one are increasingly challenging this dichotomous view (Schofield 2016).

Thus, in having to internalize and then reconcile these tensions between the self's constructions and the expectations imposed by social norms, involved fathers employ emotional bordering. As some fathers have explained this process of protecting themselves from feeling 'too much', and thereby losing a rational grip over not only their parenting responsibilities, but also their masculine role identification, it can be reasoned that in not allowing their emotions to guide them into what they perceive to be 'taboo' territories, men are reconstructing a traditional masculine identity, albeit on less sexualized terms. And the evidence suggests that these negotiations take place primarily at an emotionally reflexive level.

---

[16] Note, however, that it has been argued that fatherhood is not as 'morally policed' as motherhood (Miller 2010).

2 Doing Love: Fathers' Emotions in Relation to Their Children 63

If emotions are to be understood as a set of practices (Scheer 2012) and love defined as a type of 'doing', then emotional bordering is a relational practice employed to manage emotions, the outcome of which is fed back into to social environment. In time, borders can be raised (rigid) or dissolved (loose) according to the relational boundaries set by fathers' agency and their engagement with the various close relationships surrounding them. Nonetheless, experiencing love as a 'new' emotion implies that sudden shifts take place within the structure of the borders surrounding fathers' emotionality and that these can be stretched and expanded as emotions mingle with each other and relational boundaries are blurred. Feeling rules (Hochschild 1979) contribute thus to how relational boundaries are created, and emotional bordering is employed, and these processes have been shown to vary according to culture (Wouters 1989).

An example of 'stretching' his emotional borders is given by Malcolm (Scottish, resident, 42). He describes how the birth of his children interfered with the strong affection he had for his partner and the surprise he felt at realizing he could 'love more' than he imagined:

> I even remember because my son – the first-born – my wife went through a very long labour and seeing somebody that I loved in that situation I thought I am going to resent this child for putting her through that. But the second I saw him and just got a hold of him just everything washed away. And it really takes you back. Again, the same thing I thought when my wife was pregnant with my little girl I thought I fell back and there was no way I can love that child as much as I love this one. Again 'No. You can!' because it's a little girl, you get into that so it is quite an emotional time. But to describe it, I think it's almost indescribable, it's something you have to experience.

Malcolm had a higher sense of emotional freedom as he transitioned to fatherhood and discovered he could be more emotionally open. In this sense, in becoming a father, there was a space created where feeling rules which marked interactions which his children matched the emotional experience to the emotional standards, describing what the appropriate way to feel is: in this case that once you have children you should love them and you should love all your children equally and not have favourites. Here, borders were created in a process of internalizing feeling rules

64   A. Macht

and externalizing appropriate emotional expressions. Significant in his quote is also the 'internal conversation' (Archer 2010) he was having with himself expressed through restrictions and allowances ('No. You can!'), emphasizing that Malcolm did not just emotionally absorb 'feeling rules' in a passive manner, but that a dynamic process began, in which he engaged in emotion bordering to dissolve some of his stoicism and allow himself to *love more*.

Emotional Bordering in Time

In the expansion and contraction of emotional borders, time seems to play an important part. With age, what at first was experienced as a larger emotional freedom becomes a slowly solidifying emotional border, leaning more towards stoicism, despite intimate resistance. Patrick (Scottish, resident, 42), a father of two daughters who bordered on intimacy, describes the frustration he felt the moment his oldest daughter made him aware not only that she is physically different than him but that because of her gender he had to emotionally prepare for an inevitable reduction of their displays of affection:

> With Morgan (…) she came over and sat with me and cuddled into me and said 'I do love you daddy', and I said 'That's good, I love you too' and she said 'But I think I like mummy more than I like you' [laughter]. 'Right, ok' I said 'Why are you telling me this? What's your reason?' and she said 'Well because I've noticed I'm like mummy and I'm not like you'. So I said 'Oh, right' and she said 'And I think mummy and I probably can talk more about that, than I can with you'. At the time, I was quite emotional when she said that because I thought well (…) she's preparing me for the fact that actually she will turn into a woman and therefore she is not like me and that transition will take her a degree away from me and bring her close to my wife as she matures and gets older. Of course my relationship with both my daughters is going to change so that was quite an emotional moment. More emotional for her maturity and saying it, but also from my own perspective in that I know that the time will come where how I display my affection towards my daughters is going to change. It's going to have to, as she is not going to be a girl anymore. She'll be turning into a woman.

2 Doing Love: Fathers' Emotions in Relation to Their Children 65

What Patrick is describing is that he can only allow himself to feel intensely in the 'emotional space' afforded by the relationship with his own daughters and constructed in a moment of intimate self-disclosure. He was made aware of the time limit and the reduced emotional space (built through tactile and embodied displays of affection with his daughter) which had to diminish. In this process of 'bordering', he was also helped by his daughter's agency. This again denotes how relational boundaries are established through the body and influence the appearance of emotional borders as well. It has been shown that children can adopt gendered themes from a young age while also having the power to recreate these gendered narratives, by blending meanings to suit their purposes (Änggård 2005). In this context, his daughter's growing awareness of entering a period of a heterosexual definition of self would gradually restrict access to her habituated expressions of love with her father, particularly the physical ones. However, there is an unspoken rule that parents gradually reduce their interaction with their children as these grow older to allow them to grow up and form different social relationships (Jamieson 1998), so the quote can be seen in this context as well. Nonetheless, I am drawing attention to how this process also contains a power exchange between the father and the child, as emotional bordering incurs fathers' emotion management of their children's awareness of gender identity, and, as such, this is a child-led emotional exchange as well.

Conclusion

This chapter focused on how paternal love functions both at the level of language and the body. Involved fathers define their love for their children as a relationally constructed emotion described as powerful, new, spontaneous and unique. Fathers' emotional vocabularies were rich and professionalized, and such a finding further challenges the idea that men do not have a language for emotions. Moreover, fathers of both cultures preferred to build intimacy through practices of love (such as co-sleeping, showing tenderness, cuddling them, being there with them, reading their bodily cues and responding to them) in an embodied process of 'give-and-take'. Love became meaningful in time as a relationship, as involved fathers got to know their children and it was described as a verb, a type of 'doing', as both groups preferred to engage in practices of love rather than verbal expressions of love. To preserve the continuation of a masculine sense of self, fathers dissociate the language of love from their identities, preferring to emphasize the active characteristics of their love. They also sometimes contradictorily present in their discourses, essentialist understandings of love, although they value love as a relationship and provide data which support the social construction of their paternal love.

To an extent, therefore, paternal love challenges the repressive model of stoic masculinity and helps men embody and work through the emotional demands of the intimate fathering role. However, since love was primarily defined as a form of action, as men underlined the importance of *doing* love over putting love into words, paternal love appears as a masculinized type of interaction. Findings reveal that both groups of fathers believed that being loving had good effects on themselves as individuals and improved them. A small group of three Romanian fathers were uncomfortable with saying the word 'love' or with thinking of themselves as 'loving' fathers. This chapter has shown support for the argument that fathers value having a long-lasting relationship with their children and are in touch with their own emotions and those of their children's (Lupton and Barclay 1997). Based on this, I present in the next chapter how, in the process of establishing intimacy with their children and experiencing love, fathers shape their role according to the emotional bordering strategies received from their own parents.

References

Aboim, S. (2010). *Plural Masculinities: The Remaking of the Self in Private Life.* Farnham: Ashgate Publishing Co.

Änggard, E. (2005). Barbie Princesses and Dinosaur Dragons: Narration as a Way of Doing Gender. *Gender and Education, 17*(5), 539–553.

Archer, M. (2010). Routine, Reflexivity, and Realism. *Sociological Theory, 28*(3), 272–303.

Brennan, A., Marshall-Lucette, S., Ayers, S., & Ahmed, H. (2007). A Qualitative Exploration of the Couvade Syndrome in Expectant Fathers. *Journal of Reproductive and Infant Psychology, 25*(1), 18–39.

Brownlie, J. (2014). *Ordinary Relationships: A Sociological Study of Emotions, Reflexivity and Culture*. Basingstoke: Palgrave Macmillan.

Burkitt, I. (2014). *Emotions and Social Relations*. London: Sage.

Cancian, F. M. (1986). The Feminization of Love. *Signs: Journal of Women in Culture and Society, 11*(4), 692–709.

de Boise, S. (2015). *Men, Masculinities, Music and Emotions*. Basingstoke: Palgrave Macmillan.

Doucet, A. (2013). A "Choreography of Becoming": Fathering, Embodied Care, and New Materialisms. *Canadian Review of Sociology, 50*(3), 284–305.

Doucet, A. (2017). *Do Men Mother? Fathering, Care, and Domestic Responsibility* (2nd ed.). Toronto: University of Toronto Press.

Duncombe, J., & Marsden, D. (1995). Can Men Love? 'Reading', 'Staging' and 'Resisting' the Romance. In L. Pearce & J. Stacey (Eds.), *Romance Revisited: Part 2* (pp. 238–250). London: Lawrence & Wishart.

Edin, K., & Nelson, T. J. (2013). *Doing the Best They Can: Fatherhood in the Inner City*. Berkeley: University of California Press.

Elias, N. (1939/2000). *The Civilizing Process: Sociogenetic and Psychogenetic Investigations* (Trans. E. Jephcott). Oxford: Blackwell Publishers.

Feldman, R. (2012). Parent-Infant Synchrony: A Biobehavioral Model of Mutual Influences in the Formation of Affiliative Bonds. *Monographs of the Society for Research in Child Development, 77*(2), 42–51.

Gabb, J. (2013). Embodying Risk: Managing Father–Child Intimacy and the Display of Nudity in Families. *Sociology, 47*(4), 639–654.

Gabb, J., & Fink, J. (2015). *Couple Relationships in the 21st Century*. Basingstoke: Palgrave Pivot.

Giddens, A. (1992). *The Transformation of Intimacy: Sexuality, Love, and Eroticism in Modern Societies*. Stanford: Stanford University Press.

Hall, O. C. E. (1995). From Fun and Excitement to Joy and Trouble: An Explorative Study of Three Danish Fathers' Experiences Around Birth. *Scandinavian Journal of Caring Sciences, 9*, 171–179.

Haraway, D. J. (2003). *The Companion Species Manifesto: Dogs, People, and Significant Otherness*. Chicago/Bristol: Prickly Paradigm/University Presses Marketing.

Henwood, K., & Procter, J. (2003). The 'Good Father': Reading Men's Accounts of Paternal Involvement During the Transition to First-Time Fatherhood. *British Journal of Social Psychology, 42*(3), 337–355.

Hochschild, A. R. (1979). Emotion Work, Feeling Rules, and Social Structure. *American Journal of Sociology, 85*(3), 551–575.

Holmes, M. (2010). The Emotionalization of Reflexivity. *Sociology, 44*(1), 139–154.

Jamieson, L. (1998). *Intimacy: Personal Relationships in Modern Societies.* Cambridge: Polity Press.

Jamieson, L. (1999). Intimacy Transformed: A Critical Look at the Pure Relationship. *Sociology, 33*(3), 477–494.

Jamieson, L. (2011). Intimacy as a Concept: Explaining Social Change in the Context of Globalisation or Another Form of Ethnocentrism? *Sociological Research Online, 16*(4), 1–13.

Kemper, T. D. (1978). *A Social Interactional Theory of Emotions.* New York: Wiley.

Kimmel, M. S. (2008). *Guyland: The Perilous World Where Boys Become Men.* New York: Harper Collins.

Lamb, M. E. (Ed.). (2010). *The Role of the Father in Child Development* (5th ed.). London: Wiley.

Lupton, D. (1998). *The Emotional Self: A Sociocultural Exploration.* London: SAGE.

Lupton, D. (2013). Infant Embodiment and Interembodiment: A Review of Sociocultural Perspectives. *Childhood, 20*(1), 37–50.

Lupton, D., & Barclay, L. (1997). *Constructing Fatherhood: Discourses and Experiences.* London: Sage.

Mead, G. H. (1934). *Mind, Self, and Society: From the Standpoint of a Social Behaviourist.* Chicago: University of Chicago Press.

Miller, T. (2010). *Making Sense of Fatherhood: Gender, Caring and Work.* Cambridge: Cambridge University Press.

Nielsen, H. B. (2017). *Feeling Gender: A Generational and Psychosocial Approach.* London: Palgrave Macmillan.

Padilla, M. B., Hirsch, J. S., Munoz-Laboy, M., Sember, R. E., & Parker, R. G. (Eds.). (2007). *Love and Globalization: Transformations of Intimacy in the Contemporary World.* Nashville: Vanderbilt University Press.

Ranson, G. (2010). *Against the Grain: Couples, Gender, and the Reframing of Parenting.* Toronto: University of Toronto Press.

Ranson, G. (2015). *Fathering, Masculinity and the Embodiment of Care.* Basingstoke: Palgrave Macmillan.

Reeser, T. W., & Gottzén, L. (2018). Masculinity and Affect: New Possibilities, New Agendas. *NORMA, 13*(3–4), 145–157.

Robinson, V., & Hockey, J. (2011). Embodiment: Masculinity and the Body. In *Masculinities in Transition. Genders and Sexualities in the Social Sciences.* London: Palgrave Macmillan.

Rochlen, A. B., Suizzo, M., McKelley, R. A., & Scaringi, V. (2008). "I'm Just Providing for My Family:" a Qualitative Study of Stay-at-Home Fathers. *Psychology of Men and Masculinity, 9*(4), 193–206.

Sampson, C., & Atkinson, P. (2013). The Golden Star: An Emotional Repertoire of Scientific Discovery and Legacy. *The Sociological Review, 61*, 573–590.

Scheer, M. (2012). Are Emotions a Kind of Practice (And Is That What Makes Them Have a History)? A Bourdieuian Approach to Understanding Emotion. *History and Theory, 51*, 193–220.

Schofield, A. (2016). Hard Bodies, Soft Hearts: Mixed-Race Men as Muscular Daddies in the Films of Vin Diesel and Dwayne Johnson. In E. Podnieks (Ed.), *Pops in Pop Culture* (pp. 125–140).

Seidler, V. J. (2006). Gender, Power, Ethics and Love. In V. J. Seidler (Ed.), *Transforming Masculinities: Men, Cultures, Bodies, Power, Sex and Love* (pp. 128–142). London: Taylor and Francis.

Sharpe, S. (1987). *Falling for Love: Teenage Mothers Talk*. London: Virago.

Shirani, F., & Henwood, K. (2011). Continuity and Change in a Qualitative Longitudinal Study of Fatherhood: Relevance Without Responsibility. *International Journal of Social Research Methodology, 14*(1), 17–29.

Thorne, B. (1993). *Gender Play: Girls and Boys in School*. New Brunswick: Rutgers University Press.

Turner, B., & Stets, J. (2005). *The Sociology of Emotions*. Cambridge: Cambridge University Press.

Vandenberghe, F. (2008). Sociology of the Heart: Max Scheler's Epistemology of Love. *Theory, Culture & Society, 25*(3), 17–51.

Waitt, G., & Stanes, E. (2015). Sweating Bodies: Men, Masculinities, Affect, Emotion. *Geoforum, 59*, 30–38.

Wetherell, M. (2012). *Affect and Emotion: A New Social Science Understanding*. London: SAGE Publications Ltd.

Wouters, C. (1989). The Sociology of Emotions and Flight Attendants: Hochschild's Managed Heart. *Theory, Culture & Society, 6*(1), 95–123.

3

Memories of Love: Fathers' Emotions in Relation to Their Own Parents

Intergenerational Constructions of Self

Previous studies have shown that what seems to affect men's fathering is not only their partner's influence but also the relationship that fathers have with their own fathers (Anderson 1996; Brannen and Nilsen 2006; Brannen 2015). Additionally, we know that for fathers in dual-earner households, their engagement is influenced by their partner's occupation and hours of work, while for single-earner fathers, this is determined by the quality of the parenting that they have previously received from their own parents (Barnett and Baruch 1987). Moreover, Julia Brannen's research on English and Polish populations (2015) has shown that models of either warm or stoic emotional expression are transmitted intergenerationally from father to son. Therefore, an involved father's consideration of love (and its consideration as a 'conditional' or 'unconditional' relational exchange) may arise from his adherence to forms of stoicism potentially rooted in the father's upbringing, as Brannen writes: 'emotional undercurrents echo down the generations' (p. 106, Brannen 2015). Contrary to psychoanalytical views (Freud 1919; Bowlby 1969), sociological perspectives denote changes through time in how fathers

© The Author(s) 2020
A. Macht, *Fatherhood and Love*, Palgrave Macmillan Studies in Family and Intimate Life, https://doi.org/10.1007/978-3-030-20358-0_3

manage and transform emotional patterns from their past into their present experiences. Intergenerational transmission is a temporal process, described as: 'what is transmitted by different family generations over time and the life course. Transmission covers a variety of phenomena including assets, values, political beliefs, social mobility and social status (...) important also are the moral and emotional bonds forged between generations' (p. 12). I aim to focus in this chapter especially on the emotional bonds that Julia Brannen mentions and explain how they are understood by fathers to be transmitted in their fathering. While bordering is a horizontal process of raising and lowering emotional borders by shifting towards and reversing from stoicism to love according to social circumstances in the present (on an imagined emotional spectrum), intergenerational transmission happens vertically as a range of personal attributes are transmitted from grandfathers/grandmothers to mothers/fathers to sons and daughters down generational lines. Both bordering and transmission occur as part of the experience of being socialized in, what for many is the first social group an individual is born or adopted into: the family. However, I understand emotional bordering as linked more to fathers' agency than intergenerational transmission is, largely because the latter is an external and to some extent structural process that functions mostly in unconscious ways.

As they interact, these processes do not happen in the same way or serve the same purpose for all involved fathers. It has been argued that this transmission is not always evident; it can happen in subtle ways so that a certain resource passed on by one generation may be used in a different way by the next generation (Brannen and Nilsen 2006). In my research, involved fathers adapted their past emotional experience (or *memories of love*, through which I mean particular emotive childhood memories from the whole experience of being parented and growing up, which are reflected upon and used as models for the embodiment in the presence of their fathering role) to the contextually mitigating influences of their everyday lives in the present. This process required a dialogue between their reason and emotions, memory and fathering identity, as well as bridging their emotional reflexivity with emotion work; or put differently, memories of love influenced how fathers bordered emotionally, as they reconciled their provider's role with their intimate father's role. For example, Tim (Scottish, resident, 30) describes his father's role as selectively constructed from previous memories of how things felt for him in his childhood:

> I would say I'm taking the good parts maybe using them and maybe tailoring them to the way I would want but obviously learning from what I hated as a child and not trying to do, looking for the signs of like when I was upset as a child 'cause I would remember how it felt and what I went through, and maybe trying to do things a bit differently or a different outlook.

Tim balances his memories with a current and different outlook on fathering in the present. Furthermore, what emerged from the data was that fathers form their current intimate father's role in connection and contrast to previously received parenting models (and for some those of their mothers as well), through an assessment of how emotionally close or distant they were to their father (and, in some circumstances, to their mother as well). The data reflected the prominence of three categories of fathers: (a) *different* fathers, those that considered themselves distinct than their fathers because they were emotionally involved in their children's lives, (b) *ambivalent fathers*, those trying to be different but more or less unconsciously 'falling back' on what they have learned or remembered in relation to their own father's emotionality, and (c) *similar* fathers, those who benefited from warm and involved fathering in their childhood and were trying to replicate these in the present. For the different and ambivalent fathers, the changing characteristics of their fathering were the following: (a) having an increasing sense of awareness of their emotions (emotional reflexivity), (b) based on that awareness, engaging in reparation actions such as apologizing to maintain a positive relationship with their child/children (emotion work), and (c) being open to letting the child/children guide them in interactions (and fostering child's agency).

Different Fathers

This group was the predominant group of fathers from the sample. However, there were considerably more different fathers in the Romanian group than in the Scottish one[1] (only four Scottish fathers considered themselves different to their own). These involved fathers considered themselves to be *different* than their own fathers because they attempted to fill a lack, whether material or emotional, which emerged from their memories of having been parented. They also perceived their fathers as detached, stoic and too aggressive, and resolved to work against these characteristics by performing the intimate father's role in the present with their children through making changes. As in previous research, these fathers wanted to be more emotionally expressive than their fathers were with them (Brannen 2015). David (Scottish, resident, 38) vividly describes what to him are primarily emotional discrepancies between his own parenting approach compared to his own father's parenting:

> He's still quite active for a man in his mid-eighties, but there's also quite a cold kinda side to him. It's not to say that still waters don't run deep. I think he does love us all, he just doesn't express it very well. So, when I had Max I was thinking to be honest, I don't want to be like that. I want to say to my son 'I love you' and I say that all the time to him. And yeah just [being] really affectionate with him (…)
>
> Int: Why do you think you made that change?
>
> Yeah, I just think it's because of the way it made me feel. My mom was always quite affectionate and caring and sensitive and my dad wasn't like that. I wanted to just basically have, with Max, two parents who are sensitive and caring and he can talk to (…) My dad was just doing the best he could with the natural resources he had in him, you know, as a result of his environment and his life. So he had to be quite tough.

Contextualizing his father's parenting according to his age and the circumstances of the social environment in a given time period (post-war Britain) gives David the emotional distance to reflect on his memories of love. He situates his current focus in his fathering on warmth and expressing love, in contrast to the stoic emotionality he noticed in his father. David argues that this change was made because of how he *felt* about what was not working so well in his relationship with his father. This

---

[1] It's worth mentioning here that there were slightly more men to begin with in the Scottish sample due to the pilot study: 27 Scottish and 20 Romanian men.

underlines how the shift to intimacy is mediated emotionally, in the process of bordering.

On a different note, Alexandru (Romanian, resident, 42) reflects on the material abundance he is currently experiencing in urban Bucharest compared to his childhood spent in the rural environment around the capital. As he is now earning above his own family's previous earning capacity and could offer his daughter the material stability he lacked as a child, he also situates this in the context of shifting not only emotionally but also materially in performing a different father's role:

> I'm a different father than my father used to be. I've tried to bring something new all the time. Practically, to bring in everything that I didn't have and wanted to experience in my childhood. Maybe it's not good to offer her so much, because at the moment we offer her almost everything. We don't give her that impression, and we try to keep a distance in how she perceives things, because you can't always have everything you want (…) To give an example, she got an A at school, I was very proud of her, and I explained to her that every performance is rewarded. I promised her a karaoke set, a thing which she remembered, but I also told her I cannot buy her the set just now, but with the first occasion that I get. And she kept reminding me [laughter]. So be careful with what you promise. Eventually, of course I got her the set. So she managed to reach her goal, but we still like to keep certain elements of manipulating the child [laughter].

Iustin (Romanian, resident, 32) reflects on not only his different approach to fathering than that of his own father but also the changed socio-economic circumstances in Romania's transition from communism to capitalism, which he deems 'a different world':

> (…) my dad was more narrow-minded and tried to impose certain attitudes or whatever else he wanted to teach, on the spot. He was more aggressive. Now, I am more adaptable. I try to do as the child says. Now a days there are more sources of information and games for every age, so you can search for different things. We live in a different world than the one he lived in.

One of the main themes that emerged for different Romanian fathers was their relation to processes of *technologization* (or having access to

76   A. Macht

more information and gadgets than the previous generation and thus more choice, more 'freedom' in communication) and *psychologization* (less reliance on authoritarian techniques of parenting and navigating the choice of being a 'natural' relaxed parent or a 'perfected' or 'an improved, better' parent). For example, Vlad (Romanian, resident, 41) describes how saying 'I love you' changed in his view as a discourse in the Romanian culture:

> I think that with younger generations, let's say parents around twenty to fourty years of age, I think that they say 'I love you' more often than how I perceived this when I was a child, the way relations between parents and children were back then. Nowadays it's more like in the movies. I think people now need counsellors, coaches, psychologists and confessors more than they did in the past. But I don't think it's just typically Romanian, I think this happens across the World, as a general need.

In addition, Nelu (Romanian, resident, 34), although identifying as a different father, describes inheriting emotionally stoic tendencies from his own father. He exemplifies this by offering a memory of failing to establish emotional closeness with his father over the phone:

> I think this is a thing that I inherited because of the emotional suppression that I was exposed to, during my entire childhood. I remember one thing that I used to laugh at (...) I was away with my sister and she kept saying let's phone dad. And we phoned dad after our trip and he said 'What? Are you out of money? Why did you call me'. And I realize now that I am the same from that point of view. There is tendency that is almost natural, even if it was something that I have been taught (...) So now, I don't know. I don't identify with being dad. It's just something that I do.

Nelu was one of the fathers who resisted love and preferred to be considered his son's friend rather than father. For Scottish fathers, such as Fergus (Scottish, resident, 38), being different also meant considering temporality in his relationship with his father. He describes how memories of love (and their limitations) influence his current fathering role:

> I wonder if all dads feel that they're a bit more involved than their dad was? Partly is 'cause it's hard to remember. So yeah I feel I'm a bit more of an

involved dad, but I never really felt when I was younger that my dad was uninvolved, if he'd play golf on a Saturday morning (…) It becomes a lot more difficult when it becomes your own personal situation. See I think I'm more involved but then equally at this stage I've got no recollection of being three years old. So what I remember I've got more of a recollection of what my life was at fifteen, at which stage I was probably the one to want to have less to do with them [laughter]. It's different 'cause Katie's three and a half and I can't remember what he [his father] was like when I was three and a half. I remember of when I was fifteen.

Furthermore, Patrick (Scottish, resident, 42), also a different father, didn't think he was necessarily more intimate. Rather, he just expressed being more emotionally reflexive than his own father:

Well I think a lot of this is generational anyway but my dad was more about fun and we would see him when we were on holiday and we would associate a lot of things that we did as a family where fun things (…) I'm probably more of a disciplinarian than my dad is but I think by virtue of the fact I'm there. I think that's probably the big difference. I think I'm more aware of it and conscious of the fact that I'm doing it.

In addition, change was recorded in the way that fathers communicated to build intimacy. For example, Malcolm (Scottish, resident, 42), shows how he has changed his expressivity in time through fathering:

I do a lot more now than I did, so yes I think so. I think parenting's helped with that because of what you have gone through. You realize that your responsibilities have changed and your priorities and perspectives, everything has changed. Generally, yes I think I let people know if something's upsetting me or if I'm happy about something, or if something's pleased me. Whereas in the past I was pretty stoic and just baselined 'Don't give anything away'. But now it's far more that you have to, 'cause again with people they do pick up a lot on it. Especially with children they know if you're happy or sad and they can instantly recognize it and they know if you are very pleased with them. You wanna show it and tell them how much you love them and appreciate them, and how much you're going to miss them.

Malcolm's quote reveals change in time in how he has shifted from stoicism to more intimacy through emotional bordering. He underlines that in this process one strategy he adopts is self-disclosure, to support the unfolding of his positive relationships to his children. In his case, he felt a sense of responsibility and pressure to communicate to his children that he loves them. Not only that but Malcolm describes how he has observed that his daughter's agency employed in the relationship with her grandparents (his parents) has changed the way that they express love among themselves as family members:

> Growing up I can't remember hearing it often (…) with my parents they never really said it and it was quite a generational thing. And now my daughter is talking to them and saying 'I love you' all the time and they go 'Yeah, we love you too'. So I can see just how it impacts.

These descriptions complemented previous arguments from the literature where even saying 'I love you' could be classified as a form of emotion work (Gabb and Fink 2015):

> an act of love through which to implicitly communicate apologies, thanks, regrets and goodbyes, conveys acceptance of a partner for who s/he is, or diffuses stress and tension. Saying and hearing 'I love you' in tense situations could be enormously effective in managing potential conflict within the home. (p. 57)

In the quote above, Malcolm's daughter through her initiative and use of an emotional vocabulary is loosening the stoic borders raised by the generational transmission of restrictive emotionality. Tensions between transmission and bordering might be resolved through child-led activities, which produce love and closeness between family members who would otherwise not relate from an emotional perspective. In this way it could be that, children play an important role in intimate communication by creating new expectations of love in the family's changing set of expectations. However, adopting a different role than their own fathers was not an easy route, as it required sustained emotional bordering.

Similar Fathers

The second category of *similar* fathers was the smallest; there were five men who self-labeled themselves as such (George, Ciprian, John, Gordon and Stewart). These men had positive memories of love and revealed that they were not embodying 'new' roles but were replicating previous good parenting models from their own family. As such, they practised in the present the positive and warm parenting they received in the past and offered examples which included both their mothers and their fathers. For example, George (Romanian, resident, 46) explains how his role as an intimate father for his teenage adoptive son is merely a rendition of intergenerationally transmitted patterns that he became aware of in time:

> I recognize things that I do now, and I remember that he used to do them as well. For example, before I was married, when I was alone, I wouldn't have imagined that I could sit at the dinner table and not touch my food until the moment that my child finishes eating, just to make sure I can give him some more to eat if he wants to (…) I remembered that he used to do similar things and I realized that probably this is what it means to be a parent. To put the other's good above your own (…) I took this model from my parents and I merely tried to improve it a bit.

In addition, Stewart (Scottish, non-resident, 53), a self-professed similar father, describes how his fathering was influenced by his adoptive father rather than his biological one:

> Everything I've actually learned about parenting has actually come from (…) well the person I actually call my dad – who obviously isn't my biological dad – he had two kids from a previous relationship as well, so it was similar to the circumstances that I actually found myself in (…)

At 53 years of age and with his third child from a second marriage, Stewart also reflects on how he is attempting to embody the intimate father's role at an older age. He does this by considering his age in contrast with his own father's age and learning from previous emotionally positive and negative experiences:

(...) when you're a child you are steered by and governed by how you were parented and that leads on to when you are an adult and you become a parent yourself. The only guidelines you actually have is how you were parented yourself. And a lot of times, people say 'my mum used to do this and my dad used to do that, and I absolutely hated it, and if I ever have children I'll never do that myself'. Right, everybody does it. So, it's a learning experience. To learn from all the things that weren't negative, but also the positive things (...) Most people when they get to my age are actually thinking of heading towards their retirement, not to the rest of it now. But I've lived my life and I'm going through this again. It's a rebirth and I'm delighted.

Moreover, John (Scottish, resident, 36) also reflected on age-related fathering by comparison to his father:

My dad was always busy and I think if I was to really nit-pick I would say I would have liked a bit more time with him, and I maybe didn't realize how open I could've been with him, as a teenager and things you're going through stuff thinking that they don't understand. But in time I realized that they actually do. I was the youngest of five, so my parents were slightly older and I think that can really change the dynamic as well. Maybe that's why I was used to my dad coming home and saying 'Oh, I'm really tired!' 'cause not only was he busy, but he was old (...) You're almost like a mirror of your parents in some respects.

Lastly, Gordon (Scottish, resident, 36) thought he wanted to be like his father, although he was worried that he was *less* involved:

He was very involved and very engaged. He was a very positive role-model. How do I differ? It's a bit of a tough act to follow, I would say. Because I work full-time, I do try to be around. I do try to help out. I do try and make dinners. I definitely change plenty of nappies, but I know for a fact I'm not around as much as he was when I was little (...) just purely because financially, it's different times. We don't have the sort of disposable income that they did, so I'm not sure that they'll have the same (...) but I don't know 'cause they're still so young. Certainly, I'm not around as much as my dad was. I know that.

Due to the distinct familial and financial discrepancies he experiences now, in comparison to his childhood (when his father went on an indefinite medical leave from his birth onwards), Gordon describes his concerns about not being able to provide as properly for his children as his dad did; according to him, he and his brother also had better educational opportunities while growing up. He is faced now with a well-paid but hour-intensive job and having to raise his two sons in economically austere times, mostly through breadwinning fathering. He bemoans the lack of the same gratuities and subsidized activities that he and his brother had in his childhood. These quotes reflect how even similarity is a complex emotional experience in intergenerational transmission and does not necessarily lead to adopting the intimate father's role in the present.

Ambivalent Fathers

The third category comprised ambivalent fathers, who were mostly from the Scottish group; slightly less than the large group of different fathers, and considerably more than similar fathers, ambivalent fathers were perhaps the most theoretically interesting to investigate. These were fathers trying to be different but consistently found themselves falling back on an unconscious emotional pattern. I would interpret this as trying to maintain an emotional connection to their father, which would not be easily be shrugged off, because of a feeling of pride and a shared sense of continuity with their father's masculinity (even if that type of masculinity was aggressive or toxic). Ambivalence could also be linked to affective practice or, in this case, how fathers *do* love, and Ian Burkitt's supports this by explaining how emotions trickle down into the present from our past biographies:

> Affective practice (…) carries forward the moods, feelings and values that come from our past biography, orienting us within the present and towards the future (…) these are disruptive possibilities that will no doubt spark a range of ambivalent, contradictory and alternating emotions – fear, excitement, resistance and longing for the new – working themselves out in complex ways as they attempt to both close us off from, and open us up to, the change that the future brings. (Burkitt 2014, p. 171)

Burkitt reflects in his quote on a state of *emotional ambivalence* in relation to temporality, which denotes how the past meets the presents in constructing the future in fluid ways, by influencing emotions and constructing identities. Furthermore, in Julia Brannen's research (2003) ambivalence in the context of the father's identity is discussed as an ongoing tension between continuity and change: 'Ambivalences have to be managed; they are not resolvable' (p. 101). What this means is that conflicts between reproduction and innovation are inherent within crafting the fathering role in relation to masculine emotionality, as these roles arise from within the nexus of power, relating, sexuality (and I would add, emotions) that construct family lives. To my mind then, this ambivalence is created through the process of emotional bordering, as fathers shift from stoicism to increased love, by reflecting on their memories of love (so on their past emotions) and matching these in their current relationships by working through any doubts or worries. This complex process might entail emotional 'rollercoaster moments', which nonetheless have the potential to help fathers embody the intimate role and *move* them from traditional stoic fathering.

In this research, ambivalences appeared mostly in the Scottish than in the Romanian fathers' accounts and were closely resembling what Anthony Giddens described as a push towards increased democratic conducts in intimate relationships (1992). These changes clashed with the dominant form of stoic masculinity, at times unconsciously performed by fathers in circumstances where paternal power was affirmed through aggression (Connell 2005). For example, Nicholas (Scottish, resident, 38) reflects on how he is adapting prevalent cultural stereotypes regarding love from his childhood, to his intimate form of fathering, with his daughter:

> (…) in the common British collective, you earn your father's love and you have your mother's unconditional love. But I don't feel that way. She doesn't have to earn my love (…) Generationally, I think it's interesting (…) You wanted the respect of your father more than you wanted the love of your father.

Some fathers focused on both parents as core figures for how they parent their own children in the present. Logan describes a form of ambivalence he experiences from both of his parents and how his daughter's relational initiatives are slowly changing his emotionality through their everyday intimate interactions:

My mum and dad and my grandparents, they're quite reserved. I can remember thinking (…) that I couldn't remember the last time I hugged my dad. And that's quite a sad thought and there's not a great deal of value put on it (…) I'll probably end up the same. The thing is you naturally hug a little kid all the time. It just comes up. They follow you. You hug them. You put them to bed and you hug them. It happens all the time, whereas it will happen less often when they're fifteen and they don't want you near them (…) I guess looking back on your own experience – you put value on.

On the other hand, the themes which appear in the narratives of Romanian fathers include (a) *engaging in a process of building a reflexive self* and (b) a focus on transforming *one's own masculine aggression* and improving communication with the children (i.e. 'civilizing' those negative tendencies inherited from their own fathers). In this manner for both groups, intimate and interdependent power (which I expand upon in Chap. 3) coexisted with democratic exchanges in the relationships in which fathers reproduced their intimate role.

For example, Lucian (Romanian, resident, 38), the father to a three-year-old son, expresses a more ambivalent view of how his fathering flows into his present identity as a dad by also underlining his son's agency in helping him border towards increased intimacy:

I've realised that actually I also do the same mistakes, that I too have a problem with saying to him [that he loves him] – and I actually know why, because I too was raised in a family in which there wasn't much talk about emotions, and sometimes they would explode in a powerful way. So it is. Probably, the generation of our parents was in general less open to such things [clears throat]. I don't know, maybe we're managing now to open up more, even verbally [smiles]. Besides, I believe that Pavel understands very well what I feel for him, we hug, we caress, recently I've noticed that – I think in the last week or two – he started caressing my face; it's a sign of tenderness, but I'm not sure how conscious he is of it, and how learned this is. But even if he lacks a full understanding, he still does it, because he sees how I react, that I like it.

In other parts of the interview, Lucian expands on the context of his family, in which emotions were usually repressed; he was one of the fathers who resisted love, discussed in Chap. 2. His relationship with his father was one of evident authority, in the unfolding of which Lucian received regular physical punishments. Having acquired some psychological knowledge from attending parenting courses, Lucian was aware of a potential transmission of this pattern of relating, and he was trying not to replicate the toxic fathering he had received. This shows the influence of psychologizing discourses (Illouz 2012) on how Lucian's self as a father is shaped by emotional bordering. He found it difficult to incorporate intimacy into the rigid emotional borders he had been taught to maintain through self-described emotionally intense and physically demanding interactions with his own father, which resulted in increased stoicism. However, he had achieved a middle ground of bordering due to his son's ability to lower Lucian's intergenerationally transmitted rigid bordering, by relating to him with tenderness. The intimacy created in the present with his son can allow for change to happen, as Lucian finds himself responding positively to his son's practice of love. Lucian's example brings forth the 'creative tension (…) between processes of reproduction and innovation' (Brannen 2003, 3.1) in the achievement of intimate fathering.

The intergenerational transmission of love feeds into men's identity formations as involved fathers, constructing new *memories of love* which fathers rely upon to build their own intimate role and reflexively assess how loving they can be with their children as they preserve their masculinity. When the quality of these memories of love seemed to be reflected upon negatively, fathers assessed their involvement as being *better* than their own fathers. Overall, most fathers aimed towards changing, if not their entire approach, then at least some aspects of their fathering from the ones they mentioned they received from their own fathers (even similar fathers mentioned some improvements). Some fathers preferred to rely solely on direct interaction with the child and learning how to father through *trial-and-error* rather than relying on their relatives' advice on parenting, mostly because of the outdated nature of the information they received from their parents; this finding echoes previous research on fathers (Backett 1982).

3 Memories of Love: Fathers' Emotions in Relation to Their... 85

Less ambivalence was noticeable in the Romanian group of fathers. There was clarity that their types of fathering were distinct from their parents in bringing up the children, also because of the resources available at their disposals, after the fall of communism. But the new consumerist abundance had to be navigated with care (because of an increase in car traffic on public roads for example). In this careful assessment, using common sense in how one distributes this new material abundance in relation to instilling generosity in children were skills to teach their children about an overall sense of value, as Bogdan (Romanian, resident, 50) describes:

> We have tried to offer him – at least from my part as a father – I was raised at the countryside, and at the countryside, even during Ceauşescu's times, everything was rather limited. We used to be very happy if we got a piece of candy. I have tried as a parent, to give him things which I couldn't have. Just not in an exaggerated way, but within the limits of our possibilities, and to impose limits so as not to harm him (…) so that he won't become dependent (…) to teach him to give to someone else too, to share with someone else a toy, a piece of candy, a biscuit.

In addition, some Romanian fathers mentioned changes in relation to being left mostly on their own in their childhoods, to providing increased protection for their children in the present, as Liviu (Romanian, resident, 36) mentions:

> During winter-time grandma would come and stay with us, in the city. I was mostly brought up by my grandparents. I remember that in the first grade, when I was at the same age as my twins, I used to get a key around my neck – just like in that famous saying. In the first days my dad would take me to school. He worked, so I would rarely see him (…) I remember that I was the same age as my son and my daughter are now and I would go to school all by myself. Which I find completely bewildering now, what I was able to do and now I keep saying 'Oh my God, how can you leave the children alone around here!?' I don't know how we used to be [pause] either we are now much more protective of them, or our parents were a bit irresponsible.

For Liviu, reflecting on his childhood experiences brings about feelings of wonderment in the present and links to his desire and responsibility to protect his children better. Liviu's childhood story was echoed by a couple of other Romanian fathers, who mentioned growing up with their grandparents (or being raised mostly by them in some instances), which tends to happen for some Romanian families even nowadays, although the trend is decreasing in urban areas. The difference is that instead of spending time at the countryside where their grandparents would live, for contemporary families, the grandparents come to live in the city and provide a support service similar to that of professional childminders, only that it is unpaid, while both parents have to work during the day. This arrangement is hardly based on gender-egalitarian beliefs but on economic scarcity and a desire to have trust-worthy childcarers in the family home.

Bordering between Well-Being and Stress

An interesting aspect to fathers' embodiment was the practice of self-care. This adjacent finding appeared only in some accounts, although for fathers from both cultures. Those fathers that spoke of self-care seemed keenly aware of the need to take care of themselves in order to be there in the long-run for their children, not only relationally but also physically. Research has shown that younger children influence their father's bodies through the wear and tear of caregiving (Ranson 2015), even if they do so to a much lesser extent than with mothers. The involved fathers in my study spoke of practising self-care with a long-term perspective in mind and mostly through letting go of certain bad habits.[2] It could be then that involvement in childcare might positively contribute to men's health.[3]

Based on role considerations in relation to their own parents and the emotional bordering necessary to embody their new role in the present, fathers resorted to specific strategies of emotional bordering in emotionally

---

[2] For an in-depth discussion of how children's agency influenced fathers' health and well-being, see Macht A. (Macht 2019a, b) *The role of emotions and children's agency in improving fathers' health*, in Marc Grau-Grau and Hannah Riley Bowles 'Elevating Fatherhood', Springer (under review).

[3] This shows that, to a certain extent, fatherhood offers the opportunity to resist the practices of risk-taking and denial of treatment, which are harmful to men's health, and yet are assumed to uphold certain types of tough masculinity (O'Brien et al. 2009).

3 Memories of Love: Fathers' Emotions in Relation to Their... 87

stressful situations where the child was 'acting up' or there was some risk to the child's safety: (a) controlling their own emotions and sometimes hiding them from children to assert the image of a strong, stoic father or (b) expressing them and acting to change the feelings of the child, to assert care and intimate fathering, or (c) combining both stoicism with intimacy, in being their children's 'friends' (this strategy involved as well delegating the problem-solving to their partner). Generically, the aims of these bordering strategies were (a) to convert bad feelings into positive ones and (b) to restore calm after a tense emotional episode, without disrupting the relationship.

This shaped practices of love in many forms through compensatory embodied interactions such as using humour and being patient. For example, David (Scottish, resident, 38), an *ambivalent* father, describes how he uses humour as a type of emotion work to help sustain his son's routines and preserve positive closeness in the slightly frustrating situation of being challenged by his son:

> Sometimes rather than repeatedly saying something to the point of raising your voice, what I find is almost quite good is to distract them almost with something quite random. So I've this thing I do with Ethan if he's not listening or answering I put on this funny voice so I say let's see what I'm saying 'Ethan, do you want to come brush your teeth now?' If he doesn't answer I say it again, then I put on this funny voice (…) I count down from three to one and I go 'Three, two, one, Ethan do you want to brush your teeth [quickly said]' and he quite likes that, then he snaps back and says 'Why did you say that?', 'Because you wouldn't answer me; Come on let's go and brush your teeth' and he comes along. So this little sort of trick that you learn (…) you learn to know your child basically and what makes them tick and when they're likely to start acting up.

Lucian (Romanian, resident, 38), father to a four-year-old boy, describes an episode when his strategy of using humour to express his feelings was reflected to him by his son:

> I don't know, sometimes you express them also in a joke you know, or while playing. You tickle each other, you roll around, you mock-smack each other's bottoms, or mock-kick each other, but all for fun (…) Generally, I think we also manage to have laughs. He laughs a lot! (…) At one point I

remember how he made some jokes in a conscious way. (…) he said something and afterwards he said 'I was joking' [laughter]. And I said 'Okaaay' [looks surprised].

Humour could also take the form of sarcasm for fathers. Research has shown that fathers tend to employ sarcasm as an aggressive communication strategy with their children, irrespective of gender (Beatty and Dobos 1993).

Ewan (Scottish, resident, 36), a different father, recounts how, to him, a father's involvement relies on an emotional commitment to wanting to know his daughter, which is expressed through careful and embodied emotional bordering:

> You have to really intend to develop a relationship. Because they're so small and their world is so limited. You have to really not intrude but get into their world and make sure that they know who you really are – so, on a practical level, just taking every opportunity. If you change her nappy you don't do it like that [acts detached, as if he's not touching what he's supposed to touch] but change it like that [leans into the recorder and stares at it interested, while making quick movements with hands]. You make sure that it's a positive experience.

In his account, Ewan employs emotional bordering rather than emotion work because it is not only *what* he does but also *how* he does it that matters; in his perspective, caring for his daughter entails being emotionally involved. Also, while establishing emotional intimacy with his daughter in the acts of changing her nappy, he is also maintaining relational boundaries.

With older children, consistently more emotional reflexivity and self-disclosure is necessary in order to emotionally connect with them. For example, Mihai (Romanian, resident, 43), a *similar* father, has learned to read his son's moods and slowly bring out through patience and communication the relational dilemmas his son is experiencing:

> Well, I try to let him simmer down. Recently, he also started to let me simmer down too [laughter]. He understood. This seems to me to be the best method, because eventually it does happen that we all have some bad days

> (…) For example, I sometimes pick him up from his grandma's, because he goes there since the school is close to her place. I pick him up in the evening and I can see from how he walks down the stairs all the way until he reaches the car. And just by looking at him walking [he can tell] and I say 'How was it?' he goes 'Mmmm, fine'. We drive and then halfway through our trip, he starts to tell me that today he spoke with I-don't-know-whom and it made him really upset. And I say 'What has he done to you?' And then he tells me. If I would've forced him to speak to me on the spot, I wouldn't have gotten anything from him.

Therefore, emotional bordering is not only embodied but also reliant on a certain control of emotions which can be positively expressed as patience and planning. This included waiting for children to develop so they can do more age-appropriate things together, but also biding time and allowing their children to solve their own problems, by gently guiding them through conversation. This finding goes in line with research on the intergenerational transmission of emotional patterns between fathers and sons (Brannen 2015) but contradicts the view that men seldom support one another through intimate communication, preferring instead to physically engage in shared activities (Kimmel 2008). Despite 'doing love' in relation to their children and partners in different ways, fathers also talked about the fluid borders between these two forms of love, even if they did not value their verbal expressions of love as much as they preferred actions (as discussed in Chap. 2).

Involved fathers' role constructions (as similar, ambivalent or different to their own fathers) influence how they bordered emotionally, through their everyday practice of putting in the emotional work to sustain relationships. However, if emotion work describes how they maintained closeness and love in their interactions with other family members, bordering points towards how fathers reflected on the emotions they controlled and released in close interactions and how these formed part of their intimate father's role or had to be readjusted to fit the chosen role according to the corresponding situation. These emotional moments are akin to what previous research on fatherhood called 'rollercoaster moments' (Åsenhed et al. 2014). They are the emotional ups and downs described by fathers in the process of caring for their children, which are generally initiated by the child and as usually involving considerable stress. Such negative emotional experiences would bring out ambivalences. In relation to this, fathers also described the importance of taking care of their own physical needs such as having eaten and gotten enough rest. Furthermore, Gavin, an ambivalent father (Scottish, resident, 53), describes how emotional bordering, referred to here as 'coping', is spurred on by domestic work in everyday interactions with his children:

> You invest a lot of time and effort in trying to get them to do the right thing. A lot can be very repetitive and that can be quite hard work. Again it comes back again to how well-rested you are, how well you cope with that. But I think you don't ever lose sight of [the fact] that they are your children and you are doing it for a reason. You persevere at things.

However, it was not only being a well-rested father that helped maintain positive feelings but also having well-rested children. If both family members were well-rested, this could help contain negative moments and the surge of emotionally transmitted ambivalences and maintain emotional intimacy between fathers and children, as Ian describes:

> It's very important and well rested kids are good kids and you can do anything with good kids, they're resilient if they had a good sleep, the only thing I've really learned from all of these books is make sure your kids get a good sleep they will be resilient to anything during the day, they can cope with it because they're not tired.

Therefore, maintaining a positive close relationship included intimate fathering and child's agency, and it was described by some Scottish and some Romanian fathers as a mutual process of relating emotionally to their children from a well-rested, re-energized place. Much like the group of men who reflected on how their health was improved by having a child in the first chapter, Gavin refers to being rested, which points towards practices of self-care that sustain an embodied emotional bordering. It has been previously discussed that emotion work is performed through the body, as emotions arise physically and require interpretation (Chandler 2012); in much the same way, emotional bordering expresses itself through the body, in constructing relational boundaries. Fathering then doesn't involve only tapping into emotional responsibility but also into embodied and temporal resources.

Emotional Bordering During Conflicts and Bad Days

To resolve conflicts, calm their children down but also control their own potentially negative outbursts of emotion, fathers would reason through their children's behaviour and contextualize it. In this sense, they took on the responsibility for the momentary charged emotional situation to preserve the notion of the child's 'purity of intention' (Jamieson 1998; Lupton 2013), dismissing the potential of anything being inherently 'bad' about the child. They also attributed bad days to their own lack of being able to make use of emotional reflexivity, rather than their children's especially bad behaviour or capacity to test the fathers on purpose. For example, Florin (Romanian, resident, 35) describes such an occurrence:

> More often I see difficult moments as a provocation, and I feel like I want to snap (să răbufnesc[4]). But I stop, because the blame is with me, she has nothing to do with it. I then automatically come back to normal. I erase what happened and focus on what I have to do. I stop everything and maybe this is why I spoil her too much.

Florin describes applying emotional management to avoid snapping at his daughter and thereby damaging their connection. In this episode, he employs emotional reflexivity in becoming aware that his daughter is not acting out on purpose to annoy him; as such, he borders on stoicism to paradoxically perform the involved father's role and maintain intimacy. Other strategies to resolve 'emotionally heavy' moments were (a) remaining *patient and calm* and (b) shifting to physical displays of affection rather than verbal explanations, further reinforcing the doing of love.

---

[4] The original Romanian term.

What is interesting to observe is that fathers seem to be describing that emotion work is embedded within the process of emotional bordering, and how it emerges indeed as a practice (Scheer 2012). This work was necessary in situations where emotional reflexivity was temporarily stunted or when practical decisions were necessary, although it could also be complemented by it. It could be ascertained that contrary to Arlie Hochschild's (1979, 1983/2003) understanding of 'surface' and 'deep' acting in emotion work, the use of emotional bordering enhances this previous concept by alerting social actors to the fact that a processual interaction is taking place. Thus, social relations are created as two social actors internalize and externalize their emotions through communication and embodiment, in circumstantial and spontaneous ways.

In this sense, emotional bordering becomes the process of intimately relating through emotions, as much as in the act of relating, emotions are created and lived out. It is for this reason that feeling rules are not just emotional rules 'floating about' in society; they are imposed by and fine-tuned in social interactions by people for other people. Feeling rules are linked to gender norms (Connell 2005) and can emphasize tension points where there are differences in the interests of social actors. This leads to misunderstandings and conflicts as opposing emotions meet and cannot blend (e.g. frustration with joy, anger with love) and have the capacity to temporarily unbalance the relationship. For example, Ben (Scottish, resident, 57), a father who strongly considers himself *different* than his own father, admits to 'drawing on inner reserves' when his children are testing his patience in difficult moments. If he is angry with them, he resorts to *apologizing* to his daughter, as a strategy of emotional bordering:

> It's like drawing on reserves. You can lose it with your children. You can get angry and pissed off with them. You can and I think that's fine. I think it's important that you do actually, because I think they need to see that you are also a human with (…) you're not a robot (…) and also apologize to each other. I mean I apologized to my daughter this morning. I was a bit grumpy with her 'cause she just didn't get her shoes on quick enough and we were late for school and it was my fault, because I dallied you know [deep intake of breath] and I got grumpy and she got grumpy and then she said 'It was

your fault!' and she was actually right and I said 'Well ok, I'm sorry' and then she said 'Sorry'. I think that's, you know, an important part of our process.

Ben describes above how guilt motivates both family members to create necessary readjustments after a conflict, in order to re-establish love since closeness was momentarily compromised in their relationship.

Possessiveness

Reflecting on possessiveness[5] in fathers' emotional discourses, revealed the intermingling of love and power in intimate relationships. In these cases, possessiveness was intimately linking the child's whole being to the father's sense of self and was preponderantly incorporated into how Romanian fathers constructed love and how they legitimated it, compared to Scottish fathers. Possessiveness was shown by exclamations such as 'he's mine/my child', but which had to be tempered. For example, Nelu (Romanian, resident, 34) associated possessiveness with an 'ego boost' which had to be kept under control:

> Yes, I tell him I love him but I don't know how to tell him. I have a feeling of attachment. We are together, we love each other, and we do things one for the other. Theorizing this doesn't work for me. He's simply my son and I love him. I'm not trying. Even if I have some tendency I try to stomp this genetic tendency down, this 'He's my boy!' [makes a grumpy, determined voice] because I don't think it's fair. It creates some premises (…) I'd prefer it, if he is himself whoever he might become and then I try not to think of it as 'He's my boy!' [grumpy, determined voice again]. Only when I'm joking, yes.

This could have been Nelu's means to convey to me, during the interview, the prevalent Romanian value of modesty (Voicu 2008), as his character trait, and especially in how he understands his son in relation to

---

[5] Kemper (1978) does also refer to power as a sense of 'possession' that binds two romantic partners together, a theory I explore in the next chapter.

allowing him the accomplishment of 'natural growth' (Lareau 2003). The concept of possessiveness, in the context of parent-child relationships, might be related to an increase in closeness and intimacy, as it has been shown that in romantic relationships, experiencing jealousy and control can be linked to an intensifying emotional intimacy (Attridge 2013).

Unlike Romanian fathers, the narratives of Scottish fathers tended to emphasize a growing individualism in their children; they would generally refrain from using possessive pronouns but hint more at how they saw themselves 'reflected' in their children and, interestingly, in their youngest child, who was often deemed as 'more emotional'. Patrick (Scottish, resident, 42), a father of two girls, describes how his younger daughter's emotional intensity constitutes for him a 'looking-glass self' (Cooley 1902 in Cook and Douglas 1998):

> With Celeste, it's very powerful. For example she's watching a programme, and it was a film – they put a rabbit in a pram and shoved it down the hill – and she was in floods of tears 'cause she thought the rabbit would die. But it's a very similar way to how I would've reacted at her age and I remember it distinctly watching programmes and feeling exactly the same way. So, of course that erupts emotionally for me. She doesn't want people to get hurt and it's all very aware. She's just there, there's no middle-ground. Whereas with Morgan it's very thoughtful and she's worked out what she's going to say and there's no immediate burst of emotion, which on an intellectual level I think it's powerful. But then with Celeste it's very instant. It's right there! And that totally catches me by surprise, and I start to feel emotional as well. I think it's quite overpowering (…) in a nice way, but it's different.

The 'looking-glass self' refers to the process of becoming an individual, through seeing the self in a constant reflection with other people's emotions and opinions (Cooley 1902 in Cook and Douglas 1998). Through the process of socialization, and by adhering to social norms, in interactions with others, culture also plays a big contribution to the development of the self. If children are usually intensely subjected to such socialization, in the quote above, Patrick also refers to how his daughter's emotional outburst find a reflection within himself, denoting the processual nature of feelings rather than assuming they are merely individualized 'interiors' (Burkitt 2014). Another important outcome is that his

3 Memories of Love: Fathers' Emotions in Relation to Their... 95

daughter is described as holding an emotional power 'over' him, overpowering him in a way which is deemed as pleasant, constituting a mutual emotional affinity. Like Kemper's theorization, Patrick confers status to his youngest daughter by valuing her emotionality; through this, he is matching her value to the memory he has of himself at her age. By finding it a good match, he can transfer some of his power to his daughter, and in the process, valuing her emotionality and loving her more.

Nonetheless, it was not only emotional intensity which could be 'mirrored'. In time, fathers of older children described how their initial feelings of nurturance and love turned into pride for their child's achievements, as they reached adolescence. Mihai (Romanian, resident, 43) recounts below how his love turned into pride, in a quote where is 'engendering'[6] the expectations he has from his son—he wants him to be successful, intelligent and popular with girls by reinforcing heteronormativity, while simultaneously expressing his positive hope for his child's future, in his capacity as a caring father:

> Now it's more a sense of pride [laughter]. I mean I'm thinking if he has good results, that he has a girlfriend, who is not the first and won't be his last [laughter] and that in general when he likes something he manages to do it well. He catches on quickly. Yes, it's pride and I hope that, I don't know (…) I hope to see him finally becoming a successful guy.

In the following quote, Ray (Scottish, resident, 51) describes how he sees himself in his son, while raising him to be 'better' than him, by protecting him:

> He's everything. He's my life (…) He's like a mini-me and that can be used in a negative way as well as a positive way, as is like a wee version of me that's growing up and I don't want him to become 'a me' but I want to make him better than what I am. I want him to become a better person than me. Become the person that I couldn't be. So he can be anything. He

---

[6] Here, I am using the term in a slightly playful manner. 'Engendering' is defined as the archaic form of 'begetting an offspring', particularly of a father (https://en.oxforddictionaries.com/definition/engender). Simultaneously, I am also trying to argue that Mihai is 'gendering' his expectations in relation to his son, as he wants his son to be a 'successful guy'—therefore, the term is employed in the sense of 'begetting/creating gendered expectations'.

can do anything (…) and I want the best for him (…) That's how I would describe it. As loving him and protecting him, keeping him away from the things that are wrong.

Through such resemblances, fathers see a portion of their own selves in their children, revealing a sense of interdependence which creates closeness in their relationship. They are also correcting some emotional patterns received from their own parents, and transmitting to their children a different set of values. Even if these continued to remain gendered: for girls, it emerged that there was an emphasis on protection and increased control, which might send the message of the limits of their power in what continues to be a 'man's world'. By expanding emotional bordering to include emotions such as possessiveness and pride into the 'love complex', these are then processually recreated in interactions with the child.

Separations

Other contexts which highlighted instances of emotion work were those of separations. Since love for the child was described as an active form of love, and reliant on embodied interactions, I was curious to understand what fathers felt when they were away from their children and if their love changed during such circumstances. Fathers across culture agreed that love was a constant feeling even if it wasn't shown all the time. Hugh (Scottish, resident, 36) described it as 'ebbing and flowing' in different ways since his focus fell on other preoccupations, such as work, when he wasn't close to his family members.

Separations could be grouped into (a) daily expected separations (dropping them at nursery or school and being at work), (b) slightly longer ones (going on trips for work, children attending camping trips or having separate holidays so parents could spend some time together) and (c) permanent ones (divorce). In this context, a father's use of emotion work was more intensified or diminished according to the type of separation experienced. Distances influenced fathers' emotional bordering, as missing their children gradually loosened the rigidity imposed by stoic bordering. Men relied on emotion work to prevent from feeling disconnected from their children but also because any emotional anxieties created by such separations had to be kept at bay; worry would reinforce intimacy but the emotional anxiety it created would invade the stoic construction of their masculine identities, which was something men described that they had to protect themselves against; the construction of masculinity based on the control of anxiety has been previously discussed in the literature (Pleck 1981). Ian (Scottish, resident, 36) kept control over any feelings of worry by making sure everything is alright at home before departing on a work-related trip:

> I've been away for work for about two or three weeks at a time and yes it's definitely there (…) though I think I can, I am able to compartmentalize it, if you'd like. For example, [when] I was in Australia last summer for two weeks, I wouldn't say I physically missed them every minute of the day. When I came back I was so pleased to see them, but I never worried about them while I was away. I certainly didn't feel any less love for them (…) Again, I think that's kind of a symptom of building the environment at home. I feel like I can leave them there – obviously with their mum as well – and the whole everything is clockwork (…) I feel they're protected in the bubble I've created for them. I don't feel that the emotional strain is there, if I have to leave them for any period of time.

Ian describes how a routinized stable home environment helps him perform emotion work by controlling negative feelings such as worry and maintaining love. He also was reproducing the masculine account of a middle-class man of reason (Connell 2005) while also letting me know that he is a 'good father'. What exists throughout his account is the invisible support of his wife, whose presence at home while he is away ensures that the 'bubble' of protection he has created for his family is maintained. Furthermore, Nelu (Romanian, resident, 34), who was in a stable residential relationship with his wife and had close contact with his son, acknowledged that when he experiences separations from his son, he reasons through his feelings and comes to the conclusion that he's not really missing his son, even if he continues to think of him:

> Yes, as long as I know that he is safe and ok, I don't have (…) I mean the feeling of missing someone to me is just a state of anxiety. I hope nothing bad happens, and that our separation will not be a definitive one, that the child will allow me back into the home [grimaces] but aside from that as long as I know that that he is alright, that he's playing [it's fine].

Nelu's emotional bordering in relation to missing his son is done to keep any anxiety at bay; he even marks the moment with a joke. By having prior emotional knowledge of generally being on good terms with his son and of the temporary nature of their separation, Nelu transforms any potential negative emotion into love. Even if some fathers were worried about the outcomes of the separations, they were surprised to find out that their children reacted positively to the time spent apart. Working through a temporary feeling of loss was done by reconsidering the child's emotional detachment from them as a sign of a growth in their autonomy and a confirmation that stoic parenting gives rewards. For example, Emil (Romanian, resident, 37), the father of two daughters, describes how this took place with Sabina, his eldest daughter[7]:

> When she was three years old, I sent her by herself to a camp. My girl went to a camp with other children and their nursery (...) she was the youngest kid in the group because all the other children were over five years old and she was delighted to prepare her own luggage, to go there and make the fire. She didn't even want to talk on the phone with us because she was feeling too good.
>
> Int: And how did you experience being away from her?
>
> Difficult, very difficult (...) but easy at the same time. We were those kind of parents who took Sabina everywhere with us, all the time (...) it was stressful because we thought 'What is our child going to do? She has never been anywhere on her own without us, she hasn't slept anywhere else'. But at the same time it was relaxing because we've managed for a week to go out, see some movies, take care of us (...) For her, it was a moment of 'Wow, I can do it!' (...) she came home grinning from ear to ear.

In certain situations, fathers were not comfortable with being away from their children. This seemed to be irrespective of child's gender, although it appeared preponderantly with little children. Hamish (Scottish, resident, 52) describes below what he experienced the first time his daughter and partner had to travel without him. The situation of being away from his daughter made him realize how emotionally connected he

---

[7] Sabina was four years old at the time of the interview.

was to her. This was not a comfortable realization, as it came shrouded in anxiety:

> I was going to meet them off the train when I first came back – and this was the first time I've been apart from her a long time – and it was just this incredible release of emotion just because I got to be missing her so much after so few days. So I think that was the most striking thing about it. It was the first time that I realized how emotionally tied I was to her. And I've gone through that again a couple of times since. I had to be apart for extended periods, but also there are some times you can get some crazy idea in your head which provokes completely irrational emotions. You have fears about terrible accidents which I was quite glad to hear that I'm not the first who goes through it. It's that: 'Will you get a grip man! You've just constructed that terrible situation in your head. There's no reason to suspect that will ever happen, so just stop it.

Hamish portrays how the fear of losing someone he is connected to emotionally was what created the worry. Worry thus is constructed in an interdependent manner, as an emotion which supports paternal involvement. Therefore, accounts which refer to male anxiety as something that is locked 'within' (Pleck 1981) do not seem to portray fathers' complex emotional experiences as sustained intimate interactions with others in their family. Even if apart, time spent away from the child had a certain limit, determined by feelings of impatience and missing the child for both parents, as Ovidiu (Romanian, resident, 34) describes:

> Last week we were away without him. We left on a Friday and came back on a Sunday. Already on Friday night it felt as if we tore away from him, and I know it sounds different – but it was good for us to be able to focus just on us as a couple. By Saturday we already missed him quite profoundly and by Sunday we were almost mad to see him.

In other situations, the father acted as the main source of emotional support when the child's mother had to be away. Mark (Scottish, resident, 36) describes how because his partner had to tackle a personal family issue, he went through a period of taking on more involvement in his son's life. This, in turn, not only helped him learn more about the level of his involvement as a father but also liberated his wife from the weight of maternal expectations for intensive involvement (Hays 1996):

> My partner spent a lot of time away, sorting things out, going and seeing her mum every day before she died and all that kind of stuff. That was pretty emotional because my son (…) at the time he couldn't understand why his mum wasn't there. It was the first time that she'd been away for more than a night or two. She was away for quite a few weeks. So that was a bit different and difficult and it got to the point where, he wouldn't settle at night because his mom wasn't there. So yeah that was pretty tough, but we got through it (…) because of my job I have to be very organized and I just had that as part of his daily routine. I'd get all of his clothes out, days in advance (…) so I got into a routine very quickly: picked him up from nursery, got home, gave him his dinner, put him in the bath and just changed in his room and get everything ready for him, doing little bits and bobs (…) So yeah, that was quite a tough time but in the same way it's quite a good thing because now she is a lot more confident and happier to be away from him.

In his wife's absence, Mark took on not only more domestic work but also more emotion work. He resolved his own emotional upheaval at seeing his son missing his mother and resolved it and made his relationship with his son stronger, as Mark admits that 'we got through it'. The aim of this emotion work was also to make his partner feel happier. This shows how father-child emotion work is embedded within larger practices of love in the family such as those that involved the mother as well, even when she is not physically present. It's important to mention that unlike most Scottish fathers I interviewed, Mark and his partner did not have support from their kin network nor did they employ any childminders.

Distances could affect the emotional connections between fathers and their children, but reunions offered opportunities for relational reparations and re-establishing intimacy. While describing that he is certainly able to 'compartmentalize' his emotions when away from his family, Rod (Scottish, resident, 37) found himself in the uncomfortable situation of having to 'pay back' emotionally for temporarily having lost touch with his children. He explains how the intensity of the emotional bond he shares with his eldest son seems to diminish once he is away, and how he has to work at 'rebuilding' it once he returns home:

(…) I don't like being away, because then I come back and you definitely have to have a bonding rebuilding with the kids. And more so with Harry as well 'cause I sense he has a bit of 'Well you disappeared for a week. I'm fine so I get on, on my own. Don't feel you have to.' So, we rebuild that again (…) I feel you need to be physically there, for it to stay on a constant high.

Rod's quote points towards the demands of intimate fathering which conflict with the provider's role, and the need to keep working at maintaining a positive and close emotional connection to his son. Intimacy might then be rejected by some fathers who not only feel it is threatening their stoic emotional bordering (and, by extension, a sense of their masculine self) but because the amount of emotion work and emotional reflexivity required to foster intimate connections contradicts the rational demands of their work-load and the emotional detachment necessary to their work-mobility. Other involved fathers bridge separations through media devices such as smartphones and laptops. What I have referred to as a 'fathering from afar' practice was also replete with emotional contradictions. Logan (Scottish, resident, 34) discusses the tensions implicit in trying to find time for himself and time with his daughter, as he both misses her when he is away and yet feels simultaneously relieved from the responsibility of having to be there for her:

Occasionally I get sent to Dublin for a day or two. The first time that happened – that would've been when she was about four months – and at that point I really wasn't getting a lot of sleep, because she was up every two or three hours in the night all the time (…) so actually on an objective level I was really looking forward to being away for a couple of nights and getting a full night's sleep [and] what I actually did with myself when I was away, was sit and look at photos of her on my phone. That was odd and I was really aware of it (…) so I face-timed home to Rosie and Maeve. It's funny because we show her videos on phones and iPads and (…) she watches them, which means that instantly she doesn't realize when we do Facetime, whether it's a video or it's real. When she realizes that she's interacting with you she completely lights up, starts shouting at you and point and scream. She runs off with the iPad or the phone, she runs off with you (…) and then she'll kiss the screen and it's just really nice. So I find that for even being away for a day, you miss her.

Media devices certainly help in fostering emotional connections between social actors, in shifting and uncertain times (van Dijik 2013), but utilizing them could also function as a double-edged pathway, since it can entail the parents' higher surveillance of their children. Physical distance was also described in relation to a feeling that love was slowly 'dying', which added to situations of permanent relationship breakdown and the disappointment of not living up to expectations of intimate involvement. In such cases, father's emotional bordering was essential for bridging the divide and maintaining the loving relationship.

Worry

Challenging stoic bordering was a theme that appeared often throughout involved fathers' narratives and across culture: worry. Worrying was described as an emotion that preserved love but also could justify paternal control, much like possessiveness. David (Scottish, resident, 38), a father of two young children, explains love's connection to worry:

> I'm excited about the potential that they have (...) and at the same time there's this other thing which is like a lifetime of worry, you know? And it comes part and parcel, it's inextricably kinda interwoven, but that's just the nature of the beast you know? You can't separate them (...)

Ovidiu (Romanian, resident, 34) situates his worry in the context of his closeness to all family members, rather than as an individualized emotion, as David does above. He also describes being afraid of his own reactions sometimes:

> I think I'd be more afraid of my own expressions and actions. Worrying is indisputable and your fears are extremely profound and emphasized, because whatever happens to the child has an extremely influential effect on you. (...) I mean whatever was to happen to myself or my wife, we would be able to go over it easier than over any other event that would affect him.

3 Memories of Love: Fathers' Emotions in Relation to Their...   103

Tim (Scottish, non-resident, 30) describes that worry, much like love, can lie in the little things that constitute the everyday:

> (…) it's even stupid stuff. Like when he is upstairs in his room, I'll be worried about him and 'what if somebody climbs in the loft and he disappears?' and then you ran up the stairs and he's asleep. Or I get up to go to the toilet and you poke your head in his room and he's there and maybe peed himself [laughs] but it doesn't matter, he's still there you know. Things like 'Is he breathing?'. All sort of stupid paranoid stuff comes in your head.

Fathers believed love and worry coexist even if some to a larger and others to a lesser extent. There were variations in the causes of worry across culture. Interestingly, it was not actual fear in the present as the motivating cause of their worries but as something projected imaginatively as to what might happen in the future if something were to escape outside of their immediate control. Overall, Scottish fathers seemed remarkably more worried about their social reality and the world at large harming their child. Malcolm (Scottish, resident, 42) exemplifies this:

> (…) the first time they say 'Can I go to the shops myself?' you go [makes expression of horror]. 'No you can't!' And you sit there behind the bins looking to see if they're ok [laughter]. But they're ok. They do it, they're fine and I think worry does drive a lot of the things you do and it is bound into that. If you love somebody you don't want it damaged, so you worry about it, I suppose. But then you don't want to worry too much and control it, and you don't let it flourish to become what it can be. So it's difficult to strike the balance. There's a big grey area.

In addition, such as in Martin's case – who was the only father in the sample to take a similar amount of paternal leave as his partner (six months) – he changed how much he felt he could work in a week, due to worrying over his son:

> I spend quite a lot of time with Flynn over the past six months and it's quite hard coming back to work, 'cause he wasn't there all the time. It was like something's missing. But now that I know he's enjoying nursery, it's a little bit easier 'cause you don't worry about it so much. So yeah, it was nice

having that time off and spending it with him. Up until now definitely he's very much a daddy's boy and I don't know if that's because I spent so much time with him, like from six months to now. Whereas normally it would be the mother and I know most kids are more inclined to their mothers than their dads, but he definitely prefers me to his mum.

Because a group of five Scottish fathers included in the study were single parents engaged in different types of custodial arrangements with their ex-partners, they referred throughout their narratives of feeling worry because of their child's mother and her perceived negative influence or her current living arrangements, which might negatively influence their children's well-being and their relationship. Aside from this, they shared similar concerns about their children's physical safety and thinking of their well-being. For Romanian fathers, worry was mostly related to (a) the child getting ill and (b) the child putting himself at risk. However, Liviu (Romanian, resident, 36) describes having to control worry so as not to seem overprotective. He also underlines the importance of humour in dealing with negative emotions such as worry:

> (…) because the more you love the bigger your worries are, but you try not to worry for every little thing. To say 'Oh my God!' and suffocate them. You try and overcome it, I mean you try not to make things difficult (…) I try to let them fall down sometimes. I try to let them get some scrapes. Yes, I try even if it's harder. You kinda restrain yourself. Sometimes you make jokes 'Oh my God! Where have you been??' [said in a funny pitch]. As they're growing older I'll be like 'But where are they going? With whom are they going?' So I'm curious to know how they will react.

Most Romanian involved fathers shared that in these situations, they felt 'useless'. In these unexpected situations, fathers had to renounce their stoic image and display a certain degree of vulnerability, as they were faced with losing emotional control. Worry in these accounts helped sustain love because its presence was directly supporting the intensity of paternal love. However, in order to worry about the child, he or she had to be constructed as 'vulnerable' and in need of protection. As argued in earlier sections, feeling closeness can paradoxically also amplify control and possessiveness.

3 Memories of Love: Fathers' Emotions in Relation to Their... 105

For Scottish fathers, worry had the positive side of becoming a marker of displaying emotional involvement rather than detachment and underlined the immediate lowering of the stoic border into nurturance. John (Scottish, resident, 36) exemplifies this by showing how worry is blended with possessiveness and anger in terms of how much he loves his daughter in such a 'rollercoaster' moment:

> There was a time when Emma went to a friend's for a sleep-over and it was one of her firsts. I think she must've been about four or five, and I was a bit unsure I was like 'Hmmm I dunno. She maybe be a bit young'. She went to the sleep-over and we got a phone-call a couple of hours later that she had got her fingers stuck in the door and the tip of her finger was hanging off. Boy was that emotional! I was like 'Right. Raw raw raw' [laughter]. So her friends' mum had taken her to the hospital and I went to the hospital to get her and the range of emotions I had was just 'I'm mad at you! I'm worried about you! I feel upset because you're hurt and I'm going to protect you and nothing like this is going to happen to you ever again' and just quite a rollercoaster. All because she hurt her finger. I mean they fixed it and they stitched it back together, but it was all 'I'll do anything for you. Do you want me to get this? Do you want me to get that? Do you need a magazine? Here's a new cuddly toy?'. So it was kind of the sadness of wanting to protect her, the anger at somebody who let it happen – who obviously didn't let it happen but was supposed to be looking out for them (…) I hadn't experience that before. It was 'You are my girl and I am going to raaawww!'

However, by facing danger despite feeling powerlessness, fathers regained a feeling of power if they responded by rising to social expectations of dominant masculine conduct in order to overcome momentary obstacles. This situation would seem to reproduce hegemony rather than transform it, a point echoed in the literature on masculinity (Hearn and Šmidova 2015), but it also shows the reflective and relational character of men's power in intimate settings. In the following chapter, I expand on some of these contextual aspects of fathers' power and analyse how it functions as an emotion within the love relational complex in fathers' relationship with their children and their romantic partners.

Conclusion

This chapter reflected on the links between intergenerational transmission and emotional bordering by analysing how fathers' relationship with their children is influenced by their own parents. By reflecting on memories of love (i.e. the love that they received from their own parents or its absence), involved fathers adopt different ways of bordering emotionally to create three potential fathering identities: ambivalent, different and similar. In addition, everyday moments of high emotional intensity or 'rollercoaster moments' have highlighted involved fathers' emotional bordering in maintaining closeness and preserving the love that they feel for their children. Conclusively, the extent to which these strategies have been handed down (or resisted) from their own parents and actively negotiated in the present with family members contributes not only to the ongoing relational reparations needed to preserve loving closeness to their children but also to the ongoing reproduction of fathers' masculinity and their stoic discourse. Furthermore, worry was mentioned often in relation to emotion work and was understood as playing an important part in enacting control and protection in how fathers *fathered*. Some cultural differences were noted: as Scottish fathers seemed to be preponderantly worried about external and potentially harmful sources of danger in their children's environment while Romanian fathers were more worried that if their children were left unsupervised, they would get sick and put themselves at unnecessary risk.

With their children, they can use humour, physical touch, apologies and patience in order to diffuse conflicts and emotionally border into the intimate father's role. If involved fathers' love is mainly understood as a set of emotional practices, and these practices are intergenerationally transmitted, then different and similar fathers were more comfortable than others in expressing their emotions to family members while ambivalent fathers acknowledged that they have learned to do so in time. Such findings support Ian Burkitt's view of emotions as constituting a complex (2014) since the examples given by fathers' show how their emotions are created in sets of different relationships with each family member. Furthermore, fathers' worry and emotional vulnerability provide further evidence that contest the omnipotence of male power and remind that the 'myth of male invincibility' has its limitations (Pleck 1981).

References

Anderson, A. M. (1996). The Father–Infant Relationship; Becoming Connected. *Journal of the Society of Pediatric Nurses, 1*, 83–92.

Åsenhed, L., Kilstam, J., Alehagen, S., & Baggens, C. (2014). Becoming a Father Is an Emotional Roller Coaster: An Analysis of First-Time Fathers' Blogs. *Journal of Clinical Nursing, 23*(9–10), 1309–1317.

Attridge, M. (2013). Jealousy and Relationship Closeness: Exploring the Good (Reactive) and Bad (Suspicious) Sides of Romantic Jealousy. *SAGE Open, 3*(1), 1–16.

Backett, K. C. (1982). *Mothers and Fathers: A Study of the Development and Negotiation of Parental Behaviour*. London: Palgrave Macmillan.

Barnett, R. C., & Baruch, G. K. (1987). Determinants of Fathers' Participation in Family Work. *Journal of Marriage and Family, 49*(1), 29–40.

Beatty, M. J., & Dobos, J. A. (1993). Direct and Mediated Effects of Perceived Father Criticism and Sarcasm on Females' Perceptions of Relational Partners' Disconfirming Behavior. *Communication Quarterly, 41*(2), 187–197.

Bowlby, J. (1969). *Attachment and Loss – Vol. 1: Attachment*. New York: Basic Books.

Brannen, J. (2003). Towards a Typology of Intergenerational Relations: Continuities and Change in Families. *Sociological Research Online, 8*(2), 1–11.

Brannen, J. (2015). *Fathers and Sons: Generations, Families and Migration*. Basingstoke/New York: Palgrave Macmillan.

Brannen, J., & Nilsen, A. (2006). From Fatherhood to Fathering: Transmission and Change among British Fathers in Four-Generation Families. *Sociology, 40*(2), 335–352.

Burkitt, I. (2014). *Emotions and Social Relations*. London: Sage.

Chandler, A. (2012). Self-Injury as Embodied Emotion Work: Managing Rationality, Emotions and Bodies. *Sociology, 46*(3), 442–457.

Connell, R. W. (2005). *Masculinities* (2nd ed.). Berkeley: University of California Press.

Cook, W. L., & Douglas, E. M. (1998). The Looking-Glass Self in Family Context: A Social Relations Analysis. *Journal of Family Psychology, 12*(3), 299–309.

Freud, S. (1919). *Totem and Taboo: Resemblances Between the Psychic Lives of Savages and Neurotics*. London: Routledge & Sons.

Gabb, J., & Fink, J. (2015). *Couple Relationships in the 21st Century*. Basingstoke: Palgrave Pivot.

Hays, S. (1996). *The Cultural Contradictions of Motherhood*. Yale: University Press.

Hearn, J., & Šmidova, I. (2015). The Multiple Empires of Men. *Gender, Equal Opportunities Research, 16*(1), 74–82.

Hochschild, A. R. (1979). Emotion Work, Feeling Rules, and Social Structure. *American Journal of Sociology, 85*(3), 551–575.

Hochschild, A. R. (1983/2003). *The Managed Heart: Commercialization of Human Feeling*. Berkeley: University of California Press.

Hochschild, A. R. (2003). *The Commercialization of Intimate Life: Notes from Home and Work*. Berkeley/London: University of California Press.

Illouz, E. (2012). *Why Love Hurts: A Sociological Explanation*. Cambridge: Polity Press.

Jamieson, L. (1998). *Intimacy: Personal Relationships in Modern Societies*. Cambridge: Polity Press.

Kemper, T. D. (1978). *A Social Interactional Theory of Emotions*. New York: Wiley.

Lareau, A. (2003). *Unequal Childhoods: Class, Race, and Family Life*. Berkeley: University of California Press.

Kimmel, M. S. (2008). *Guyland: The Perilous World Where Boys Become Men*. New York: Harper Collins.

Lupton, D. (2013). Infant Embodiment and Interembodiment: A Review of Sociocultural Perspectives. *Childhood, 20*(1), 37–50.

Macht, A. (2019a, Forthcoming). Travelling Feelings: Narratives of Sustaining Love in Two Case Studies with Fathers in Family Separations. In L. Murray et al. (Eds.), *Families in Motion: Ebbing and Flowing Through Space and Time* (pp. 19–37). Bingley: Emerald Publishing.

Macht, A. (2019b). Shifting Perspectives: Becoming a Feminist Researcher While Studying Fatherhood and Love. *Vitae Scholasticae: The Journal of Educational Biography, 35*(2), ISSN: 0735-1909/eISSN: 0735-1909.

O'Brien, R., Hunt, K., & Hart, G. (2009). 'The Average Scottish Man Has a Cigarette Hanging Out of his Mouth, Lying There with a Portion of Chips': Prospects for Change in Scottish Men's Constructions of Masculinity and Their Health-Related Beliefs and Behaviours. *Critical Public Health, 19*(3–4), 363–381.

Pleck, J. H. (1981). *The Myth of Masculinity*. Cambridge, MA: MIT Press.

Ranson, G. (2015). *Fathering, Masculinity and the Embodiment of Care*. Basingstoke: Palgrave Macmillan.

Scheer, M. (2012). Are Emotions a Kind of Practice (And Is That What Makes Them Have a History)? A Bourdieuian Approach to Understanding Emotion. *History and Theory, 51*, 193–220.

van Dijik, J. (2013). *The Culture of Connectivity: A Critical History of Social Media*. Oxford: Oxford University Press.

Voicu, M. (2008). Religiosity and Religious Revival During the Transition Period in Romania. In B. Voicu & M. Voicu (Eds.), *The Values of Romanians 1993–2006: A Sociological Perspective* (pp. 144–170). Iasi: The European Institute.

4

Love and Power: Fathers' Emotions in Relation to Their Romantic Partners'

Paternal Love and Maternal Love

Previous research considered how both mothers and fathers participate in reproducing certain forms of masculinity (Brandth and Kvande 1998). For example, there is a higher likelihood for fathers to be involved if two conditions were met in the establishment of family intimacy: (a) if they had a high level of assumed involvement in family life, even before having a family, and (b) if their involved fathering role was supported by their partner (Cohen 1993). Nonetheless, men continue to be perceived as 'feminine' if they choose to express their feelings openly (de Boise 2015). In heterosexual couples, fatherhood exists in relation to motherhood and can be shaped by either 'maternal gatekeeping' (Gaunt 2008) or maternal support and facilitation (Formoso et al. 2007; Darling-Fisher and Tiedje 1990). However, the process is mutual, as other findings reveal that in post-divorce arrangements, the mother's gatekeeping exists in relation to 'paternal banking' (Moore 2012).[1] These findings prompt the general

---

[1] As Mead writes: 'Take the simple family relation, where there is the male and the female and the child which has to be cared for. Here is a process which can only go on through interactions within this group. It cannot be said that the individuals come first and the community later, for the individuals arise in the very process itself, just as much as the human body or any multi-cellular form

© The Author(s) 2020

A. Macht, *Fatherhood and Love*, Palgrave Macmillan Studies in Family and Intimate Life, https://doi.org/10.1007/978-3-030-20358-0_4

question, that if emotions have been theorized in relational ways,[2] then how is masculinity shaped by emotions in men's intimate lives?

Adam (Scottish, resident, 38) describes a triadic interaction taking place in how intimacy is maintained in his family, where the relationship with his partner influences his relationship with his three-year-old son:

> I think we're very close, but it changed our relationship in that a lot of time is now dedicated to him (…) I do like that because I also see qualities in my partner that I haven't seen before. For instance, I have experiences of being a dad that I didn't have before that I sometimes like and sometimes it's very difficult. Yeah it's just an aspect that I suppose enriches my life, but you know it's a relationship, a caring relationship that just adds to something I didn't have before, which is very nice.

What also emerges from Adam's quote is how his son's presence in his life helps him see his partner in a new light. Bearing this in mind, I asked fathers during our interviews to describe how they understand love for their family members and what they think paternal love is in comparison with maternal love. My assumption was that if these men strongly identify with their involved fathers' roles, they would experience their love in similar ways to how their partners would. I was also curious to hear their thoughts on whether there were more differences or similarities between romantic and paternal love. Unsurprisingly, their narratives reveal mostly differences between a father's and a mother's love. For example, Will (Scottish, non-resident, 36) named the distinction quite clearly as 'mom's love is cotton wool and dad's love is tough love'. Moreover, Vlad (Romanian, resident, 41), the father of an 11-year-old daughter, explains below how he sees the maternal and paternal roles as different but that feeling love is a shared and similar emotion:

---

is one in which differentiated cells arise. There has to be a life-process going on in order to have the differentiated cells; in the same way there has to be a social process going on in order that there may be individuals' (1934, p. 189).

[2] Arising from and forming bodily relationships between self and others and between self and the world (Ahmed 2014; Burkitt 2014).

4 Love and Power: Fathers' Emotions in Relation to Their...

Yes, well there's a big difference. The mother is the mother and the father – in her case – is a play-partner [laughter]. There is a difference, of course there is, she takes Veronica [his partner] as the 'authority'. I think the feeling of being parent is as powerful both for the mother and for the father, just that paternally the feeling is differently than maternally and it is so powerful that it cannot be measured. It just exists and that is it (…) It's different. [At his daughter's birth] I was somewhere around her, gravitating, and it cannot be any other way. I was clearly a support to her [his partner] but at the same time I also felt that she was a support for me too [laughs] because I had to manage things somehow.

Maternal love for Vlad was conceived from a biological premise: by reducing mothering to its biological embodiment, Vlad justifies his opinion that women are evolutionarily different ('more loving', 'giving') and that this is an argument strong enough to justify how mothers share a *special bond* to children since they carry the baby inside their body for nine months. In Vlad's view, these differences are assumed to be natural and cannot be conceived as socially constructed. Despite situating his role as a father and his partner's role as mother in essentialist terms, he continues by describing the mutual support they gave each other after his daughter's birth and how love for him grew as an emotion in time. In addition, Malcolm (Scottish, resident, 42), the father of two, mentions that his love is different but not less intense than the love that his partner has for their children:

I remember the first time he came through the door, with Abel after he was born and we just put him on the ground in his seat and it was 'Well what do you do now?'. So it's very much just make it up as you go along (…) there's nothing I'm sure my wife wouldn't be able to describe or articulate her emotions around having children and the love she has for them. In the same way I find it difficult, it's a very difficult thing to do. I don't think mine is any less (…) I can empathize with her as much as I love the children, but I don't know if it's the same thing.

However, Gavin expressed the view that *'I think with mums, you know that's a bit of a natural thing gravitational force'*, and the examples offered in support of this were moments when children turned to their mothers when feeling tired or frightened. Such gendered discourses where enhancing fathers' power, as there is little that is considered instinctive about fatherhood, while for women, motherhood is still represented as essential to their feminine identity and inborn (Dermott and Miller 2015). Lucian (Romanian, resident, 38) describes that in his role as a father, his love is different than his partner's. He argued that this is because his son needs to experience both types of (gendered) love:

> I laughed at her for this one, because 'you're the mother you would excuse him anything'. You see this is also an example which tells you that I am slightly stricter. I try to push him 'come on, do more' while Maria is 'whatever you do you are wonderful, everything is perfect!'. I think he needs both, he needs this base, of the kind of love which is 'you are good no matter what' so that he can have the confidence to do things.

Lucian's belief is that it was the mother's nature to accept everything and love the child for who he/she is, and his role as a father is to be critical and push the child to do more; he found these gendered ways of loving, complementary and working well together as they each fulfilled his son's presumed different emotional needs. For Lucian, who was one of the fathers who resisted love, the child's emotionality was, therefore, constructed as 'complex' while parents' emotions were organized according to him between a mother's love and a father's role. His reflections connect to what Stephanie Shields (2002) wrote in relation to the emotional aspects of gendered power:

> Because concepts of emotion and emotionality are differently applied to women and men, the gendered emotional scheme inevitably connects to systems of power. Feminist ethnographies reveal the intersection of emotion and gender as a critical locus for revealing how a culture incorporates emotion into its system of social organization. (p. 9)

Therefore, for most Romanian fathers, the prerogative to love unconditionally was mostly delegated to their partner, who, in their view, could love 'unrestrained' because they are women and, through this, build the child's confidence.

In addition, three participants thought that there wasn't any difference in the way things are felt in terms of both parents' love for their children but argued that there were distinctions in how love is *cultivated* (implying it is a learned process[3]). These three fathers explained that, according to them, there was a clear difference between maternal and paternal love, with terms such as *'it's evolutionary'*, *'it's in the nature of man to seek the mother'*, *'I cannot love like a woman'* and so on. As Patrick recounts:

> So my wife had already worked out before she told me, she already made a connection with the child's that's growing inside her and that's something that I can't as a man really understand. So, from that point I think there is a huge bond between a mother and a child that a man can't understand. However when the child is born I still think and I have never, ever experienced such a rush of emotion as when I did when both of them were born. Quite amazing! Quite unlike anything I've ever experienced or soon will experience again. I don't think that can be ignored at all. There's something happening, something primal, something very, very difficult to explain and then even from the point before birth, there's a huge protective element that comes over (…) I don't believe it's learned, it's just something that suddenly exists and it's very, very powerful and it exists for a woman as well but it is different.

The assumptions were that maternal love is superior to the love that a father can offer their children, downplaying paternal love but not their important role as fathers. By keeping the experience of love linked to stereotypical gender roles, fathers could then employ emotional bordering into increased stoicism and enact a tough form of masculinity.

---

[3] Dalessandro and Wilkins (2017) have researched how social actors gender love, how they filter the emotion through their masculine/feminine/fluid gender identity and thereby set its social parameters and limits according to age; they conclude that age has the effect that masculinity and maturity involved men considering and reflecting more on their partner's feelings 'finding maturity is an intrinsic process in which men themselves decide when it is time to stop behaving badly and to take their partners' feelings into account' (p. 114). Although it should be mentioned that emotional maturity need not coincide with old age.

Supportive and Complementary Fathering Roles

Fathers from both cultural groups tended to see themselves according to two definitions: (a) support for the mother, and (b) as complementary – they were different and provided children with distinct things than the mothers. These findings fall in line with previous research on fathering (Lamb 2010). However, when seen from a sociology of emotions perspective, the picture is complicated by the frequent contradictions in fathers' explanations, which can be interpreted as depicting an interdependent state of relating as a family member. Since fathers *border* between traditional and progressive constructions of self, it is the shifting nature of this dynamic process that is significant since this shift illustrates how social change can also begin from an emotional level.

In line with this, it is important to reflect on the meaning of 'unconditional love', signifying a love that has no 'conditions' or, said differently, a form of relating and expressing emotion that has no limitations, no boundaries or borders that might affects its fluidity. Aware of their bordering, some involved fathers reasoned that 'conditional' love is not necessarily a negative emotion, as this helped their child's social development and protected them from 'being spoiled' ('a fi răsfățat', in the Romanian equivalent). Six Scottish fathers (five of whom had separated from their wives and were non-resident) draw on different discourses to explain how fathers also contribute to parenting despite biological differences (such as their inability to give birth), as Ray explains:

> (…) a human being tends towards the mother, because you spend the first part of your life in that mother, as a part of that growing up inside the mother. So it is that maternal instinct. And in our society, that's been the way that has been. But going back to my dad's time or going back to the time when I was brought up as a kid, my dad went out to work and my mother provided the nurturing and everything. Times have changed now. There's no difference between being a single dad and being a single mum as well.

Compared to mothers' love, fathers' love, for these six men, had the role of setting relational boundaries that would help their children fit better into society. When I asked Iustin, a Romanian resident father, if his relationship with his daughter was different than the relationship his daughter shared with his wife, he instantly described how his daughter prefers his wife. He attributed this preference to the extra time his daughter spends with his wife and positioned himself in a supportive role:

> Yes, she is more attached to my wife, mom comes first. But I help her as much as I can. Anyway mom is the main person: she dictates and I help. I mean what can I say, she's my child and I love her and this is pretty much it. (…) I try to not be aggressive, I try to take care of her, but at the same time to explain to her that there are certain limits.

Iustin seems to be detaching from the father's role as he is describing it; by bordering emotionally through saying "and this is pretty much it", he is setting 'certain limits' and enacts stoicism to reinforce the good father's role.

As described in the quotes above, most fathers I interviewed viewed mother's love as different to father's love. Romanian fathers constructed sentences where the pronouns were often mixed, and it could be that this was because they were building a continuous and gendered narrative of themselves, where men were not seen as owning the capacity to love unconditionally, as it is considered 'unmanly' to delve into too much emotion since this is the woman's prerogative. Their identity appears muted, or delegated to the 'Other', and rendered many times invisible. What remained, according to most fathers, were the actions. Cultural values influenced this relational dynamic. For example, Scottish fathers were not as quick to determine the primacy of their partners' mothering as were the Romanian fathers. The first group was mostly detaching themselves from maternal expertise. Some Scottish fathers would prioritize the love they feel for their children compared to the love they feel for their partners while others would emphasize team effort. To Lewis (Scottish, resident, 39) who sees his wife as 'the immediate focal point for everything (…)', in relation to his daughter, he reflected on the role-conflict that he experiences:

> The hardest thing in parenting, to me is that balance between I'm her dad not her friend. But it would be nice to be her friend too (…) I try to keep a balance again between not killing enthusiasm and trying to keep it interesting (…) I guess it's trying to create commonality a bit you know (…) to encourage her and also make sure there's some stuff we can talk about a

little bit, as well 'cause at some point I think I'm still cool but at some point I'm not. I'm going to be 'the dad'. She's going to a teenager. The relationship will change, you know. So I'm trying to create some commonality, things that we've got common interests in.

Moreover, he shares that his mutual aim with his partner is emotionally led, as they aim to cultivate their daughter's enthusiasm:

We try to balance it because she's still eight years old so there's still a 'Can we make it enthusiastic? Interesting? and keep the enthusiasm there without taking her up on a rainy day and killing that enthusiasm?' so 'How do we nourish that enthusiasm that she's currently got?'

What Lewis also describes above is his own bordering strategy: the prerogative to be an intimate father would see him adopting the democratic and progressive role of 'friend' to his child; however, veering towards stoicism would see him adopt the authoritarian, traditional role. This distinction between being the responsible adult and being the child's friend appeared as well for a separate group of fathers who resisted love, as I have discussed in Chap. 2. Despite acknowledging that child-rearing was a mutual 'team effort', accounts of their own important contribution, intense desire to have children and examples of 'good fathering' abounded in fathers' narratives. What is important to underline is that as fathers were differentiating between their love and their partner's love, and emotionally bordered between being a stoic, authoritative father versus being an intimate, caring father, they also provided data which directly contradicted these separations, revealing how a father's role exists within barely acknowledged family interdependencies.

Interdependent Love Power

Most Scottish fathers relied on their partners' support and interventions in managing their relationship with their child/children, especially during bad days. Rod (Scottish, resident) describes how he employed *waiting* as a strategy of emotion work, done in collaboration with his wife, to help his son overcome his lack of confidence:

4 Love and Power: Fathers' Emotions in Relation to Their... 117

> The wonderful thing I've seen improving in the past year or so is his confidence. So I think naturally he'd be quite shy (…) in bigger groups of peers, at parties and such. He was quiet and quite hesitant in big social circles, for about a year it would seem (…) A good example is the school's sports day. We had that on Saturday morning. He's just in P1,[4] so effectively there's the same sort of set up[5] (…) A year ago it was overwhelming. It was too much for him, to the point that the teacher had to come and get him and ran up with him (…) And I was – wasn't annoyed with him – but I was annoyed *for him*[6] that there were other kids, these keen four-year-olds sprinting and I wanted him to be one of the enthusiastic ones. So twelve months ago there was him being overwhelmed, in tears and not being able to join in and enjoy it, and me feeling frustrated for him. While on Saturday he was amazing! He did all the races and he loved it and he came third in this, second during the races and he's feeling full of smile and concentration. Even then little things in between the races, with his classmates and he's just interacting and laughing and joking with them (…) to me it felt a huge sense of being pleased for him. The fear of a year ago was 'He's a quiet kid. He can't join in' (…) and our conscious decision last year was not to make a big deal out of it.

What comes out of Rod's quote and is relevant to an aesthetic understanding of emotions (Burkitt 2014) was how his own emotion work in relating to his son, received the support of his partner. In a mutual effort of emotionally navigating the relationship with their son, Rod pinpoints that he had to work on his emotions helped by his wife, as he felt momentarily frustrated in relation to his son's lack of achievement. Moreover, Horia (Romanian, MC, resident) describes a similar strategy of doing emotion work, collaboratively with his wife, to help his daughter's shyness:

> From the beginning – Flaviu who is the first-born – grew up a little bit more sociable than Oana. He seems to have more charm: he speaks with anyone, greets, asks questions, he is curious, he's not afraid that he is both-

---

[4] This refers to 'Primary 1': the first level of education following from nursery in the Scottish school system.

[5] Here, he refers to the building structure of the private school, which had the nursery on the same school grounds with other buildings. The competitive events organized there were a school tradition and were repeated each year with the same set-up.

[6] Emphasis my own.

ering someone. But Oana had an introverted period, of shyness, during which we couldn't do much for her except allow her to come out of it slowly-slowly. Of course, we would talk to her, we would explain things, we gave her examples. But until the effort comes from within her, to make a step forward, to get out of there, and realize she is ok, that she can interact with people, then (…) There were two good years where she seemed to have had a shell around her, which instead of toughening up, it gradually dissolved.

Both fathers emphasize that their emotion work was not enough in itself but relied on their children's agency to ultimately help overcome their emotional obstacles. In relation to his partner, Nicholas (Scottish, resident, 38) reflects on the differences between himself and his wife regarding role responsibilities:

So, I can get up at four o'clock in the morning and give her a bottle and have time with just myself and herself which I think helps produce a very strong bond very quickly (…) [but] you find out for yourself how you expand in that area: sneaking off to do something on your own, having a couple of minutes to yourself. Do I need that more than my wife? Or do I selfishly demand that more than my wife? I get to go to work each day, and you'd think I would have a separate enough life, but I still want some time to myself at the weekend. When I think about that I realize that my wife never really gets any time for herself anymore as much. And as much as I might try and provide it, she doesn't seem to need it as much as me (…) 'I'll do it tonight, you just go and get seven hours of sleep' and she says 'I can't'. Whereas when I'm given that permission, I ran out to the other room and I get those seven hours of sleep.

Nicholas is using in this way emotional reflexivity to adapt his emotional bordering, and build a narrative of choice.

Partner's Support and Emotional Contagion

Interestingly, several Romanian fathers mentioned how they are managing 'contagious' emotions, during the 'rollercoaster' moments I described in Chap. 2. The socio-psychological literature (Hatfield et al. 1993) has described emotional contagion as:

(...) the tendency to automatically mimic and synchronize facial expressions, vocalizations, postures, and movements with those of another person and, consequently to converge emotionally. (pp. 153–154)

Some fathers described resisting being 'contaminated' by the child's bad moods while they believed their partners could not do the same, since mothers were positioned in their narratives as empathetic to the child's emotions even if these were negative, as Nelu (Romanian, resident, 34) explains:

I think he has the right to his bad days. We also have them and deal with them according to how we are. My wife gets affected and then she's having a bad day if he's having a bad day (...) she's much more empathetic, but in an unpleasant way to my mind. I mean if he has a bad day (...) I try to make it as good as I can. When I can't, well that's it (...) at least I try to give him some support (...)

Nelu frames his son's conduct as a 'right', describing it through a democratic discourse similar to Anthony Giddens's description of 'pure relating' (1992) while situating his wife's 'empathy' as unpleasant and different than his stoic resistance. This might have been because his partner's emotional conduct momentarily broke through the normative expectations of 'pleasantness' imposed on female emotionality (Graham et al. 1981) but also because familial harmony was disturbed by the child's emotional outburst. Nelu, therefore, detaches from the negative situation, differentiating himself from the image of the 'nurturer' while establishing a sense of 'good-enough' fathering by conferring stoic support. Through this, he might be teaching his son how to emotionally detach from highly emotional social situations according to masculine prerogatives, and stoicism might serve as an emotional resource, handed down from father to son (intergenerationally) in the accomplishment of successful masculinity.

Moreover, emotional contagion also saw fathers positioning themselves as an 'emotional buffer' between a mother and the child. They sometimes had to intervene when the mother was exhausted, ill or physically tired, and calm the child down through embodied practices such as holding them in their arms. In this sense, emotional bordering was performed through the body. Iustin (Romanian, resident, 32) describes how he intervenes during emotional contagion to keep his daughter calm by remaining stoic:

> I try not to have her empathize with me, only when maybe I'm really ill. But again when I'm with her, she doesn't need to feel too much. She might just see that I'm a bit more moody and that's about it (…) Many times my wife takes on the feelings from the child and as in many families, I take her in my arms and with me she calms down. Because I try to impose myself a calm rhythm, so that we won't have a problem.
> Int: And how does that feel for you then emotionally?
> Emotionally, I have no problems, I try and keep as rational as possible (…) We try to balance our interaction, and to establish some rules.

Iustin describes how he resorts to gendered feeling rules during a difficult emotional episode not only to enhance his own stoic bordering but also to veer his daughter's emotions in a certain direction and to keep her calm. Therefore, emotional management is taught in moments when fathers border on stoicism, to paradoxically increase intimacy with their close family members and to maintain a good relationships with them, despite disruptive events.

Similarly, and for sons as well, Ciprian (Romanian, resident, 35) describes instances of having to control his own emotions to help deal with his two boys' feelings of fright, so as not to get the whole family anxious, thereby situating himself as the 'rational centre' in his family's life:

> Often they get some big fright and their reaction is disproportionate. They get scared quite badly and they've developed (…) something against blood and they say 'Is that blood? It is blood!' and I have to not panic and see what's really happening. I have to speak calmly, to get a grip somehow, so that they won't go, I don't know where.
> Int: So if you're calm, they're also calmer in these kind of situations?
> Well, somehow you have to be. Because you don't want panic in the entire household, and then we won't know what to do [laughter].

Ciprian's example portrays how by reinstating masculine rational control, the family is 'saved', but a resistance against the 'feminization' of feeling (Cancian 1986) has been concomitantly asserted. Conceptions of emotions as a relational energy which is effervescent and contagious have been discussed by classical sociologists, such as Emile Durkheim and Erving Goffman (in von Scheve 2011), in the context of groups, in showing how facial expressions play a role in relational interactions, as people learn to read each other's bodily cues. But the data above portrays the father as detaching from a too loving connection in moments of tension, precisely because love is perceived as highly emotional, chaotic and, therefore, a threat to the stoic masculine border even when it seems to construct an interdependent love power and add to the family's well-being.

The Love and Power Complex

In this section, I critically assess Theodore Kemper's (1978) theory of power, status and love, to highlight an alternative account of love and power as processual-constructed emotions. Kemper's theory assumed that romantic love is an emotion existing within relationships of power and status, which subordinate this emotion by constraining its expression. However, the empirical data I gathered describes love and power as mutually constituting emotions, which are both emerging from and are reproducing social relationships. Parental actions which are integral to the civilizing process (Elias 1939/2000) seem also to be underlined by emotional dynamics in which children are active co-participants. Seen from this theoretical perspective, fathers do emotion work in slightly different ways than mothers because this work is tied in with their masculinity; as such, it becomes bordering or the work required to deal emotionally with any relational issues feeds back into the construction of their masculinity and the type of fathering that they practise. This is why in an intimate, familial context, emotional bordering, as the act of creating emotional borders involves the simultaneous setting of relational limits. The emotional involvement necessary to fulfil the intimate father's role is influenced by fathers' masculine identities; the two roles are never separate. More negatively, however, the love for the child could also be used as an emotional 'band-aid' in patching up a wounded intimate relationship with their partner, to gain more credibility in public and social situations or to help continue the bond with a partner.[7]

The findings complement previous research in that men's extensive array of choices continue to come into stark contrast with their partner's institutionalized responsibilities as mothers (Williams 2011), which are not as easily subject to 'opting out'. It is important to mention that a small group of men within the sample were challenging this 'soft sexism'; they were taking on full-time and primary childcare responsibilities and combining their paternity leave with their shared parental leave provision or cutting back on hours at work. James (Scottish, resident, 39) describes his strong desire to have a child and how this impacted his degree of involvement in parenting, compared to this partner:

> I think I should probably explain that I really wanted children and Suzie didn't. So it was quite a hard decision for her (…) At that time I'd say that in our relationship I was suffering a lot because I was really unhappy. I really wanted to know what it felt like to have that relationship with her, with a daughter or a son (…) in the early months he really needed his mother's comfort. Just to be close to her. So, it definitely developed but I think the last six months when I was off work it's when we really bonded and he became more interactive and more interested (…) to the point where as I say he now prefers me to his mum most of the time.

What fathers alluded to was a focus on child's preference which sometimes created minor conflicts between parents, as the intimate father's role was prioritized over intensive mothering and vice versa.

Fathers' intimate paternal power rested on an interdependent exchange of emotions and interactions with their close ones, and on the links between power and love. When love is considered together with power as emotions that exist within and maintain relationships (Heaney 2011), then interdependencies are illuminated. This is because in analysing 'love power' we need to consider what love does, not only what love is (Fergusson and Jónasdóttir 2014). A study by Christensen, Hockey and James (1999) convincingly portrayed how a man's claims of independence

---

[7] Judith Halberstam (2018) draws attention to 'the new sexism embodied by sensitive men' (p. 19).

4 Love and Power: Fathers' Emotions in Relation to Their... 123

rested on a carefully balanced relational act made up of tiny structural dependencies with other people, to whom he was connected in his role as a father, a husband and employer, and an ageing individual. Therefore, in intimate relationships, power can exist at the intersections of dependence and independence, or what has been termed interdependence (Smart and Neale 1999) and highlights as well how gender intersects with age in fathering (Gardiner 2002). Interdependent intimate power is theorized in the literature as:

> (...) an essentially relational concept. Put simply, for an individual to be dependent requires another for them to be dependent on. At an analytic level, dependency therefore necessarily entails a social connection which can be constituted both through mutual and reciprocal relations as well as the more hierarchical relations traditionally noted between an independent and a dependent person. Furthermore, dependency may be constructed across a variety of domains – material, social, economic and political dependency – and different connections may be made by different people across and between these different domains (...) This allows dependency to be understood as a fluid state of affairs such that people can be seen to move in and out of relations of dependency at different points in their lives. How, why and in what manner they do this may, in part, be a function of particular power relations. (Christensen et al. 1999, pp. 173–174)

The quote above shows that it is difficult then to describe father-child activities in isolation from the mother's influence, particularly when analysing the experiences of mostly coupled/cohabiting men. Patrick (Scottish, resident, 42) draws attention to the emotional bordering he employs, in how he has constructed clear differentiations between 'liking' and 'loving' his children. He makes a conscious decision to separate the experiences in difficult moments, as for him they do not always coincide. In moments of losing control, Patrick also refers to his reliance on his partner's support:

> You know sometimes I don't particularly like them: if they're being difficult or if they're not doing what they should be doing or if they're being a pain in the neck and not being nice (...) I would love to say 'Oh well I applied that logic to it and I think about it' but of course it wasn't always the case

and I react emotionally and I shout, send them to their room and get them to think about it you know, because I'm annoyed. Sometimes it's very difficult to take a step back and say 'Right ok, I am now annoyed' and they're annoyed and this is not a good situation. It's explosive. But it's quite good because my wife and I are aware of when these situations escalate – and you know that 15 minutes later you're going to feel terrible (…) So it takes just one of us to say you know 'Let me sort it out'.

If love for their children was experienced as empowering and potentially transformative, the experience of loving their children in the context of their partner's care and love made for unequal differentiations. Love for their children, at times, was presented as different in intensity to the love they felt for their partners and it was framed around a discourse of 'unconditionality'. This discourse incorporated elements of responsibility, a stability of emotional connection built in time and 'loving because they did not have a choice'.

Their reasoning on the topic revealed that involved fathers had an interdependent power in the family, mediated by the quality of the relationships with other family members. Interdependent power is dynamic and productive, created relationally through social interactions; it is stimulated by strong emotions such as love. Interdependent power has value, not necessarily as a display of 'manliness', as gendered power can be. On the contrary, interdependence can provide a refuge from the traditionally assumed and individualized account of male power (Connell 2005).

However, this problematizes other aspects such as mother's power in intimate bonds. The structure of patriarchal societies sees women hold intimate power mostly through interdependence, which often plays out in their role as mothers. Mothers are assumed to hold dominion over interdependent and intimate power mostly with their children, as they can only gain access to men's type of patriarchal power in limited ways (or not at all in certain situations) since their power is also continuously socially subverted in other public roles (Allen 2008). Women might feel that the only relationship where they have some power (with their children) is being exploited by men, paradoxically through their involved and intimate fathers' role. In this way, men are presumed to gain power in another different area of social life, where women, through their mothering, play a central role.

Through intimate involvement in their children's lives and supporting their partner's mothering, involved fathers can not only increase their social privileges but also resist patriarchal prerogatives. This was sometimes fraught with tensions. Reminiscing on their transitions to their role as fathers, most men described how they had to cope with changes in the relationship with their partner such as diminishing the amount of quality time spent with her and having full access to her emotional resources by having to compromise and accept being 'second best' in the household. In having multiple choices in the process of 'acting responsibly', fathers exerted their power, through either delegating their parenting to their partner or diminishing the power imbalance by sharing it with the partner, which is in line with other work presenting the delegation of emotional responsibilities (Hochschild and Machung 1990). What complicates the picture is that empirical evidence has shown that emotional responsibility (Doucet 2013) is not only determined by the ways in which parents 'hold on' to their children but also the ways in which they carefully 'let them go', and fathers in particular can display responsibility, in this way linking it to an increase in children's autonomy; even when this could be perceived as a lessening of intimacy. Instead of envisioning love as the opposite of power, as Kemper initially theorized them in his explanations of romantic love, I understand love and power as emotions that are linked together through relating, in an emotional stickiness that creates interdependencies.

Culture matters in this respect. For example, in Romanian families, paradoxically, even if the woman is subordinated to the role of the mother and wife, and has little public power, she owns considerable private power in that she is usually managing the finances of the family and the distribution of hers and her husband's income. Mothers are also expected to take over the practical decision-making in all matters concerning the family's life, whether social or material (Popescu 2009). Therefore, for Romanian men, identifying with the intimate father's role poses gendered power issues, as threats to good mothering appear if men attempt to shift roles. This is especially significant as Romanian women seldom acquire opportunities for public or political power (Popescu 2004). As Ovidiu mentions:

I think that with women, with wives and mothers, it's a little bit taboo. I mean it's hard to say to a mother how to raise her child, and if you don't do this with a little diplomacy, then you risk creating a lot of adversity.

In addition, children's agency plays an important role in how this power is distributed in the family. From the data I gathered, I found that between family members, interdependent power circulates in relation to love in three possible ways: (a) it is sometimes child-led, as children pick up on relational tensions and mirror those back emotionally to their parents, as they 'play' one parent against the other; (b) fathers' power is established through their capacity to choose – they can decide not to participate intimately, and even if they share in the responsibilities for caring, they can also relinquish support of the mother; they can also choose to work more hours away from caring responsibilities and reconstruct good fathering through providing; and finally, (c) in interactions with others (such as during the interviews with me), fathers conceive of their intimacy with the child as more important than the intimacy shared with their partner, in an attempt to display their power. This means that their traditional role as a provider is reinforced through the supplementation offered by the discourse of intimate fathering, without necessarily having this translate into their everyday, domestic practices. To fully embody the intimate father's role, men must match practices of intimacy with the discourse of paternal love, which remains for many fathers a challenge as the data excerpts illustrate. Concerning the child-led aspect of interdependent power, I draw from Ion's interview. He is the father to a four-year-old son, and in the quote below he explains how his son goes through periods of preferring one parent to the other, thereby restricting his close involvement when he prefers his mother:

There are moments, when for example, now he is in a ,mom' period and he is telling me frequently that he doesn't love me any more, that he doesn't want to be my friend. He is his mom's friend. But just as well he also had a dad period when he was telling her 'I don't love you, I don't know now', etc. Now next week it is his birthday and his latest thing is 'I won't invite you to my birthday!'

According to a Kemperian understanding of power, Ion describes how his son, who is given a high status in the relationship he shares with both of his parents, is perceived as using this status to create power games between them. But as an emotionally involved father, Ion's love for his son is employed to over-ride feelings of threat and gain a humorous understanding of his son's incipient practices of wielding power in relating to his parents (i.e. the power to decide who can and cannot be his friend). From the perspective of interdependent love power, such an example shows that it is not only parents who exert 'power over' their children, but also children learn how to 'play one parent against the other' in the process of asserting their will, thereby contributing to some of the emotional tensions experienced between family members. And this was evident across culture. For example, Stephen (Scottish, non-resident, 35) describes a similar situation:

> (…) Especially if they see us two to be different – if the mother and father are together – but when we are separated, she can play one off the other 'I'm telling my mummy' or 'I'll tell my daddy'. When she's with me, if she falls she'll cry for her mummy, and with her she'll cry for her daddy. So it's just the way they work, or the way she does really.

For these fathers, intimate power dynamics involved a competitive presentation of the self, in which they position themselves as better than their own fathers and they differentiate from their partners' emotionality despite considering her as superiorly apt at caring. This performance of 'good fathering' also includes a feeling of being 'undeserving' of their children's love in some cases because they fail to be as emotionally close to them as they would like. Love's power serves the purpose of increasing the child's emotional value, above other intimates, and falls in line with the discourse of unconditional love. If love for their children was experienced as empowering and potentially transformative, the experience of loving their children in the context of their partner's care and love revealed unequal differentiations between family members, which again took place at an emotional level.

Romanian fathers were especially keen to emphasize they did everything related to their children in unison with the partner, and sometimes even with the help of extended kin, as Liviu, a resident father of twins, portrays:

> We used to take turns, with my wife or my mother-in-law. They would either change her and I would change him or the other way around. It almost came by itself that thing of 'OK, I need to step in, I can't let them do everything alone'. It was simply an instinct. For us, it didn't matter that it was I, or my wife, or my mother-in-law. We were all there together with them in the front line (...) And I can remember when I used to prepare their powder milk formula it was the same. We were all the same team. I can't say it was you and then I. I wasn't pushing anyone aside to step it. We were all there, side by side.

Most Romanian fathers mentioned they received some sort of help from grandparents in caring for their children, even if distance and economic costs are constructed as a barrier for wider kin involvement; interdependent love power could, therefore, be extended to the wider kin network.

Emotional Responsibilities

Furthermore, interdependent power between partners can also be exercised through relinquishing emotional responsibilities[8] (Hochschild and Machung 1990). Some participants expressed a combination of sharing emotional responsibility and delegating it to their partners; in having multiple choices in the process of 'acting responsibly', fathers exerted their power. Power as an emotion is largely employed in the construction of the father's and the mother's authority as a 'naturalized' point of disciplining and socializing the child into cultural conceptions of what it means to raise 'a good child' ('good' in this sense means compliant, warm and friendly).

---

[8] According to Doucet, emotional responsibility (2015) comprises emotional attentiveness and childcare competence, and it is not only determined by the ways in which parents 'hold on' to their children but also the ways in which they carefully 'let them go'.

4 Love and Power: Fathers' Emotions in Relation to Their... 129

For example, even if he considers himself to be emotionally involved in educating his son to be open and tender, and sees himself as far removed from traditional models of masculinity, Ovidiu (Romanian, resident, 34) gives an account of detaching from his son during difficult times:

> When I'm having a difficult day or when it's harder for me, I think I'm more closed off or we don't communicate as much as we do. The periods that we spent together are still as lengthy, but I'm not as involved in his activities and then my wife gets more involved. But I am present in a way or another, next to him, but not as attentive or as close to him, but [I'm] near him.

Ovidiu mentions that he replaces verbal intimacy with physical presence during trying days. Being 'involved' was clearly then an option. A discursive loop of construction and choice appeared that intimately benefited fathers more than mothers; who were described as unproblematically loving and continuing to provide 'second shifts' in the family (Hochschild and Machung 1990). Power plays and delegation of responsibility for care were concomitant with emotional support and collaboration, further asserting how love and power are intertwined as emotional and relational experiences. Horia (Romanian, resident, 32) describes how his wife helps him at times to border emotionally with the aim of encouraging his daughter to overcome her shyness:

> From the beginning – Flaviu who is the first-born – grew up a little bit more sociable than Oana. He seems to have more charm: he speaks with anyone, greets, asks questions, he is curious, he's not afraid that he is bothering someone. But Oana had an introverted period, of shyness, during which we couldn't do much for her except allow her to come out of it slowly-slowly. Of course, we would talk to her, we would explain things, we gave her examples. But until the effort comes from within her, to make a step forward, to get out of there, and realize she is ok, that she can interact with people, then (...) There were two good years where she seemed to have had a shell around her, which instead of toughening up, it gradually dissolved.

Both fathers emphasize that their emotional bordering relied on their children's agency to ultimately help patch any relational problems. Interdependently then, in this process, both mothers and fathers replicate their own culturally and historically dependent ideas of what it means to be a 'good mother' (Thurer 1995) and 'good father' (Henwood and Procter 2003). Through 'universalizing' love as an emotion equally shared by both parents, some Romanian involved fathers reproduce an account of gender similarity and familial cohesion, but in differentiating between maternal love and paternal love, the responsibility to provide childcare was re-emphasized as belonging to the mother since she was perceived to be more intuitively or naturally emotionally equipped to manage the children's emotional and practical demands.

Even if this increases their intimate father's identity, the responsibility to care was renounced, veering into a partner-support role while still maintaining the potential for positive interaction with their children. It is true that involved fathers are parenting in a context in which mothers are still central and considered to be naturally more nurturing and affectionate by the wider social circle, but the parent's roles are indeed socially constructed, as there is an increasing amount of considered thinking that goes into parenting and in developing a 'project of the self' (Lupton and Barclay 1997) as the data presented above shows. In the next section, I discuss how interdependent love power is employed when involved fathers resort to stoic discipline in relation to their children, even as they continue to maintain intimate fathering.

Anger and the Role of the Disciplinarian

In order to highlight the relational interdependencies between love and power, I bring into the discussion the analysis of an emotion, which has been many times considered in relation to men's power: anger (Kimmel 2013; Seidler 1998; Hearn 2013). Anger (which I discussed in Chap. 2 in relation to intergenerational transmission) is considered to represent and reproduce masculine power, as it supports the performance of hegemonic masculinity. What I would propose is that rather than upholding status, experiencing frustration can lead to an angry episode in the father-child relationship and increase the expression of power, precisely because love is temporarily suspended (or not the main focus); emotionally, however, love and power unleash a lot of relational energy between social actors. Thus, even if this situation then is likely to invade status conferral or decreasing love as Kemper argued, I would ascertain that it does not destroy it. Fathers' narratives revealed that the loving relationship can survive the exercise of power, and it can also contain it.

Norbert Elias (1939/2000) argued that social norms have the power to constrain human conducts and 'civilize' them accordingly – people learn self-restraint, which takes place with the control of violence and through knowledge. For Elias, power worked in relation to agency, self and individualization, as human agency is networked, supported by members of a close group, based on interdependencies and asymmetries. The author especially underlines how the act of providing is connected to power: 'A group's capacity to provide, perhaps to ration or to withdraw and generally to control the means of fulfilling social requirements of a survival unit (and thus of other groups) is the mainstay of that group's power ration' (Elias 1987, p. 235). If one conceives of the family as a group, then the one who usually fulfils the role of the provider not only has the most power but also can *share* the most power.

For example, Charlie (Scottish, MC, resident), the father of two daughters, is aware of and clearly asserts that '*gender equality is important for me*'. Although rationally this seems ideal, emotionally, Charlie experiences tensions. He works through this ambivalence by resorting to emotional bordering. He describes how an angry outburst has made him reassess his high standards for being a perfect parent and a good provider and the high expectations he had of his daughters. Spending long hours in his stressful job had the advantage of furthering his career but was also disconnecting him from his family. What alerted him to this course of action were the changes he noticed in his youngest daughter's behaviour towards him:

> I think due to fatigue, lack of sleep, general amount of stress, I was very short-fused and I remember once just losing my temper shouting at the eldest one, and the smallest one took herself away (…) that was the real

trigger for me. It was like 'Why are you away?' she said 'You're scaring me' I said 'Well that's it. I'm not doing that, I'm not being a scary dad'. So that's taught me (...) and I think that was very (...) that was probably one of the most emotional, sort of negative emotional aspects in the last year I think (...) it was a real catalyst for change. I do not want my child finishing this, to go away from me, *ever* [his emphasis].

As the father of two daughters aged five and seven, he initially experienced a lot of stress but decided to just enjoy spending time with his daughters while cutting back on work. The changes he has made were propelled by a series of emotional moments where he couldn't continue to uphold emotional stoicism. To Charlie, expressing anger was not the problem but the fact that he noticed that unloading his negative emotions onto his children might damage the quality of the relationship with them and thereby would reduce closeness. In that moment, as well as being branded a 'scary dad', he failed to live up to the idea of the 'good father'. In spite of the fact that Charlie *thinks* it's good for the girls to have their mother as a female model with a strong work ethic (as he would like his children to have similar options when they reach adulthood), the account above denotes the emotional ambivalence he experiences in the process of changing emotionally towards more gender-equal and democratic forms of relating to his daughters.

Similarly, in Malcolm's account (Scottish, MC, resident), in spite of his best intentions, there is a layer of finding a justification for his emotional outbursts in front of his children. He goes on to explain that the reason for losing control is the fact that he cares so much ('because you love them'), denoting a breach in his stoic emotional border brought on by emotionally intense situations, such as his children finding themselves in danger:

I don't think they're bad just for the sake of being bad. And similarly as parents I think you need to know when to step out or step back and realize that you're not yourself. So I'd probably do things differently if I was more or less emotional (...) and it depends, I mean probably the times when I've shouted at them or when I got very angry is normally a reaction to them doing something which puts them at risk – when you see these horrible situations and you're so wrapped up in them and because you love them so much you don't want to see anything bad happen to them. When you do, you overreact [shifts in chair]. See, it's all tied up in one reason, which is how you react to what they're doing, because you love them, yeah.

As Malcolm describes, it's all a matter of seeing things from your child's perspective, but through this, he is also reinforcing his stoic bordering. He employs a certain emotional reflexivity in trying to understand how his own self interacts with that of his children, by legitimizing his anger through the discourse of 'the vulnerable child'. He re-creates himself in a position of power in what was an emotional and chaotic moment which momentarily contravened his role of a rational man. By lowering the emotional border into a justification of love, Malcolm regained a sense of power.

Furthermore, Fergus (Scottish, resident, 38), a father of two preschool children, explains how he must apply emotional discipline to himself in order to appear authoritative to his daughter, thereby constructing 'respect' in his relationship with her. This process is not clear-cut but rather emotionally demanding and replete with tensions:

I've enforced myself to be disciplined with Mia. I've given her a yellow cup – it's not a big deal, you can have your own meltdown if you want – but I'm not going to give you a purple cup, you know? I give that as an example 'cause it sounds like a little thing when you think. Actually it doesn't cost me anything if I can get the purple cup but then she starts thinking she just gets what she wants. Actually my natural inclination would just be like 'Oh my god, I don't want to see you sad. I'll get you the other one' so, I'll go and get her the other cup. (…) but you almost have to force yourself to be a little bit detached, especially on the disciplined side 'cause your natural inclination is not to be at all (…) It's almost because it's unconditional that you have to enforce a sense of discipline in terms of the way that you bring them up – if I sound like a really disciplined father I'm probably not – I think it's almost because you can't love them too much. You have to be careful (…) As I said if anything the challenge is to try and be a bit more disciplined with them when you think they're just taking the mickey about something.

Finally, it's important to consider that embodied interactions could also have a negative side in relation to how power as an emotion is expressed through physical discipline. For example, there were instances of smacking mentioned, and mostly these appeared in Romanian fathers' accounts. Remus (Romanian, resident, 35) describes how he occasionally employs smacking and rationalizes it by emphasizing the importance of a civilizing norm that has been broken:

> I'm a little strict. But anyway I like to think I'm a continuation of my wife who is really not that strict and we somehow complete each other. I really feel like all this thing that came over us with 'Don't shout at your child, don't smack your child' is relative. I mean if I smack their bottoms, that doesn't mean that I beat them up, it just means that I drew their attention to something and I had to underline it somehow.

Remus locates the responsibility of enforcing discipline into a collective 'we', as he sees his fathering connected to his partner's mothering in complementing ways: he can, therefore, remain stoic, all while reinforcing the good and intimate father discourse through an occasional delegation of his disciplinarian role. Echoes of authoritarian upbringing persist in fathering practices, even if nowadays it seems that simply the threat of impending violence – shown in shouting at children – is deemed strong enough to discipline 'unruly' behaviours.

In Scotland, the traditional idea that the father was the disciplinarian who delivered the serious punishment upon his arrival at home is now circumscribed to the realm of folk memory according to Lynn Jamieson (2005). This could also be due to the rising strength of the judicial protection of children's rights in the UK (Children and Young Peoples Scotland Act 2014). The child as it is constituted in modern discourse is increasingly seen as a person with agency and human rights, particularly in the Western world. Conceptualizing the boundaries of childhood is culturally dependent, where there are other cultures who continue to use physical and verbal violence to discipline their children, as this is considered the normative practice of good parenting (Selin 2013). It is, however, difficult to know how restrained such conducts are in the private realm of personal lives, in spite of media coverage and feminist activist work persistently reporting on such cases of abuse (Powell and Scanlon 2014).

Returning to the data at hand, observations revealed that if the child would misbehave, and communication could not produce a positive change, then involved fathers would resort to physical control to manage their children's emotional outbursts. This control was expressed in picking children up, holding them and distracting them; it did not need to be negatively coloured. It was also echoed in the interviews such as in Gavin's and Iustin's accounts as their physical power was needed to pick the children up, play with them and carry them when their partners were not able to do so. Embodied involvement with the intimate father prerogatives also showed that through certain 'body techniques', men would reinforce their power and the general expectation that men are strong (Ranson 2015). It remains important to consider both the positive and intimacy-building aspects of male embodiment in the context of fatherhood, alongside the negative aspects which remain inherited from an authoritative model of stoic fathering.

Male intimate violence, whether verbal or physical (Breines et al. 2000; Edwards 2006; Hearn and Pringle 2006; Hearn 2013), in family contexts, can exist through an understanding of masculinity as powerful and needing to be reinforced when its authority is weakened. A reversal of men's power positioning can give way to the rage and frustration they might feel in close relationships; therefore, father's rage tells us something about how the father's power – or its absence – operates in intimate relationships. Mentioning and reflecting on angry moments in their path towards accomplishing intimate fathering served as a discursive device employed by some fathers to inform me that the reproduction of a courteous demeanour was not far from the reinstating of a dominant masculinity, whenever necessary in their close relationships. Despite being loving as fathers, anger continued to be an emotion tied in with their masculinity and sense of power.

But the emotion of anger is not maintained on a static, stable basis; it suffers transformations, and one of them is its turning into warmth and love, as the rigid emotional border is lowered into intimacy, through subsequent interactions. In this sense, child's emotionality could thwart father's attempts to exert power. Martin (Scottish, resident) who previously took six months off to be with his newborn son in his first year of life, as part of a caring arrangement with his partner who is also working full-time. He took on the responsibility of care as he explained that this was based on his rather than his partner's strong desire to have a child. In the quote below, he describes how his attempts at being strict are interrupted by his son's age and crying:

> I try to be strict but it's quite hard with a baby so young, because they don't really understand. You can find yourself getting quite frustrated and shouting at him, but that usually has the effect of making him cry, as opposed to making him do what you want him to do.

Momentarily, his position of full-time caregiver (although an enjoyable and chosen role) is not aligned with his masculine image (that of an 'active' man who enjoys going rock-climbing). By responding to his son's tears with aggression (normally considered a masculine strategy to reinstate power), Martin finds that this is not an appropriate strategy. He is also not fully comfortable to react with the tenderness apparently befitting a nurturing father, since this would pose an ongoing challenge to Martin's definition of self, as a proponent of traditional Scottish masculinity. However, through such interactions with his son, a process of change is underway, within which his *power over* his son becomes a *power with* (Allen 2008), and ideally would shift in time as their relationship develops, from control to cooperation.

Control as Closeness

The limits of the intimate father's role by comparison to previous stoic and detached models could be highlighted when one considered intimate control. In the father-child relationships, intimacy and love served mostly to maintain positive interactions which could then be used to maintain control over the child. Alexandru (Romanian, resident, 42), the father of a school-aged daughter, thinks it's an advantage to live in a time where one can benefit from 'an explosion of information' because the one *'who has the knowledge, holds the power'*. He applies a rather Foucault (1983) understanding of the role of knowledge in determining his power

4 Love and Power: Fathers' Emotions in Relation to Their...

as an informed modern parent, who engages together with his partner in the cultural reproduction of intensive parenting. He shared that he enjoys supervising his daughter's educational progress and exposing her to many different activities (such as karate, football, fashion shows, ice-skating). For Alexandru, a measure of subtle control is needed to keep his daughter balanced and focused on her trajectory of expected educational achievements. He details in this quote how he shows love by being involved to such an extent that it risks appearing strict or controlling, which is according to him preferable than being seen as an indifferent parent:

> You have to pay close attention, because from what I've seen they can easily burn-out. This is why it's good to keep your eyes on her [laughter]. To stay behind her, but not so that she can feel you are there always. Because when a child feels watched, she will try to do exactly what is forbidden (…) Every day I go with her and I leave her in her school bench. I walk all the way until the classroom, a thing which bothered her current teacher. Yes, because she told me I need to let her be slightly more independent. But she's not a very robust character. She's petite. We're also not very tall [laughs] and only from a desire to protect her and to carry her backpack, which weighs around five to six kg. To have her wear it on her shoulders from such a small age seems a bit too much to me. So as long as I can do it, then why not? I think it's a minor thing, but they drew my attention to it (…) although I did explain that for my child's safety and health I will always do everything that I'm allowed to do. Since walking into the school is permitted to parents on the basis of showing an ID and being given a badge, as long as this possibility exists, I will keep doing it. When there won't be any possibility, then we'll do something else.

Alexandru links his need for protectiveness to his daughter's gender. By acting in such a way, he not only exercises the characteristics of the ideal type of involved father but is also socializing his daughter into a traditional type of femininity as he states in another part of our interview that: 'in general, girls are a little bit docile (…) a girl is always seen as a more delicate person calmer.' Alexandru's example details how power can also be framed as ongoing negotiations and boundary-setting surrounding one's access to certain places (Edwards et al. 1999). His desire to protect and display responsibility is not considered to its full extent as possessiveness but is framed as protection and care. Despite receiving advice from a teacher on developing his daughter's autonomy, Alexandru reinforces his daughter's interdependence, but he does so by disempowering her, in a discursive account of expressing love through protection. He does not seem to link his daughter's education with the potential development of a certain autonomy, which can provide empowerment from masculine control (Presser and Sen 2000). However, this does reflect the literature, which argued that gendered, feeling rules are passed on from parents to children in the family according to sex-role models (Chodorow 1978) and are reinforced through gendered education in public places, such as the school (Thorne 1993).

Ewan (Scottish, resident, 36) defended his stance during the interview as a deeply involved father, when I remarked on his desire to 'watch' his child grow. He deflected this by emphasizing the 'active' nature of his fathering:

> (…) but not 'watching her grow' but 'growing with her', being with her when she grows. I think that phrase is often used in itself. It feels like a detachment and it's very much a dad thing 'Oh, I'm really looking forward to watching them grow up' (…) Maybe it's just part of where the English language, it is tied in with the culture and everything else. But it feels to me very much at the heart of that emotional detachment. So, it's not on the same level and you want to be involved. Whereas watching them feels like watching them from above and you're not really seeing it from their perspective.

These two fathers were actively and passionately working against emotional detachment, in establishing their intimate father's role, and this meant as well an increase in their control. Ewan described how impressed he was with his daughter's fragility at birth, shown by his recounting of a memory of 'holding her in my palms'. By contrast as she is now three years old and is acquiring the capacity to speak, there are more challenging interactions taking place:

> I think the harder things when she's really challenging you and to control your own frustration and she can just wind you up and you're really trying not to get angry because otherwise it just sets a precedent of starting you

know? If you shout at someone then it just becomes normal to just shout that's not where I want it to be, so my mom's friend, my godmother she said when she was raising her kids 'Look, you're gonna have fifty battles every day so just fight two' and I was like 'That's great, that's brilliant, that's such good advice!' So you go like 'yeah, fine whatever' you give up on most of it without showing that you've (…) without even creating a confrontation 'cause as soon as you do it becomes competitive and Anni wants to beat me and whatever the negotiation is or whatever the altercation is, if you don't even enter into it, it doesn't matter, it's gone. I'm not showing that it's bothering me, it's not serious and you just let it go, and another couple of things if you really feel it matters and that chain is on depending on whether I slept the whole night or she woke up three times, how calm you are [laughs] but yeah just try to focus on what's important and sometimes it's more about controlling her own frustration than anything difficult about how she is feeling.

Here Ewan is describing how Anni is fragile but can also be demanding, and it is not altogether coincidentally that control as closeness emerged as a sub-theme, mostly in examples of father-daughter interactions. The child can be vulnerable and empowered in relation to the father but also in how the father himself experiences strong same emotions in relation to the child, supporting a processual view of emotionality. Discourses of intensive parenting construct the child as affection and protection-needy (Lupton 2013). However, it is not always true that children are disempowered and vulnerable (Valentine 1997), as children manage to have an important influence over their parents and, many times, guide paternal behaviour, as I've also shown in previous sections focused on child-led agency. Nonetheless, it is true that paternal overprotection can stifle a child's self-confidence (Flouri 2005); so paradoxically, what might be perceived as detachment in the stoic provider's role can form a potential strategy of raising autonomous and capable children (Brussoni and Olsen 2013). In such cases, an emotional border towards increased stoicism with strict relational boundaries could also, paradoxically, create democratic arrangements between fathers and children, confirming that perhaps stoic fathers might be better emotionally 'equipped' to let their children go as they reach adulthood (Doucet 2015).

Conclusion

The findings presented in this chapter reveal how involved fathers hold a hierarchical understanding of love, and yet their narratives also foreground their interdependent love power in relation to their romantic partners and their children. Even if the requirements of a selfless, successful parenting identity and those of unconditional love invite parents to put the love for their offspring above their romantic love for each other, by maintaining opinions of biological differentiation and 'otherness', involved fathers continue to reproduce a patriarchal form of power, by emotionally subordinating their partners. Scottish fathers see themselves as rather distinct from their family members and emphasize autonomy while Romanian fathers blur the boundaries of their close relationships with those of their father's role into a collective 'we'. Both groups adopts the discourse of the intimate fathering, even as they continue to express traditional and stoic beliefs in relation to their partners.

The chapter also presented an interdependent account of love and power as mutually shaping emotions which are created within close family relationships. Power enhances emotional bordering by helping socially construct masculine emotionality on a spectrum, from intimacy to stoicism. Researching paternal love is essential to theoretically unlock obstacles in the way of gender change but also poses new theoretical dilemmas, as the gender conflict and emotional asymmetry in intimate life mentioned by Duncombe and Marsden (1995) can be increased by the fact that it is difficult to logically argue with affirmations based on love. In this intimate context, a father's unconditional love, even though it is generally considered a positive characteristic for children's lives, can also have a shadow side due to its subtle blend with paternal power. Furthermore emotional bordering shows how unconditional love should be limited by boundaries in order to be perceived as 'healthy' or 'appropriate'. Conclusively, love was a *risk* for fathers of both cultures. Therefore, despite increased involvement, too much emotional closeness can have the negative consequence of over-employing paternal control, as love was not altogether fully incorporated into their diverse forms of masculine emotionality.

References

Ahmed, S. (2014). *The Cultural Politics of Emotion*. Edinburgh: Edinburgh University Press.

Allen, A. (2008). Rethinking Power. *Hypatia, 13*(1), 21–40.

Brandth, B., & Kvande, E. (1998). Masculinity and Child Care: The Reconstruction of Fathering. *The Sociological Review, 46*, 293–313.

Breines, I., Connell, R., & Eide, I. (Eds.). (2000). *Male Roles, Masculinities and Violence: A Culture of Peace Perspective*. Paris: UNESCO Publications.

Brussoni, M., & Olsen, L. L. (2013). The Perils of Overprotective Parenting: Fathers' Perspectives Explored. *Child: Care, Health and Development, 39*, 237–245.

Burkitt, I. (2014). *Emotions and Social Relations*. London: Sage.

Cancian, F. M. (1986). The Feminization of Love. *Signs: Journal of Women in Culture and Society, 11*(4), 692–709.

Children and Young People Scotland Act. (2014). Available from http://www.legislation.gov.uk/asp/2014/8/pdfs/asp_20140008_en.pdf. Accessed 12 Mar 2019.

Chodorow, N. (1978). *The Reproduction of Mothering: Psychoanalysis and the Sociology of Gender*. Berkeley: University of California Press.

Christensen, P., Hockey, J., & James, A. (1999). 'That's Farming, Rosie...': Power and Familial Relations in an Agricultural Community. In J. Seymour & P. Bagguley (Eds.), *Relating Intimacies: Power and Resistance* (pp. 171–188). Houndmills: Macmillan.

Cohen, T. F. (1993). What Do Fathers Provide? Reconsidering the Economic and Nurturant Dimensions of Men as Parents. In J. C. Hood (Ed.), *Men Work and Family* (pp. 1–23). California: Sage.

Connell, R. W. (2005). *Masculinities* (2nd ed.). London: Allen & Unwin Academic.

Dalessandro, C., & Wilkins, A. C. (2017). Blinded by Love: Women, Men, and Gendered Age in Relationship Stories. *Gender and Society, 31*(1), 96–118.

Darling-Fisher, C. S., & Tiedje, L. B. (1990). The Impact of Maternal Employment Characteristics on Fathers' Participation in Child Care. *Family Relations, 39*(1), 20–26.

de Boise, S. (2015). *Men, Masculinities, Music and Emotions*. Basingstoke: Palgrave Macmillan.

Dermott, E., & Miller, T. (2015). More than the Sum of Its Parts? Contemporary Fatherhood Policy, Practice and Discourse. *Fathers, Relationships and Societies, 4*(2), 183–195.

Doucet, A. (2013). A "Choreography of Becoming": Fathering, Embodied Care, and New Materialisms. *Canadian Review of Sociology, 50*(3), 284–305.

Doucet, A. (2015). Parental Responsibilities: Dilemmas of Measurement and Gender Equality. *Journal of Marriage and Family, 77*(1), 224–242.

Duncombe, J., & Marsden, D. (1995). Can Men Love? 'Reading', 'Staging' and 'Resisting' the Romance. In L. Pearce & J. Stacey (Eds.), *Romance Revisited: Part 2* (pp. 238–250). London: Lawrence & Wishart.

Edwards, T. (2006). *Cultures of Masculinity*. London: Routledge.

Edwards, R., Ribbens, J., & Gillies, V. (1999). Shifting Boundaries and Power in the Research Process: The Example of Researching Step-Families. In J. Seymour & P. Bagguley (Eds.), *Relating Intimacies: Power and Resistance* (pp. 13–42). Houndmills: Macmillan.

Elias, N. (1939/2000). *The Civilizing Process: Sociogenetic and Psychogenetic Investigations* (Trans. E. Jephcott). Oxford: Blackwell Publishers.

Elias, N. (1987). The Retreat of Sociologists into the Present. *Theory, Culture and Society, 4*(2–3), 223–247.

Fergusson, A., & Jónasdóttir, A. G. (2014). *Love: A Question for Feminism in the 21st Century*. New York: Routledge.

Flouri, E. (2005). *Fathering and Child Outcomes*. Chichester: Wiley.

Foucault, M. (1983). The Subject and Power. In H. Dreyfus & P. Rabinow (Eds.), *Michel Foucault: Beyond Structuralism and Hermeneutics* (pp. 208–226). Chicago: The University of Chicago Press.

Gardiner, J. K. (2002). Theorising Age with Gender: Bly's Boys, Feminism, and Maturity Masculinity. In J. K. Gardiner (Ed.), *Masculinity Studies and Feminist Theory: New Directions* (pp. 90–118). New York: Columbia University Press.

Gaunt, R. (2008). Maternal Gatekeeping. *Journal of Family Issues, 29*(3), 373–395.

Giddens, A. (1992). *The Transformation of Intimacy: Sexuality, Love, and Eroticism in Modern Societies*. Stanford: Stanford University Press.

Graham, J. W., Gentry, K. W., & Green, J. (1981). The Self Presentational Nature of Emotional Expression: Some Evidence. *Personality and Social Psychology Bulletin, 7*(September), 467–474.

Halberstam, J. (2018). *Female Masculinity* (2nd ed.). Durham: Duke University Press.

Hatfield, E., Cacioppo, J. T., & Rapson, R. L. (1993). Emotion Contagion. *Current Directions in Psychological Science, 2*(3), 96–99.

Heaney, J. G. (2011). Emotions and Power: Reconciling Conceptual Twins. *Journal of Political Power, 4*(2), 259–277.

Hearn, J. (2013). The Sociological Significance of Domestic Violence: Tensions, Paradoxes and Implications. *Current Sociology, 61*(2), 152–170.

Hearn, J., & Pringle, K. (2006). Men, Masculinities and Children: Some European Perspectives. *Critical Social Policy, 26*, 365–389.

Henwood, K., & Procter, J. (2003). The 'Good Father': Reading Men's Accounts of Paternal Involvement During the Transition to First-Time Fatherhood. *British Journal of Social Psychology, 42*(3), 337–355.

Hochschild, A. R., & Machung, A. (1990). *The Second Shift: Working Parents and the Revolution at Home*. New York: Avon Books.

Jamieson, L. (2005). Boundaries of Intimacy. In J. Campling, S. Cunningham-Burley, & L. McKie (Eds.), *Families in Society Boundaries and Relationships* (pp. 189–207). Bristol: Policy.

Kemper, T. D. (1978). *A Social Interactional Theory of Emotions*. New York: Wiley.

Kimmel, M. S. (2013). Is It the "End of Men", or Are Men Still in Power? Yes! (Response to Article by Hanna Rosin in This Issue). *Boston University Law Review, 93*(3), 689–697.

Lamb, M. E. (Ed.). (2010). *The Role of the Father in Child Development* (5th ed.). London: Wiley.

Lupton, D. (2013). Infant Embodiment and Interembodiment: A Review of Sociocultural Perspectives. *Childhood, 20*(1), 37–50.

Lupton, D., & Barclay, L. (1997). *Constructing Fatherhood: Discourses and Experiences*. London: Sage.

Mead, G. H. (1934). *Mind, Self, and Society: From the Standpoint of a Social Behaviourist*. Chicago: University of Chicago Press.

Moore, E. (2012). Paternal Banking and Maternal Gatekeeping in Post-Divorce Families. *Journal of Family Issues, 33*(6), 745–772.

Popescu, L. (2004). *Politica Sexelor (Gender Politics)*. Bucuresti: Maiko.

Popescu, R. (2009). *Introducere in Sociologia Familiei: Familia Romaneasca in Societate Contemporana (Introduction to the Sociology of Family Life: The Romanian Family in Contemporary Society)*. Bucharest: Polirom.

Powell, F., & Scanlon, M. (2014). The Media and Child Abuse. *Discover Society, 13*. Available from http://discoversociety.org/2014/09/30/the-media-and-child-abuse/. Accessed 17 Mar 2019.

Presser, H. B., & Sen, G. (2000). *Women's Empowerment and Demographic Processes: Moving Beyond Cairo*. Oxford: Oxford University Press.

Ranson, G. (2015). *Fathering, Masculinity and the Embodiment of Care*. Basingstoke: Palgrave Macmillan.

Seidler, V. J. (1998). Masculinity, Violence and Emotional Life. In G. Bendelow & S. J. Williams (Eds.), *Emotions in Social Life: Critical Themes and Contemporary Issues*. London: Routledge.

Selin, H. (2013). *Parenting Across Cultures: Childrearing, Motherhood and Fatherhood in Non-Western Cultures*. New York/London: Springer.

Shields, A. S. (2002). *Speaking from the Heart: Gender and the Social Meaning of Emotion*. New York: Cambridge University Press.

Smart, C., & Neale, B. (1999). 'I Hadn't Really Thought About It': New Identities/New Fatherhoods. In J. Seymour & P. Bagguley (Eds.), *Relating Intimacies: Power and Resistance* (pp. 118–141). Houndmills: Macmillan.

Thorne, B. (1993). *Gender Play: Girls and Boys in School*. New Brunswick: Rutgers University Press.

Thurer, S. (1995). *The Myths of Motherhood: How Culture Reinvents the Good Mother*. New York: Penguin.

Valentine, G. (1997). My Son's a Bit Dizzy, My Wife's a Bit Soft: Gender, Children and Cultures of Parenting. *Gender, Place and Culture, 4*(1), 37–62.

von Scheve, C. (2011). Collective Emotions in Rituals: Elicitation, Transmission, and a "Mattheweffect". In A. Michaels & C. Wulf (Eds.), *Emotions in Rituals and Performances: South Asian and European Perspectives on Rituals and Performativity* (pp. 55–78). London: Routledge.

Williams, S. (2011). Chaotic Identities, Love and Fathering. *Folklore: Electronic Journal of Folklore, 48*, 31–54.

5

Discussion

Analysing the accounts of 47 Scottish and Romanian involved fathers revealed both the importance they place on love as an element of their fathering and the significance of their active fatherly love for their masculinity, even if love remains secondary to how they understand their emotions and identities. Men love their children *by doing* and, therefore, perform a masculinized version of love, understood here as an *active emotion*. However, involved fathers are interdependently linked to their family members since their love and power co-construct each other in the intimate realm, as David Morgan and Carol Smart argued in their previous research with English populations. As the findings of this research show, intimate fathering is not done 'purely' as Anthony Giddens argued, but it is an everyday practice in which men fall back on providing and emotional stoicism in a contradictory relational process.

This final section provides an integrated commentary on the data presented in the previous chapters and summarizes the main points of the analysis and how emotional bordering brings a unique contribution to knowledge. The over-arching idea is that by understanding love and masculinity not as separate and unrelated experiences but as existing in a relational exchange, in the socially constructed relational space where two

© The Author(s) 2020

A. Macht, *Fatherhood and Love*, Palgrave Macmillan Studies in Family and Intimate Life, https://doi.org/10.1007/978-3-030-20358-0_5

145

or more people interact with each other, a multidimensional account is put forth of how emotions contribute to the forming of gendered identities.

The analysis has emphasized the value of applying Ian Burkitt's idea to the collective and multi-relational characteristics of how some involved fathers construct their emotional selves. This awareness of multidimensional selves could be the reason why gender change is stalling since it needs to undergo transformations on plural levels, as gender identities are emotionally and relationally situated. Further implications for policy and the place of these findings in the debates surrounding love, fathering, masculinity and family life are mentioned by considering this new evidence and its limitations.

Relational Masculinity and Love: Summary of Contributions and Limitations

The main aim of this book was to provide an in-depth and sociological account of paternal love while considering masculinity in relation to non-sexual/non-romantic love. As such, the readers can attest better whether I achieved this aim. The book is, nonetheless, one of the first of its kind. Moreover, by exploring culture, age, relationship status and intergenerational transmission through the accounts of a heterogeneous group of fathers, a multitude of fathering experiences were represented; this formed a multidimensional account of how a small group of contemporary European fathers understand and practice the emotional and relational transitions from stoicism to love, and from traditional to intimate fathering. The main finding which emerged is that *paternal love is a form of action*, something fathers do in order to feel. As such, it is a different interpretation of Eric Fromm's understanding of love as recognition, which refers primarily to the establishment of a sense of intimacy between individuals (i.e. seeing into the Other). When viewing love as action then a dynamic account comes forth which portrays love as a process of relating, which contains both moments of intimacy and moments of detachment. Love can be re-energized by absence and stoicism; these emotional experiences do not have to 'kill' love as Kemper argued in his structural account of romantic love and power (1978). Such fluctuations of feeling in personal relationships *move* the relationship, allowing it to grow or dissolve. Contrary to Theodore Kemper's view that love is merely a positive emotion easily destroyed by power plays, love can contain power and power contains love in the relational *love complex* where two people construct their identities and live out their everyday lives.

In my work of recording and interpreting men's experiences of paternal love, I might have merely captured their experiences of parenting or caregiving or just their ways of talking about affection. Asserting with certainty what are the clear boundaries between love and care remains difficult. At times, acts of care can be an escape from love (Hollway 2006) or love can emerge from the decision to care for someone (Fromm 1956). In other circumstances, practices of love and relating do not necessarily involve practices of care. However, powerful emotions such as love can *move* social actors into practices of care (Macht 2019).

Nonetheless, considerable effort was employed both in the design of the research, during its data collection stages, as well as during the data analysis phase, to elicit rich and ethical narratives and remain close to the data provided by fathers. Love appeared in this book as it was lived, interpreted and understood by them. During our conversations, fathers engaged in thoughtful considerations of the role of love in their lives; for some, it was the first time they talked about paternal love with a stranger. Even if love, at times, proved elusive to grasp, the study is nonetheless a comprehensive and empirically supported first attempt at linking masculinity, fatherhood and love in a cultural comparison with two usually overlooked groups of European men. I have applied Ian Burkitt's theory to two specific and overlooked cultural contexts: the Scottish and the Romanian family context. Surprisingly, the data analysis revealed several similarities between the two cultures that contravene cultural stereotypes and what I initially assumed were decisively different ways of experiencing emotions in intimate relationships. I was surprised to uncover more similarities in how both groups adopted the discourses of the love-based family and that of intimate fathering.

Emotional bordering reveals the complexity of masculine emotionality and cements our understanding of it as a flexible social performance, one which can reinforce hegemonic masculinity or render it vulnerable and porous. Emotional bordering relies on instances of emotional management, but it is slightly different, as it can involve the opposite of managing emotions, as in the act of letting go and feeling them. Emotional management coordinates actors to carefully express their emotions in a professional or in a private setting (Theodosius 2006) and involves a certain degree of choosing what to 'display' in a process which is both cognitively and emotionally mediated. However, by bordering, fathers actively create boundaries between their self and their close family members, according to an emotionally reflexive compromise between the reactions of the people they interact with in a given social context and their own agency. This shifting between emotional borders as relational boundaries requires emotion work and emotional reflexivity, as I discussed throughout the book's substantive chapters.

Chapter 1 was focused on involved fathers' vocabularies, expressions of love and the embodiment of their love in relation to their children. It provided data excerpts that revealed that fathers of both cultures build intimacy through practices of care which evolve into practices of love. This happens through engagement or doing things together with their children, both domestic and leisurely activities. For some fathers, paternal love was presented initially as a powerful emotion, an instinct, but for most, it became meaningful as a relationship in time (particularly if fathers had more than one child and older children). Love occurred relationally, through a process of mutual 'give-and-take', and it became meaningful as fathers got to know their children, through spending time and doing things together with them. Paternal love to them was a form of action.

Relating to their children was marked by communication (mutual self-disclosure) and embodied involvement (especially with younger children), as important ways of *doing love*. Despite this, fathers did not consider themselves to be 'talking subjectivities' or 'communicating selves'. As they described that they value love as something that they do rather than talk about, they were hinting at how they blended their masculine identities with their father's role. This blending took the form of what I have tentatively termed 'emotional bordering' and have illustrated how this takes place for men across public and private places and in relation to a child's gender and age. Slight nuances appeared in that verbal declarations of love were preponderantly preferred by Scottish fathers while Romanian fathers preferred to engage in visible, active displays of love. However, Scottish fathers also tended to dispose of a wider variety of father-child activities outside of the home that they could engage their children in and, thus, were in a better position to define how they can practice love in visible, material ways.

Similarly, Chap. 2 presented data excerpts from fathers' narratives to further deconstruct the idea that the father's role is a unidimensional identity. It portrayed divisions between both Scottish and Romanian men in how they 'modelled' their role on that of their fathers and, at times, even their mothers, and they reflected on love from their own parents. Chapter 2 brought further evidence to demonstrate how in maintaining close relationships with their children, involved fathers engage in emotional bordering in relation to their own parents, especially their fathers. Again, several similarities could be perceived across culture. Findings show that there are three main ways in which being emotional in the context of parenting is transmitted intergenerationally, mirroring, to some extent, the findings of Julia Brannen's research (2015). These three typologies are (a) fathers who are ambivalent, (b) different and (c) similar to their own fathers in how they expressed love. *Ambivalent fathers* described having to learn how to become more loving in time but finding themselves 'falling back' into familiar patterns while *similar fathers* believed that they reproduced the same parenting and emotional ethos of their family; lastly, *different fathers* were certain that they were warmer and more intimate with their children. Ambivalent and similar fathers were more preponderant in the Scottish group while different fathers were more often found in the Romanian group; this could be a consequence of the different economic systems in which Romanian fathers grew up compared to the one in which they are raising their children, that being communism rather than capitalism.

A few Scottish fathers argued that it is not only their father but also their mother that shaped their current emotional patterns and, again, a different, small group of Scottish men confessed to feeling more comfortable than other fathers about expressing negative emotions in intimate relationships. Father's emotional bordering intervenes here to mark a compromise struck between the father's role as a disciplinarian (traditional and hegemonic) to that of the friend (democratic and intimate). An interesting discovery was noted by a small group of Romanian men, who struggled with love and the role-expectations traditionally associated with the fathering identity, such as discipline and authority; they considered themselves their children's 'friends'. Their experiences further underlined the deeply socially constructed character of paternal love and its slow transformation towards democratic (although not necessarily more enhanced) intimate relating. Conclusively, the chapter engages with Burkitt's theory of emotions as social relations to attempt to explain why this might have been and discusses that paternal love is not simply a granted relationship but that it can suffer changes. The analysis highlighted with excerpts from interviews, illuminated thematic similarities and differences between ages and cultures, to demonstrate how fathers' emotional bordering impacts upon these different social categories and is limited by them.

Lastly, Chap. 3 discussed how most involved Scottish fathers have positioned the father-child relationship above the mother-father relationship, which leaves space for a series of unequal practices of intimacy, nonetheless interpreted as positive. Surprisingly, it was the group of Romanian men who 'struggled with love' who clearly prioritized their relationship with their partner over that with their child, while the remainder tended to mix the agency of their fathering role with their family's collective 'we' and discerned their roles as one of self-confessed support for their children's mothers. Because of this complex relational dynamic, I argued that involved fathers' power is not only a relationship but also an emotion in much the same way as love is experienced not only as an emotion but also as a relationship. The emotional bordering between stoicism and intimacy employed by involved fathers is used consequently to leverage between feeling 'powerful' and feeling 'powerless' (or vulnerable) in the experience of emotionally connecting to their child/children.

Both Scottish and Romanian men mentioned that in working on their emotions in relation to the child, they are helped by their partner. However, an interesting difference appeared, in that some Romanian fathers described a process of resisting an emotional contagion of negative feelings, which took place between the mother and the child during emotional 'rollercoaster moments' and which reinforced their stoic bordering. Children as well participated in men's process of working on their emotions, by distracting, calming and energizing their fathers; this took place across gender and at child's different ages. Lastly, emotion work was employed in how men bordered their emotionality in that there was a push-and-pull dynamic between emotional detachment and emotional warmth. Again, and much like in the previous chapter, the evidence emphasizes fathers' attempts at detaching from past models of authoritarian and stoic fathering by engaging in physical (embodied) and verbal expressions of love.

Overall, fathers' accounts point to one highly important characteristics of love—it is something they have learned to do, in time, by getting to know and interact with their children. If one would generalize from these findings, love is something that men learn to do in time by taking actions for others. However, the readers need to remember that this is a qualitative piece of research and, therefore, generalizability is limited. Here is where the concept of emotional bordering helps us understand exactly how they do that, by establishing the boundaries of masculine emotions. Bordering comprises emotional reflexivity and emotion work, which are processes necessary to sustain everyday relationships. I argue that the concept can be used in a variety of settings to explain the emotional undercurrent that could accompany identity changes (from one gender performance to another, from one cultural identity to another, from one parenting and work role to another, etc.). Involved fathers become intimate fathers, lowering the stoic border, as they prioritize their time and attention to mutual activities with the child and carve out spaces to build intimacy together. Emotional bordering helps fathers enact their intimate involvement while maintaining a close relationship with the child by engaging in necessary efforts to suppress certain negative emotions, to detach from the worry that surges occasionally and promises to engulf other positive feelings, and the anger and protectiveness that both cement the father's role and the discourse of traditional male strength.

A case is made that paternal love is not only a positive relationship, but because it is complex, it includes a paradoxical mixture of both positive and negative emotions, the overcoming of which adds to its durability and 'strength' in uncertain post-modern times; a focus on the feeling self then reveals, much as Julia Brannen reflected on how 'feelings can endure over long periods of the life course' (p. 116, Brannen). Contrary to what Beck and Beck-Gernsheim (2014) and Baumann (2003) have written about the fluidity and lack of depth of romantic love, I have argued that for these fathers, their love is a relationship that solidifies in front of adversity and becomes something 'strong' when other institutions are weakened by societal changes. And yet paradoxically, a discourse of the 'heroic' quality of their love even when faced with separations continues to reproduce hegemonic masculinity in the intimate realm.

One of the key contributions of this research is showing that emotions are central, not peripheral, in the construction of fatherhood and masculinity. Emotions can be understood as the basis for the identity-making process of masculinity, not strictly built upon emotional repression as the concept of restrictive emotionality has sustained (Jansz 2000), but in a fluid process that sees men shifting emotionally between stoicism and intimacy. This moves the conversation to how men are socialized emotionally into 'loving selves', rather than continue to focus solely on masculinity and sexuality and their links to predatory/toxic forms that regulate the links between men and children through 'the shadow of paedophilia'. In this respect, an involved father's self, which comes into being through a variety of close relationships, draws from both love and power as emotions, in the formation of either controlling/hegemonic or collaborative/democratic close relationships. In this book, I argued that in order for fathers to balance the tensions between their fathering and masculinity, between social expectations of breadwinning and increased intimacy, and how they understood the establishing of appropriate relational boundaries, fathers bordered emotionally between stoicism and love. Ian Burkitt's work, to some extent, has framed the approach I have taken in analysing the data provided by my interviews with a diverse group of European fathers, but, at the same time, I have also used my research findings to shed light on the theoretical understanding of *emotions as relational characteristics*, embedded as they are in everyday, dynamic, social processes.

Importantly, it is not only having children that determine men to be reflexive (Shirani and Henwood 2011; Finn and Henwood 2009), but children themselves as individuals seem to engage fathers into increased emotional reflexivity, and through their daily interactions help fathers lower their stoic bordering into increased nurturance and intimacy.

Children are portrayed in this research and through the involved fathers' narratives as removed from the simplified image of 'intimate subordinates' to their parents' socialization practices; they are, on the contrary, primarily described as *active agents*. Despite the literature presenting love as a passionate and destabilizing social force, which is liquefied in the post-modern landscape, paternal love is shown here to present relational stability and adds a sense of meaning to fathers' lives during brief (circumstantial or work-related) or more permanent separations (residential or legally bound). This complements previous research with similar results but mainly focused on romantic couples (Gabb and Fink 2015).

One final, yet important, contribution of this research is that it gave modern Scottish and Romanian involved fathers a voice and placed it in the twenty-first century; this is over and above what historic research dealing with fatherhood in both countries, already uncovered in terms of eighteenth-, nineteenth- and twentieth-century masculinities and fatherhood. In addition, this unique investigation of involved fathers' accounts of their quotidian experiences provides empirical support for a fully sociological construction of *paternal* love (Jackson 1993).

Emotional bordering could have a wider applicability in describing how certain borders are emotionally created around the social construction of the self in a variety of contexts. However, more research is certainly needed to develop it. One methodological shortcoming of the study is that because of time and space limitations, I was not able to interview the children and their mothers. Recording their perspectives as well would have provided new insights and would've further contextualized fathers' narratives, especially since it has been shown that fathers report more closeness than children do (Waller 2002). As this book has focused primarily on the fathers, and since motherhood much like fatherhood is a learned process (Doucet 2017; Ranson 2015), more depth and nuance can be added to the findings by investigating parenting experiences in tandem, rather than individually. Moreover, even if there are some continental similarities between Scottish and Romanian cultures subsumed as they are under a shared European heritage, it needs to be said that a comparison with Asian or African or Middle Eastern fathers might reveal more obvious cultural differences.

This research took simply one of the many views in which fatherhood and love can be researched. In the wider population, not all men are fathers and not all fathers are involved. Furthermore, not all people parent with love. Aside from these facts, the study looked at a subset of fathers from specific cultural proveniences. In addition, the generalizability of qualitative research is tricky to establish and there are ongoing academic debates on the topic (Mason 2002; Charmaz 2013). My intentions were to critically understand fatherly love in its positive as well as negative aspects. However, this does not mean that my work supports extremism of any kind, such as offering data to support any fathers' rights groups. A careful reading of the text reveals how I have highlighted some of the persisting problems inherent within patriarchal forms of fathering, particularly those expressed through stoic bordering.

This book has been an overall effort to 'de-feminize' love and consider it in relation to masculinity by reflecting on how masculine identities are layered through their emotional stickiness to others (Ahmed 2010). Studying the role of the father remains interesting because it lies then at the intersections of age, gender, culture, rationalization, capitalism and the patriarchal division of the public and the private[1]; it also stands at the border between stoicism and intimacy and also between the reality of how intimate relationships are lived versus the discursive rhetoric of what we might want them to be. Gillis' (1997) often-quoted sentence 'families we live with and live by' could, in this way, be rewritten as 'fathers we live with' and 'fathers we live by'. One of the reasons why gender-equal changes are stalling are certainly political and structural but they are also emotional, as doing masculinity (Morgan 1992; Schrock and Schwalbe 2009) and doing love reveal that men's performance of gender is tied in with their performance of emotion. Gender equality is not only about men changing themselves as personalities that must 'work upon

---

[1] Despite progress in gender relations, society in most parts of the Globe continue to be organized according to patriarchal principles, as hooks writes, 'Patriarchal masculinity requires of boys and men not only that they see themselves as more powerful and superior to women (…)'. I am using the term 'patriarchy' here being defined according to Judith Lorber's definition of 'the ideological dominance of women by men' (p. 2, 1994). It is true that the term continues to intimidate readers, however, since gender progress continues to be slow and as Browne (2012) drew attention to the fact that the current era is undergoing a 'patriarchal resurgence', the term is analytically useful in helping us consider how we can envision 'post-patriarchal futures'.

5 Discussion 155

themselves' but about the ways in which they relate to others and the social networks into which their lives are lived, which need to be changed as well, in order to support the *personal* progressive efforts of men.

Data from this research has shown that there are moments of tenderness, mutual self-disclosure, encouragement and patient waiting happening between fathers and their sons, which challenge, to a certain extent, the idea that men mostly learn how to be dominant from their fathers. Changing the ways in which men relate with other women has been the focus thus far, but importantly the time has come to change the ways in which men relate to other men in their close relationships. Such a process would, however, require men to break through personal and gendered barriers and engage with 'gender vertigo' (Risman 1998).

Despite widespread discourse predicating fathers' involvement, Johansson and Klinth (2007) remind that men developing a more caring attitude does not necessarily equate with their practical implementation of gender equality strategies within their families. On the contrary, the authors argue that men can choose a parental role and that this is an expression of their power. Fathers can thus act as 'bricoleurs' (Aboim 2010) in selecting various means of performing emotions and gender to increase social privileges. Some have shown that British fathers can indeed concede power during special circumstances such as childbirth (Dolan and Coe 2011) although only temporarily and while still maintaining power through stoic displays of masculinity in interactions with medical staff in delivery rooms. Therefore, there is a fine difference between the child-oriented and the gender-equal parenting approaches that men adopt, especially as mothers are still more involved in child-rearing than their partners (Craig 2006).

In addition, and based on Ian Burkitt's and Jonathan Heaney's work on emotions and power (and in contrast to Kemper's theory of power and romantic love), I provided empirical support for how power and love are relational and emotional experiences, lived by parents and children in the civilizing and socializing processes in which they are engaged in. So, power in relation to love can also be understood as an emotion, not only as an external structure impressing upon the intimate lives of family members. Reiterating the point, I think that emotions are not simply stuck 'within' their bodies or 'locked deep down', and they are also not only oppositional (ex. love versus hate). Understood in this way, (paternal) love becomes an everyday processual exchange where embodied interiors (a person's physiological and 'private' feelings) become normative exteriors (verbally constructed and dynamically expressed feeling rules). Fathers' narratives have shown that far from being a self-contained, intrinsic and mysterious experience, love is an embodied reality, a relational process. As such, love and power are *complexes* of emotions and mutually complementing sides of the same close relational experience. Providing and intimacy coexist precisely because of capitalism's intrusion into the private.[2] In this sense, by choosing to be more caring, men perform not only an intimate act but also a political one. As bell hooks reminds, social norms might need to be changed to value the measure of a man's worth not exclusively through his physical or mental strength but also based on their courage to love:

> The moment we choose to love we begin to move against domination, against oppression. The moment we choose to love we begin to move towards freedom, to act in ways that liberate ourselves and others. That action is the testimony of love as the practice of Freedom. (p. 298, 1994)

There is hope then that fatherhood might be one of the avenues through which hegemonic forms of masculinity can continue to be dismantled. And if this is to be done, then a relationally embedded and increasingly complex nexus of explanations is necessary, as Norbert Elias wrote:

> Only if we see the compelling force with which a particular social structure, a particular form of social interweaving, is pushed through its tensions to a specific change and so to other forms of intertwining, can we understand how those changes arise in human mentality (...) (1939/2000, p. 367)

Lastly, Linda-Anne Rebhun (2007) speaks of '(...) love as an ideal, rarely achieved but powerfully compelling as a moral archetype' (p. 117). Love can thus fulfil a dual social function, as a *value* and as a *practice*.

---

[2] For an in-depth discussion of fathers' love and capitalist commodification, see Macht (2018).

Sociologists should, therefore, analyse how this ideal is brought into being in everyday practices and what purposes it serves: Social cohesion? Social unrest? Or perhaps even social transformation? It is unwise to discount the importance of ideals such as love and their power to both move and motivate people to act in ways which are not always or immediately tied in with rational self-interest and the gratification of sexual, romantic needs. Love as a relational force could help transform social roles. In this way, it acts as a creative, relational force between what the social reality is and what it can be. I think that as such, love is an important catalyst in the study of social change, but its connection to power warns of its complex and ongoing negative implications, from intimate partner violence and child abuse to the patriarchal ideological discourses of nation-states (Fergusson and Jónasdóttir 2014).

It remains vital to explore the emotional impact of patriarchy, as a system of gendered relationships that continues to structure our social world. All social actors live within the gender order and continue to be constrained by it. However, increasingly, more men and women can contribute to accomplishing a social world where not necessarily all inequalities are transformed into 'equalities', and where diversity is flattened out, but an environment in which individuals' many potentialities of relating, and of creating intimacy, are freed from unidimensional, one-size-for-all type of restrictions. A social world in which we all have the responsibility to love and care and implement the social changes we want to see happen around us, not only through the exercise of reason or the constricting prerogatives of biology but also through the ways in which we *feel*. As Ian Burkitt reflects: '(…) emotion and our feelings about our self and world remain at the heart of everything we know and everything we are' (2014, p. 171).

References

Aboim, S. (2010). *Plural Masculinities: The Remaking of the Self in Private Life*. Farnham: Ashgate Publishing Co.

Ahmed, S. (2010). Happy Objects. In M. Gregg & G. J. Seigworth (Eds.), *The Affect Theory Reader* (pp. 29–51). Durham: Duke University Press.

Baumann, Z. (2003). *Liquid Love: On the Frailty of Human Bonds*. Cambridge: Polity Press.

Beck, U., & Beck-Gernsheim, E. (2014). *Distant Love: Personal Life in the Global Age*. Cambridge: Polity Press.

Brannen, J. (2015). *Fathers and Sons: Generations, Families and Migration*. Basingstoke/New York: Palgrave Macmillan.

Browne, V. (2012). Backlash, Repetition, Untimeliness: The Temporal Dynamics of Feminist Politics. *Hypatia, 28*(4), 1–17.

Burkitt, I. (2014). *Emotions and Social Relations*. London: Sage.

Charmaz, K. (2013). *Constructing Grounded Theory*. London: SAGE.

Craig, L. (2006). Parental Education, Time in Paid Work and Time with Children: An Australian Time-Diary Analysis. *The British Journal of Sociology, 57*, 553–575.

Dolan, A., & Coe, C. (2011). Men, Masculine Identities and Childbirth. *Sociology of Health & Illness, 33*, 1019–1034.

Doucet, A. (2017). *Do Men Mother? Fathering, Care, and Domestic Responsibility* (2nd ed.). Toronto: University of Toronto Press.

Elias, N. (1939/2000). *The Civilizing Process: Sociogenetic and Psychogenetic Investigations* (Trans. E. Jephcott). Oxford: Blackwell Publishers.

Fergusson, A., & Jónasdóttir, A. G. (2014). *Love: A Question for Feminism in the 21st Century*. New York: Routledge.

Finn, M., & Henwood, K. (2009). Exploring Masculinities Within Men's Identificatory Imaginings of First-Time Fatherhood. *British Journal of Social Psychology, 48*, 547–562.

Fromm, E. (1956). *The Art of Loving*. New York: Harper and Row.

Gabb, J., & Fink, J. (2015). *Couple Relationships in the 21st Century*. Basingstoke: Palgrave Pivot.

Gillis, J. R. (1997). *A World of Their Own Making: Myth, Ritual and the Quest for Family Values*. Cambridge: Harvard University Press.

Hollway, W. (2006). *The Capacity to Care: Gender and Ethical Subjectivity*. New York: Routledge.

hooks, b. (1994). *Teaching to Transgress: Education as the Practice of Freedom*. New York/London: Routledge.

Jackson, S. (1993). Even Sociologists Fall in Love: An Exploration in the Sociology of Emotions. *Sociology, 27*(2), 201–220.

Jansz, J. (2000). Masculine Identity and Restrictive Emotionality. In A. H. Fischer (Ed.), *Gender and Emotion: Social Psychological Perspectives* (pp. 166–186). Cambridge: Cambridge University Press.

Johansson, T., & Klinth, R. (2007). Caring Fathers: The Ideology of Gender Equality and Masculine Positions. *Men and Masculinities, 11*(1), 42–62.

Kemper, T. D. (1978). *A Social Interactional Theory of Emotions*. New York: Wiley.

Lorber, J. (1994). *Paradoxes of Gender*. New Haven/London: Yale University Press.

Macht, A. (2018). Resisting the Commodification of Intimate Life? Paternal Love, Emotional Bordering and Narratives of Ambivalent Family Consumerism from Scottish and Romanian Fathers. *Families, Relationships and Societies, 8*, 21. https://doi.org/10.1332/204674318X15384702551202.

Macht, A. (2019, Forthcoming). Travelling Feelings: Narratives of Sustaining Love in Two Case Studies with Fathers in Family Separations. In L. Murray et al. (Eds.), *Families in Motion: Ebbing and Flowing Through Space and Time* (pp. 19–37). Bingley: Emerald Publishing.

Mason, J. (2002). *Qualitative Researching*. California: Sage Publications.

Morgan, D. H. J. (1992). *Discovering Men*. London: Routledge.

Ranson, G. (2015). *Fathering, Masculinity and the Embodiment of Care*. Basingstoke: Palgrave Macmillan.

Rebhun, L. A. (2007). The Strange Marriage of Love and Interest: Economic Change and Emotional Intimacy in Northeast-Brazil, Private and Public. In M. B. Padilla, J. S. Hirsch, M. Munoz-Laboy, R. E. Sember, & R. G. Parker (Eds.), *Love and Globalization: Transformations of Intimacy in the Contemporary World* (pp. 107–120). Nashville: Vanderbilt University Press.

Risman, B. J. (1998). *Gender Vertigo: American Families in Transition*. New Haven: Yale University Press.

Schrock, D., & Schwalbe, M. (2009). Men, Masculinities and Manhood Acts. *Annual Review of Sociology, 35*, 277–295.

Shirani, F., & Henwood, K. (2011). Continuity and Change in a Qualitative Longitudinal Study of Fatherhood: Relevance Without Responsibility. *International Journal of Social Research Methodology, 14*(1), 17–29.

Theodosius, C. (2006). Recovering Emotion from Emotion Management. *Sociology, 40*(5), 893–911.

Waller, M. R. (2002). *My Baby's Father: Unmarried Parents and Paternal Responsibility*. Ithaca: Cornell University Press.

List of Participants

Scottish Fathers

Adam is a lecturer and has been living together with his partner Mia (who is Spanish) in Edinburgh for five years now. Their two-year-old son Jack was born in Scotland. Adam is the main breadwinner in the family while Mia is a stay-at-home mother.

Charlie is a doctor who lives in Edinburgh with his wife Mary and their two daughters: Tessa, aged seven, and Kate, aged five. Mary works as a medical researcher and together, the couple shares a demanding work schedule. Charlie has chosen to reduce his work hours and become more involved in fathering his daughters. The couple also receives help from childminders and Charlie's mother-in-law.

Ben works for an organization supporting Scottish fathers. He lives in Edinburgh with his wife Siobhan. Together, they have a six-month-old son. Ben also has four girls from his previous relationships, who spend half of their time in his care and the rest of the time with their mothers.

David works as a researcher in Glasgow. He lives with his wife Sara and his four-year-old son, Max, in a village near Glasgow. At the time of the interview, he was expecting another son.

© The Author(s) 2020
A. Macht, *Fatherhood and Love*, Palgrave Macmillan Studies in Family and Intimate Life, https://doi.org/10.1007/978-3-030-20358-0

162   **List of Participants**

Ewan works as an accountant in Edinburgh. He lives with his partner Pia, who is Greek, and their three-year-old daughter Anni. At the time of our interview, Ewan was expecting his second child and his partner was on maternity leave.

Fergus works as a manager in Edinburgh. His wife Katie works full-time for the same company and in a similar senior position. They have two children Mia (three years) and Adam (six months). Fergus reduced his working week to four days once his first-born arrived but got back to full-time employment when Mia went to nursery and he received a promotion. At the time of our interview, he was scheduled to take parental leave with Adam in the summer.

Gavin was unemployed at the time of the interview. He previously worked as a manager in Edinburgh. He considered himself a full-time, stay-at-home father while his wife Betty works as a doctor. Together, they have three children: nine-year-old Lucy and four-year-old twins Eva and Robbie. Gavin went back to full-time employment, three months after our interview. He continues to share housework with Betty and takes shifts in picking up their children from school.

Gordon is a lecturer, living in Edinburgh with his wife Tora, who is a part-time designer. Together, they have two boys: three-and-a-half-year-old Ian and six-month-old Maxwell. Because his wife works nightshifts, Gordon frequently takes the boys to father-child playgroups at the weekends so that his wife can have some time for herself.

Hamish was unemployed at the time of our interview due to budget cuts in the company in which he worked. He had previously worked as an engineer. He is living with his partner Constance, who is a teacher, and together they have a two-year-old daughter, Jessica. His partner became the main breadwinner in the family and, consequently, Hamish spent more time doing childcare. He receives help a day a week from the child's grandmother.

Hugh works as a manager in Edinburgh. His wife works full-time in the same company, in a similar role, and together, they have two boys, Emmett (five-year-old) and Oliver (three-year-old). During the week, the boys are looked after by a childminder.

Ian works as an investment professional in Edinburgh. His wife also works full-time in a similar position. Together, they have two children Annabel (seven years) and Tom (four years).

James works as a manager in Edinburgh and his wife Pam is currently a stay-at-home mother to their three-year-old son Hamish and one-year-old daughter Sophie. John has been living in Scotland since he was eight years old but has Irish heritage. The family receives lots of help from their relatives who live near their home.

John works as an accountant in Edinburgh. He is married to a photographer and together they have three children: Ben (six years), Emma (seven years) and Tania (one year). His wife's schedule is more flexible and, therefore, she ends up spending more time taking care of the children. John is the family's main breadwinner.

Keith works as a consultant in Edinburgh. He has a nine-year-old son Terry and a seven-year-old daughter Miranda. At the time of our interview, he was in the process of divorcing from his wife, who lives with the children in England. Keith commutes every weekend down South to be with his children. At the time of our interview, his work contract was soon to expire, and he was preparing to buy a flat to move down South to be closer to his children.

Lewis works as a computer specialist in Edinburgh. He is married to Marissa, who also works full-time and together, they have an eight-year-old daughter, Fionna. Lewis sent me an email after our interview to elaborate on the practical ways in which he is working towards financially ensuring his daughter's future.

Logan works as a solicitor in Edinburgh. He is living with Rosie, who works part-time, and together, they have a one-year-old daughter Maeve. The little girl is going to nursery two days a week and on Wednesdays, she's being looked after on rotation by her two grandmothers.

Malcolm works as an investment professional in Edinburgh. He is married to Connie who works part-time as a researcher. Together, they have two children, 11-year-old Abel and 9-year-old Kathy.

Mark works as a team leader for a company in Edinburgh. He lives with his partner Deborah, who also works full-time, and their three-year-old son, Reese. Once a month, Mark's mother would drop by to take care of her grandson for some hours, otherwise, the child attends nursery. Mark had to care on his own for his son a couple of months last year while his partner travelled due to wider family-related reasons.

Martin works part-time as a computer specialist in Edinburgh. He lives with his wife Thea who works full-time and their 14-month-old son

164   List of Participants

Benjamin. Prior to Benjamin's birth, Martin mutually decided with Thea to each take six months off and be with the baby. After spending six months with the baby, Martin returned to work but shortened his work-week to four days.

Nicholas works as an engineer in Edinburgh. He is married to Danielle and together, they have a six-month-old daughter Celeste. The process of conceiving his daughter involved in-vitro fertilization treatment over a period of five years. Because of this, since Celeste's birth, his wife decided to stay-at-home and look after their daughter, and Nicholas became the family breadwinner.

Patrick is a computer specialist in Edinburgh. He lives with his wife Ann-Marie who also works part-time, and they live in a village near Edinburgh. He has two daughters, eight-year-old Morgan and five-year-old Celeste.

Ray has been his nine-year-old son's primary caregiver for four years. His son, Scott, was diagnosed with autism the year prior to our interview. Before that, he had been a contact father for Scott since his birth due to the legal arrangements in place after he separated from his ex-wife. Ray used to work as a manager for a shipping company in Edinburgh but had lost his job when he became a carer.

Rod works as an investment professional in Edinburgh. He is married to Rona who works as a teacher and together, they have three children: five-year-old Andrew, three-year-old Skye and three-week-old Rowan. They receive regular help from his parents, who had come to live with them while his wife was pregnant.

Stephen, who was unemployed at the time of our interview, saw himself as a 'part-time' father who managed to overcome an addiction to drugs. He is the father of five-year-old Michelle, who he can see every weekend. Together, they attend father-child groups. Recently, he has been reconnecting with his estranged father.

Stewart is the full-time carer of his three-year-old son Matthew. He is retired and has a 33-year-old daughter from a previous marriage. He used to work as a manager in constructions and owned a shop. Last year, he had separated from his second wife Kiera, Matthew's biological mother. Stewart took care of the family's three boys before he lost custody of his two non-biological sons last year. At the time of the interview, Stewart was engaged in court proceedings because his ex-partner appealed for sole custody over Matthew.

Tim works part-time as a supermarket assistant. He lives with parents in Edinburgh and is a single parent to six-year-old Johnny. Tim has been separated from his partner since around the birth of his son. At the time of the interview, he was in court proceedings to have his weekly contact with his son extended and was attending night classes to gain a higher education certificate.

Will was, at the time of the interview, on an extended sick leave due to a serious medical condition. He previously worked as a sports instructor He is the father of 17-year-old Carla and 6-year-old Toby. Two years ago, he went through a divorce and is presently living with his parents. He can see his youngest child only at weekends. His teenage daughter and her boyfriend visit him regularly.

Romanian Fathers

Alexandru works as a computer specialist. He lives in Bucharest with his wife Catalina, who also works full-time for a large corporation, and together, they have a seven-year-old daughter, Ana. The couple cannot rely on help from relatives in raising their daughter since both sets of parents live outside of Bucharest.

Bogdan works in a factory. He has been living in Bucharest since he was 16 years old. He is married to Rodica, who works in retail, and together, they have an eight-year-old boy, Cornel. Cornel is attending school and spends most of the afternoons by himself until his parents return from work since the family has no additional childcare support.

Ciprian works as a computer specialist in Bucharest. Despite living a relatively middle-class life, Ciprian defines himself as 'working class'. He is married to Tania, who also works full-time for a company and together, they have two six-year-old twin boys, Liviu and Horia. The couple receives help from Ciprian's sister-in-law who comes sometimes to baby-sit at weekends.

166 List of Participants

Daniel is an engineer and is married to Magda who works part-time for an online company. They live in Bucharest and together they have a four-year-old boy, Paul, who goes to nursery a couple of days a week and is looked after by their relatives the rest of the week.

Emil is the executive director of his own company. He is originally from Iași but has been living in Bucharest for most of his adult life. He is married to Catinca and has a four-year-old daughter Sabina, and a three-month-old baby, Iulia. He brings his children to work regularly as his company has a child-friendly environment.

Florin works as an engineer in Bucharest and lives with his wife Selma, who also works full-time. He is the father of two-year-old Mădălina. At the time of our meeting, he was expecting another baby boy due in the fall. Mădălina is cared for by her grandparents while her parents are at work.

George works as a computer specialist in Bucharest. He has a 15-year-old biological girl, Cerasela, from a previous marriage but hasn't been in contact with his daughter for almost two years now, due to legal arrangements. He has remarried and is now the non-adoptive father of his wife's 17-year-old son, Andrei (since the boy's biological father lives in another country). They have been living together in a house as a family for three years now.

Horia is an actor. He lives in the suburbs of Bucharest with his wife Doina, who is also an actress. Together, they have three children: four-year-old Oana, five-year-old Flaviu and one-year-old Teo. Horia and his wife have a childcare arrangement that allows them individually the freedom to pursue creative work projects.

Ion works as an executive director for a company in Bucharest. He is married to Tina, who is also employed full-time in a company, and together they have a four-year-old son Matei. During workdays, Matei goes to a private nursery in the city.

Iustin works as an engineer in Bucharest. He is married to Daniela, who also works full-time, and together, they have a two-year-old daughter Miruna. During the week, Miruna is being looked after by Iustin's mother-in-law and, sometimes, his father.

Lucian works as an engineer in Bucharest and is in a relationship with Maria, who is a stay-at-home mom. Together, they have a three-year-old son called Pavel.

Liviu works as a car mechanic in Bucharest, where he lives with his wife Selma, who also works full-time. Together, they have twins Elena and George who are both six years old and are preparing to enter school in the fall. The twins are looked after by his mother-in-law during the day.

Mihai works as a computer specialist in Bucharest, where he lives with his wife Georgeta and his 14-year-old son Andrei. He was looking forward to seeing his son passing an important exam to enter high school in the fall.

Nelu is an animal trainer. He lives in Bucharest with his wife, Ada, a stay-at-home mom to their three-year-old son Lucian. At the time of the interview, Lucian was just two months away from starting nursery.

Ovidiu works as an economist in Bucharest where he lives with his wife Flora, who also works full-time. Together, they have a two-and-a-half-year-old son, Vlad. During the workweek, their son is looked after by his grandmother.

Petre is a pilot who lives in Bucharest with his wife Ana-Maria, who is a stay-at-home mother. Together, they have a two-year-old son, David. There aren't receiving any help from grandparents who are both still in full-time employment, but Ana-Maria occasionally hires help from nannies.

Remus works as a manager in Bucharest. He lives with his wife Camelia and two daughters: seven-year-old Cătălina and five-year-old Flori. His wife worked as a notary in the past but decided to become a stay-at-home mother once she had their second child.

Sergiu is a supply worker who lives in Bacău. He commutes between Bacău and Scotland for work. He went through a divorce last year, after which his ex-wife Clara relocated his two children 15-year-old Matei and 11-year-old Anca to another European country where she could find work. Sergiu has seen his children only a couple of times in the year prior to our interview because commuting is expensive.

Vlad is a painter living in Bucharest. He is the father of ten-year-old Roxana and lives together with his partner Mia, who also works part-time. After the birth of his daughter, Vlad decided to settle his art workshop at home, so that he can spend more time with his daughter and have the family closer together.

Vasile is a bus driver who lives in Bucharest. He is married to Catinca and together, they have a two-and-a-half-year-old boy, Dragoş. His wife is staying at home to take care of his son, as their relatives live far away and cannot provide care. Vasile works roughly 12 works a day on the road, which leaves him with very little time to spend with his child, but he had plans to switch jobs soon, to reduce his workload and spend more time with his family.

References

Aboim, S. (2010). *Plural Masculinities : The Remaking of the Self in Private Life*. Farnham: Ashgate.

Abrams, L., & Breitenbach, E. (2006). Gender and Scottish Identity. In L. Abrams, E. Gordon, D. Simonton, & E. Yeo (Eds.), *Gender in Scottish History Since 1700* (pp. 17–43). Edinburgh: Edinburgh University Press.

Ahmed, S. (2010). Happy Objects. In M. Gregg & G. J. Seigworth (Eds.), *The Affect Theory Reader* (pp. 29–51). Durham: Duke University Press.

Ahmed, S. (2014). *The Cultural Politics of Emotion*. Edinburgh: Edinburgh University Press.

Allen, A. (2008). Rethinking Power. *Hypatia, 13*(1), 21–40.

Anderson, A. M. (1996). The Father–Infant Relationship; Becoming Connected. *Journal of the Society of Pediatric Nurses, 1*, 83–92.

Änggard, E. (2005). Barbie Princesses and Dinosaur Dragons: Narration as a Way of Doing Gender. *Gender and Education, 17*(5), 539–553.

Archer, M. (2010). Routine, Reflexivity, and Realism. *Sociological Theory, 28*(3), 272–303.

Åsenhed, L., Kilstam, J., Alehagen, S., & Baggens, C. (2014). Becoming a Father Is an Emotional Roller Coaster: An Analysis of First-Time Fathers' Blogs. *Journal of Clinical Nursing, 23*(9–10), 1309–1317.

© The Author(s) 2020
A. Macht, *Fatherhood and Love*, Palgrave Macmillan Studies in Family and Intimate Life, https://doi.org/10.1007/978-3-030-20358-0

170   References

Attridge, M. (2013). Jealousy and Relationship Closeness: Exploring the Good (Reactive) and Bad (Suspicious) Sides of Romantic Jealousy. *SAGE Open, 3*(1), 1–16.

Backett, K. C. (1982). *Mothers and Fathers: A Study of the Development and Negotiation of Parental Behaviour*. London: Palgrave Macmillan.

Barnett, R. C., & Baruch, G. K. (1987). Determinants of Fathers' Participation in Family Work. *Journal of Marriage and Family, 49*(1), 29–40.

Baumann, Z. (2003). *Liquid Love: On the Frailty of Human Bonds*. Cambridge: Polity Press.

Bawin-Legros, B. (2004). Intimacy and the New Sentimental Order. *Current Sociology, 52*(2), 241–250.

Beatty, M. J., & Dobos, J. A. (1993). Direct and Mediated Effects of Perceived Father Criticism and Sarcasm on Females' Perceptions of Relational Partners' Disconfirming Behavior. *Communication Quarterly, 41*(2), 187–197.

Beciu, C. (2009). The Perception of Europeanization in Public Institutions: The Imagery of the 'Adaptation' to a New System. *Revista Română de Sociologie (The Romanian Journal of Sociologie), XX*(3–4), 193–214.

Beck, U., & Beck-Gernsheim, E. (2014). *Distant Love: Personal Life in the Global Age*. Cambridge: Polity Press.

Beigel, H. G. (1951). Romantic Love. *American Sociological Review, 16*(3), 326–334.

Bodogai, S. I., & Cutler, S. J. (2014). Aging in Romania: Research and Public Policy. *The Gerontologist, 54*(2), 147–152.

Bosoni, M. L., & Baker, S. (2015). The Intergenerational Transmission of Fatherhood: Perspectives from the UK and Italy. *Families, Relationships and Societies, 4*(2), 239–251.

Bowlby, J. (1969). *Attachment and Loss – Vol. 1: Attachment*. New York: Basic Books.

Brandth, B., & Kvande, E. (1998). Masculinity and Child Care: The Reconstruction of Fathering. *The Sociological Review, 46*, 293–313.

Brannen, J. (2003). Towards a Typology of Intergenerational Relations: Continuities and Change in Families. *Sociological Research Online, 8*(2), 1–11.

Brannen, J. (2015). *Fathers and Sons: Generations, Families and Migration*. Basingstoke/New York: Palgrave Macmillan.

Brannen, J., & Moss, P. (1998). The Polarisation and Intensification of Parental Employment in Britain: Consequences for Children, Families and the Community. *Community, Work & Family, 1*(3), 229–247.

Brannen, J., & Nilsen, A. (2006). From Fatherhood to Fathering: Transmission and Change among British Fathers in Four-Generation Families. *Sociology, 40*(2), 335–352.

Breines, I., Connell, R., & Eide, I. (Eds.). (2000). *Male Roles, Masculinities and Violence: A Culture of Peace Perspective*. Paris: UNESCO Publications.

Brennan, A., Marshall-Lucette, S., Ayers, S., & Ahmed, H. (2007). A Qualitative Exploration of the Couvade Syndrome in Expectant Fathers. *Journal of Reproductive and Infant Psychology, 25*(1), 18–39.

Browne, V. (2012). Backlash, Repetition, Untimeliness: The Temporal Dynamics of Feminist Politics. *Hypatia, 28*(4), 1–17.

Brownlie, J. (2014). *Ordinary Relationships: A Sociological Study of Emotions, Reflexivity and Culture*. Basingstoke: Palgrave Macmillan.

Brussoni, M., & Olsen, L. L. (2013). The Perils of Overprotective Parenting: Fathers' Perspectives Explored. *Child: Care, Health and Development, 39*, 237–245.

Burkitt, I. (2002). Complex Emotions: Relations, Feelings and Images in Emotional Experience. *The Sociological Review, 50*(S2), 151–167.

Burkitt, I. (2014). *Emotions and Social Relations*. London: Sage.

Cancian, F. M. (1986). The Feminization of Love. *Signs: Journal of Women in Culture and Society, 11*(4), 692–709.

Chand, A. (2016). *Masculinities on Clydeside: Men in Reserved Occupations During the Second World War*. Edinburgh: Edinburgh University Press.

Chandler, A. (2012). Self-Injury as Embodied Emotion Work: Managing Rationality, Emotions and Bodies. *Sociology, 46*(3), 442–457.

Charmaz, K. (2013). *Constructing Grounded Theory*. London: SAGE.

Children and Young People Scotland Act. (2014). Available from http://www.legislation.gov.uk/asp/2014/8/pdfs/asp_20140008_en.pdf. Accessed 12 Mar 2019.

Chodorow, N. (1978). *The Reproduction of Mothering: Psychoanalysis and the Sociology of Gender*. Berkeley: University of California Press.

Christensen, P., Hockey, J., & James, A. (1999). 'That's Farming, Rosie…': Power and Familial Relations in an Agricultural Community. In J. Seymour & P. Bagguley (Eds.), *Relating Intimacies: Power and Resistance* (pp. 171–188). Houndmills: Macmillan.

Christopoulos, A. L. (2001). Relationships Between Parents' Marital Status and University Students' Mental Health, Views of Mothers and Views of Fathers: A Study in Bulgaria. *Journal of Divorce & Remarriage, 34*(3–4), 179–190.

Christozov, C., & Toteva, S. (1989). Abuse and Neglect of Children Brought Up in Families with an Alcoholic Father in Bulgaria. *Child Abuse & Neglect, 13*(1), 153–155.

Cohen, A. (1994). Culture, Identity and the Concept of Boundary. *Revista de Antropología Social, 3*, 49–62.

172   References

Cohen, T. F. (1993). What Do Fathers Provide? Reconsidering the Economic and Nurturant Dimensions of Men as Parents. In J. C. Hood (Ed.), *Men Work and Family* (pp. 1–23). California: Sage.

Coltrane, S. (1997). *Family Man: Fatherhood, Housework, and Gender Equity.* Oxford: Oxford University Press.

Connell, R. W. (2002). Understanding Men: Gender Sociology and the New International Research on Masculinities. *Social Thought & Research, 24*(1–2), 13–31.

Connell, R. W. (2005). *Masculinities* (2nd ed.). Berkeley: University of California Press.

Constantin, M. (2012). The Comparative Interpretation of Rural and Urban Regional Ethnicity in Romania. *Revista Română de Sociologie (The Romanian Journal of Sociology), XXIII*(1–2), 89–114.

Cook, W. L., & Douglas, E. M. (1998). The Looking-Glass Self in Family Context: A Social Relations Analysis. *Journal of Family Psychology, 12*(3), 299–309.

Cottingham, M. D. (2015). Learning to "Deal" and "De-Escalate": How Men in Nursing Manage Self and Patient Emotions. *Sociological Inquiry, 85*(1), 75–99.

Cottingham, M. D., Eriksson, R. J., & Diefendorff, J. M. (2015). Examining Men's Status Shield and Status Bonus: How Gender Frames the Emotional Labor and Job Satisfaction of Nurses. *Sex Roles, 72*, 377–389.

Craig, L. (2006). Parental Education, Time in Paid Work and Time with Children: An Australian Time-Diary Analysis. *The British Journal of Sociology, 57*, 553–575.

Dalessandro, C., & Wilkins, A. C. (2017). Blinded by Love: Women, Men, and Gendered Age in Relationship Stories. *Gender and Society, 31*(1), 96–118.

Darling-Fisher, C. S., & Tiedje, L. B. (1990). The Impact of Maternal Employment Characteristics on Fathers' Participation in Child Care. *Family Relations, 39*(1), 20–26.

de Boise, S. (2015). *Men, Masculinities, Music and Emotions.* Basingstoke: Palgrave Macmillan.

Dempsey, D., & Hewitt, B. (2012). Fatherhood in the 21st Century. *Journal of Family Studies, 18*(2–3), 98–102.

Dermott, E. (2008). *Intimate Fatherhood: A Sociological Analysis.* London/New York: Routledge.

Dermott, E., & Millar, T. (2015). More than the Sum of Its Parts? Contemporary Fatherhood Policy, Practice and Discourse. *Families, Relationships and Societies, 4*(2), 183–195.

References   173

Deutsch, F. (1999). *Halving It All: How Equal Shared Parenting Works.* Cambridge: Harvard University Press.

Dewey, S. (2011). *Neon Wasteland: On Love, Motherhood, and Sex Work in a Rust Belt Town.* Berkeley: University of California Press.

Djikic, M., & Oatley, K. (2004). Love and Personal Relationships: Navigating on the Border Between the Ideal and the Real. *Journal for the Theory of Social Behaviour, 34*(2), 199–209.

Dolan, A., & Coe, C. (2011). Men, Masculine Identities and Childbirth. *Sociology of Health & Illness, 33*, 1019–1034.

Doucet, A. (2013). A "Choreography of Becoming": Fathering, Embodied Care, and New Materialisms. *Canadian Review of Sociology, 50*(3), 284–305.

Doucet, A. (2015). Parental Responsibilities: Dilemmas of Measurement and Gender Equality. *Journal of Marriage and Family, 77*(1), 224–242.

Doucet, A. (2017). *Do Men Mother? Fathering, Care, and Domestic Responsibility* (2nd ed.). Toronto: University of Toronto Press.

Duncombe, J., & Marsden, D. (1995). Can Men Love? 'Reading', 'Staging' and 'Resisting' the Romance. In L. Pearce & J. Stacey (Eds.), *Romance Revisited: Part 2* (pp. 238–250). London: Lawrence & Wishart.

Edin, K., & Nelson, T. J. (2013). *Doing the Best They Can: Fatherhood in the Inner City.* Berkeley: University of California Press.

Edwards, T. (2006). *Cultures of Masculinity.* London: Routledge.

Edwards, R., Ribbens, J., & Gillies, V. (1999). Shifting Boundaries and Power in the Research Process: The Example of Researching Step-Families. In J. Seymour & P. Bagguley (Eds.), *Relating Intimacies: Power and Resistance* (pp. 13–42). Houndmills: Macmillan.

Eggebeen, D. J., & Knoester, C. (2001). Does Fatherhood Matter for Men? *Journal of Marriage and Family, 63*(2), 381–393.

Ehrenreich, B., Hess, E., & Jacobs, G. (1987). *Re-Making Love: The Feminization of Sex.* New York: Doubleday.

Elias, N. (1939/2000). *The Civilizing Process: Sociogenetic and Psychogenetic Investigations* (Trans. E. Jephcott). Oxford: Blackwell Publishers.

Elias, N. (1987). The Retreat of Sociologists into the Present. *Theory, Culture and Society, 4*(2–3), 223–247.

Ellingsaeter, A. L., & Leira, A. (2006). *Politicising Parenthood in Scandinavia: Gender Relations in Welfare States.* Bristol: Policy Press.

Elliott, K. (2015). Caring Masculinities: Theorizing an Emerging Concept. *Men and Masculinities, 12*, 240–259.

Engdahl, E. (2018). *Depressive Love: A Social Pathology.* London: Routledge.

Eydal, G. B., & Rostgaard, T. (2014). *Fatherhood in the Nordic Welfare States: Comparing Care Policies and Practice.* Bristol: Policy Press.

174   References

Featherstone, B. (2009). *Contemporary Fatherhood: Theory, Policy and Practice.* Bristol: Policy Press.

Feldman, R. (2012). Parent-Infant Synchrony: A Biobehavioral Model of Mutual Influences in the Formation of Affiliative Bonds. *Monographs of the Society for Research in Child Development, 77*(2), 42–51.

Fergusson, A., & Jónasdóttir, A. G. (2014). *Love: A Question for Feminism in the 21st Century.* New York: Routledge/Taylor and Francis.

Finn, M., & Henwood, K. (2009). Exploring Masculinities Within Men's Identificatory Imaginings of First-Time Fatherhood. *British Journal of Social Psychology, 48*, 547–562.

Flouri, E. (2005). *Fathering and Child Outcomes.* Chichester: Wiley.

Foucault, M. (1983). The Subject and Power. In H. Dreyfus & P. Rabinow (Eds.), *Michel Foucault: Beyond Structuralism and Hermeneutics* (pp. 208–226). Chicago: The University of Chicago Press.

Fox, B. (2009). *When Couples Become Parents: The Creation of Gender in the Transition to Parenthood.* Toronto: University of Toronto Press.

Freud, S. (1919). *Totem and Taboo: Resemblances Between the Psychic Lives of Savages and Neurotics.* London: Routledge & Sons.

Friedman, M. (2014). Unpacking MILF: Exploring Motherhood, Sexuality and Feminism. *Atlantis: Critical Studies in Gender, Culture & Social Justice, 36*(2), 49–60.

Fromm, E. (1956). *The Art of Loving.* New York: Harper and Row.

Gabb, J. (2013). Embodying Risk: Managing Father–Child Intimacy and the Display of Nudity in Families. *Sociology, 47*(4), 639–654.

Gabb, J., & Fink, J. (2015). *Couple Relationships in the 21st Century.* Basingstoke: Palgrave Pivot.

Galasinski, D. (2004). *Men and the Language of Emotions.* Basingstoke: Palgrave Macmillan.

Gardiner, J. K. (2002). Theorising Age with Gender: Bly's Boys, Feminism, and Maturity Masculinity. In J. K. Gardiner (Ed.), *Masculinity Studies and Feminist Theory: New Directions* (pp. 90–118). New York: Columbia University Press.

Gaunt, R. (2008). Maternal Gatekeeping. *Journal of Family Issues, 29*(3), 373–395.

Gergely, G., & Watson, J. S. (1996). The Social Biofeedback Theory of Parental Affect-Mirroring: The Development of Emotional Self-Awareness and Self-Control in Infancy. *International Journal of Psycho-Analysis, 77*, 1181–1212.

Giddens, A. (1991). *Modernity and Self-Identity: Self and Society in the Late Modern Age.* Cambridge: Polity Press in association with Blackwell.

Giddens, A. (1992). *The Transformation of Intimacy: Sexuality, Love, and Eroticism in Modern Societies.* Stanford: Stanford University Press.

Gillis, J. R. (1997). *A World of Their Own Making: Myth, Ritual and the Quest for Family Values*. Cambridge: Harvard University Press.

Gilmore, D. D. (1990). *Manhood in the Making: Cultural Concepts of Masculinity*. New Haven: Yale University Press.

Goldberg, W. A., Tan, E. T., & Thorsen, K. L. (2009). Trends in Academic Attention to Fathers, 1930–2006. *Fathering, 7*(2), 159–179.

Goode, W. (1959). The Theoretical Importance of Love. *American Sociological Review, 24*(6), 38–47.

Goodey, J. (1997). Boys Don't Cry: Masculinities, Fear of Crime and Fearlessness. *British Journal of Criminology, 37*, 401–418.

Gordon, E. (2006). The Family. In L. Abrams, E. Gordon, D. Simonton, & E. Yeo (Eds.), *Gender in Scottish History Since 1700* (pp. 235–267). Edinburgh: Edinburgh University Press.

Graham, J. W., Gentry, K. W., & Green, J. (1981). The Self Presentational Nature of Emotional Expression: Some Evidence. *Personality and Social Psychology Bulletin, 7*(September), 467–474.

Gucht, D. V. (1994). The Religion of Love and the Culture of Marriage (La religion de l'amour et la culture conjugale). *Cahiers Internationaux de Sociologie (International Journals of Sociology), 97*, 329–353.

Gunnarsson, L. (2016). The Dominant and Its Constitutive Other: Feminist Theorizations of Love, Power and Gendered Selves. *Journal of Critical Realism, 15*(1), 1–20.

Halberstam, J. (2018). *Female Masculinity* (2nd ed.). Durham: Duke University Press.

Hall, O. C. E. (1995). From Fun and Excitement to Joy and Trouble: An Explorative Study of Three Danish Fathers' Experiences Around Birth. *Scandinavian Journal of Caring Sciences, 9*, 171–179.

Hanlon, N. (2012). *Masculinities, Care and Equality: Identity and Nurture in Men's Lives*. Basingstoke: Palgrave Macmillan.

Hanmer, J. (1990). Men, Power, and the Exploitation of Women. *Women's Studies International Forum, 13*(5), 443–456.

Haraway, D. J. (2003). *The Companion Species Manifesto: Dogs, People, and Significant Otherness*. Chicago/Bristol: Prickly Paradigm/University Presses Marketing.

Hardt, M. (2011). For Love or Money. *Cultural Anthropology, 26*(4), 676–682.

Harne, L. (2011). *Violent Fathering and the Risks to Children: The Need for Change*. Bristol: Policy.

Hatfield, E., Cacioppo, J. T., & Rapson, R. L. (1993). Emotion Contagion. *Current Directions in Psychological Science, 2*(3), 96–99.

176 References

Hays, S. (1996). *The Cultural Contradictions of Motherhood*. Yale: University Press.

Heaney, J. G. (2011). Emotions and Power: Reconciling Conceptual Twins. *Journal of Political Power, 4*(2), 259–277.

Hearn, J. (2013). The Sociological Significance of Domestic Violence: Tensions, Paradoxes and Implications. *Current Sociology, 61*(2), 152–170.

Hearn, J., & Pringle, K. (2006). Men, Masculinities and Children: Some European Perspectives. *Critical Social Policy, 26*, 365–389.

Hearn, J., & Šmidova, I. (2015). The Multiple Empires of Men. *Gender, Equal Opportunities Research, 16*(1), 74–82.

Henwood, K., & Procter, J. (2003). The 'Good Father': Reading Men's Accounts of Paternal Involvement During the Transition to First-Time Fatherhood. *British Journal of Social Psychology, 42*(3), 337–355.

Hirsch, J. S., & Wardlow, H. (Eds.). (2006). *Modern Loves: The Anthropology of Romantic Courtship and Companionate Marriage*. Ann Arbor: The University of Michigan Press.

Hochschild, A. R. (1979). Emotion Work, Feeling Rules, and Social Structure. *American Journal of Sociology, 85*(3), 551–575.

Hochschild, A. R. (1983/2003). *The Managed Heart: Commercialization of Human Feeling*. Berkeley: University of California Press.

Hochschild, A. R. (1998). The Sociology of Emotion as a Way of Seeing. In G. Bendelow & S. J. Williams (Eds.), *Emotions in Social Life: Critical Themes and Contemporary Issues* (pp. 3–17). London: Routledge.

Hochschild, A. R. (2003). *The Commercialization of Intimate Life: Notes from Home and Work*. Berkeley/London: University of California Press.

Hochschild, A. R., & Machung, A. (1990). *The Second Shift: Working Parents and the Revolution at Home*. New York: Avon Books.

Hojgaard, L. (1997). Working Fathers – Caught in the Web of the Symbolic Order of Gender. *Acta Sociologica, 40*, 245–261.

Hollway, W. (2006). *The Capacity to Care: Gender and Ethical Subjectivity*. New York: Routledge.

Holmes, M. (2010). The Emotionalization of Reflexivity. *Sociology, 44*(1), 139–154.

Holmes, M. (2014). Men's Emotions: Heteromasculinity, Emotional Reflexivity and Intimate Relationships. *Men and Masculinities, 18*(2), 176–192.

Hood, N., Peat, J., Peters, E., & Young, S. (Eds.). (2003). *Scotland in a Global Economy: The 2020 Vision*. Basingstoke: Palgrave Macmillan.

Hook, J. L., & Wolfe, C. M. (2013). Parental Involvement and Work Schedules: Time with Children in the United States, Germany, Norway, and the United Kingdom. *European Sociological Review, 29*(3), 411–425.

References   177

hooks, b. (1994). *Teaching to Transgress: Education as the Practice of Freedom.* New York/London: Routledge.

hooks, b. (2000). *All About Love: New Visions.* New York: Harper Collins Publisher.

hooks, b. (2004). *The Will to Change: Men, Masculinity, and Love.* Washington: Washington Square Press.

hooks, b. (2006). *Outlaw Culture: Resisting Representations.* New York: Routledge Classics.

Horvath, A., Thomassen, B., & Wydra, H. (Eds.). (2015). *Breaking Boundaries: Varieties of Liminality.* New York/Oxford: Berghahn.

Howson, A. (1993). No Gods and Precious Few Women: Gender and Cultural Identity in Scotland. *Scottish Affairs, 2*(1), 37–49.

Illouz, E. (2012). *Why Love Hurts: A Sociological Explanation.* Cambridge: Polity Press.

Iluț, P. (2015). *Dragoste, familie și fericire: Spre o sociologie a seninătații (Love, the Family and Happiness: Towards a Sociology of Serenity).* Bucharest: Polirom - Collegium.

Inglis, R. (1987). *Sins of the Fathers: A Study of the Physical and Emotional Abuse of Children.* London: Owen.

Jackson, S. (1993). Even Sociologists Fall in Love: An Exploration in the Sociology of Emotions. *Sociology, 27*(2), 201–220.

Jaggar, A. M. (1989). Love and Knowledge: Emotion in Feminist Epistemology. *Inquiry, 32*(2), 151–176.

Jamieson, L. (1998). *Intimacy: Personal Relationships in Modern Societies.* Cambridge: Polity Press.

Jamieson, L. (1999). Intimacy Transformed: A Critical Look at the Pure Relationship. *Sociology, 33*(3), 477–494.

Jamieson, L. (2005). Boundaries of Intimacy. In J. Campling, S. Cunningham-Burley, & L. McKie (Eds.), *Families in Society Boundaries and Relationships* (pp. 189–207). Bristol: Policy.

Jamieson, L. (2011). Intimacy as a Concept: Explaining Social Change in the Context of Globalisation or Another Form of Ethnocentricism? *Sociological Research Online, 16*(4), 1–13.

Jansz, J. (2000). Masculine Identity and Restrictive Emotionality. In A. H. Fischer (Ed.), *Gender and Emotion: Social Psychological Perspectives* (pp. 166–186). Cambridge: Cambridge University Press.

Johansson, T., & Klinth, R. (2007). Caring Fathers: The Ideology of Gender Equality and Masculine Positions. *Men and Masculinities, 11*(1), 42–62.

178   References

Johnson, J. E., & Robinson, J. C. (2006). *Living Gender After Communism*. Bloomington: Indiana University Press.

Kaufman, G. (2013). *Superdads: How Fathers Balance Work and Care in the 21st Century*. New York: New York University Press.

Kemper, T. D. (1978). *A Social Interactional Theory of Emotions*. New York: Wiley.

Kimmel, M. S. (2008). *Guyland: The Perilous World Where Boys Become Men*. New York: Harper Collins.

Kimmel, M. S. (2013). Is It the "End of Men", or Are Men Still in Power? Yes! (Response to Article by Hanna Rosin in This Issue). *Boston University Law Review, 93*(3), 689–697.

Kuhn, A. (2002). *Family Secrets: Acts of Memory and Imagination* (2nd ed.). London: Verso.

Lamb, M. E. (Ed.). (2010). *The Role of the Father in Child Development* (5th ed.). London: Wiley.

Lareau, A. (2003). *Unequal Childhoods: Class, Race, and Family Life*. Berkeley: University of California Press.

LaRossa, R. (1997). *The Modernization of Fatherhood: A Social and Political History*. Chicago: University of Chicago Press.

Lorber, J. (1994). *Paradoxes of Gender*. New Haven/London: Yale University Press.

Lupton, D. (1998). *The Emotional Self: A Sociocultural Exploration*. London: SAGE.

Lupton, D. (2013). Infant Embodiment and Interembodiment: A Review of Sociocultural Perspectives. *Childhood, 20*(1), 37–50.

Lupton, D., & Barclay, L. (1997). *Constructing Fatherhood: Discourses and Experiences*. London: Sage.

Lynch, K. (2007). Love Labour as a Distinct and Non-Commodifiable Form of Care Labour. *The Sociological Review, 55*(3), 550–570.

Macht, A. (2018a). Grounding Reflexivity in a Qualitative Study on Love with Fathers. *SAGE Research Methods Cases* Part 2, Sage. Available at http://methods.sagepub.com/case/grounding-reflexivity-in-qualitative-study-on-love-with-involved-fathers

Macht, A. (2018b). From Romanian "Soul" to English "Heart": Dilemmas of Cultural and Gender Representation in Translating Qualitative Data. *Forum: Qualitative Social Research/Forum Qualitative Sozialforschung, 19*(2), ISSN: 1438-5627/eISSN: 1438-5627.

Macht, A. (2018c). Resisting the Commodification of Intimate Life? Paternal Love, Emotional Bordering and Narratives of Ambivalent Family Consumerism from Scottish and Romanian Fathers. *Families, Relationships and Societies, 8*, 21. https://doi.org/10.1332/204674318X15384702551202.

Macht, A. (2019a, Forthcoming). Travelling Feelings: Narratives of Sustaining Love in Two Case Studies with Fathers in Family Separations. In L. Murray et al. (Eds.), *Families in Motion: Ebbing and Flowing Through Space and Time* (pp. 19–37). Bingley: Emerald Publishing.

Macht, A. (2019b). Shifting Perspectives: Becoming a Feminist Researcher While Studying Fatherhood and Love. *Vitae Scholasticae: The Journal of Educational Biography, 35*(2), ISSN: 0735-1909/eISSN: 0735-1909.

Macht, A., & Popescu, R. (2018). Romania Country Note. In S. Blum, A. Koslowski, A. Macht, & P. Moss (Eds.), *International Review of Leave Policies and Research 2018*. Available at http://www.leavenetwork.org/lp_and_r_reports/

Marsiglio, W., & Roy, K. (2012). *Nurturing Dads: Social Initiatives for Contemporary Fatherhood*. New York: Russell Sage Foundation.

Mason, J. (2002). *Qualitative Researching*. California: Sage Publications.

McCrone, D. (2001). *Understanding Scotland: The Sociology of a Nation* (2nd ed.). New York: Routledge.

McIvor, A., & Johnston, R. (2004). Dangerous Work, Hard Men and Broken Bodies: Masculinity in the Clydeside Heavy Industries. *Labour History Review, 69*(2), 135–152.

McMunn, A., Martin, P., Kelly, Y., & Sacker, A. (2015). Fathers' Involvement Correlates and Consequences for Child Socio-Emotional Behavior in the United Kingdom. *Journal of Family Issues, 38*(8), 1109–1131.

Mead, G. H. (1934). *Mind, Self, and Society: From the Standpoint of a Social Behaviourist*. Chicago: University of Chicago Press.

Meah, A., & Jackson, P. (2016). The Complex Landscape of Contemporary Fathering in the UK. *Social and Cultural Geography, 17*(4), 491–510.

Miller, T. (2010). *Making Sense of Fatherhood: Gender, Caring and Work*. Cambridge: Cambridge University Press.

Moore, E. (2012). Paternal Banking and Maternal Gatekeeping in Post-Divorce Families. *Journal of Family Issues, 33*(6), 745–772.

Morgan, D. H. J. (1985). *The Family, Politics and Social Theory*. London: Routledge.

Morgan, D. H. J. (1992). *Discovering Men*. London: Routledge.

Morgan, D. H. J. (2011). *Rethinking Family Practices*. Basingstoke: Palgrave Macmillan.

Morrison, C. A., Johnston, L., & Longhurst, R. (2012). Critical Geographies of Love as Spatial, Relational and Political. *Progress in Human Geography, 37*(4), 505–521.

180 References

National Institute of Statistics. (2018). *Social Trends for 2017*. Bucharest: INS – National Institute of Statistics Publishing Press.

National Records of Scotland. (2018). *Mid-2016 Population Estimates for Settlements and Localities in Scotland*. Available from https://www.nrscotland.gov.uk/files//statistics/settlements-localities/set-loc-16/set-loc-2016-publication-updated.pdf. Accessed 12 Mar 2019.

Nelson, S., & Mckie, L. (2005). *Child Sexual Abuse: Fracturing Family Life; Families, Violence and Social Change*. Maidenhead: Open University Press.

Nielsen, H. B. (2017). *Feeling Gender: A Generational and Psychosocial Approach*. London: Palgrave Macmillan.

O'Brien, M., Brandth, B., & Kvande, E. (2007). Fathers, Work and Family life. *Community, Work & Family., 10*(4), 375–386.

O'Brien, R., Hunt, K., & Hart, G. (2009). 'The Average Scottish Man Has a Cigarette Hanging Out of his Mouth, Lying There with a Portion of Chips': Prospects for Change in Scottish Men's Constructions of Masculinity and Their Health-Related Beliefs and Behaviours. *Critical Public Health, 19*(3–4), 363–381.

Padilla, M. B., Hirsch, J. S., Munoz-Laboy, M., Sember, R. E., & Parker, R. G. (Eds.). (2007). *Love and Globalization: Transformations of Intimacy in the Contemporary World*. Nashville: Vanderbilt University Press.

Parsons, T. (1943). The Kinship System of the Contemporary United States. *American Anthropologist, 45*, 22–38.

Paxson, H. (2007). A Fluid Mechanics of Erotas and Aghape: Family Planning and Maternal Consumption in Contemporary Greece. In M. B. Padilla, J. S. Hirsch, M. Munoz-Laboy, R. E. Sember, & R. G. Parker (Eds.), *Love and Globalization: Transformations of Intimacy in the Contemporary World* (pp. 120–139). Nashville: Vanderbilt University Press.

Pini, B., & Pease, B. (Eds.). (2013). *Men Masculinities and Methodologies*. Basingstoke: Palgrave Macmillan.

Pleck, J. H. (1981). *The Myth of Masculinity*. Cambridge, MA: MIT Press.

Polansky, N. A., Chalmers, M. A., Buttenwieser, E., & Williams, D. P. (1979). The Absent Father in Child Neglect. *Social Service Review, 53*(2), 163–174.

Popescu, L. (2004). *Politica Sexelor (Gender Politics)*. Bucuresti: Maiko.

Popescu, R. (2009). *Introducere in Sociologia Familiei: Familia Romaneasca in Societate Contemporana (Introduction to the Sociology of Family Life: The Romanian Family in Contemporary Society)*. Bucharest: Polirom.

Popescu, R. (2014). Family Policies in Romania Within the European Framework. *Journal of Community Positive Practices, XIV*(3), 99–113.

Powell, F., & Scanlon, M. (2014). The Media and Child Abuse. *Discover Society, 13*. Available from http://discoversociety.org/2014/09/30/the-media-and-child-abuse/. Accessed 17 Mar 2019.

Presser, H. B., & Sen, G. (2000). *Women's Empowerment and Demographic Processes: Moving Beyond Cairo.* Oxford: Oxford University Press.

Raiu, S. L. (2011). The Process of Globalization in Romania. *Revista Română de Sociologie (The Romanian Journal of Sociology), XXII*(3–4), 373–380.

Ranson, G. (2010). *Against the Grain: Couples, Gender, and the Reframing of Parenting.* Toronto: University of Toronto Press.

Ranson, G. (2015). *Fathering, Masculinity and the Embodiment of Care.* Basingstoke: Palgrave Macmillan.

Rebhun, L. A. (2007). The Strange Marriage of Love and Interest: Economic Change and Emotional Intimacy in Northeast-Brazil, Private and Public. In M. B. Padilla, J. S. Hirsch, M. Munoz-Laboy, R. E. Sember, & R. G. Parker (Eds.), *Love and Globalization: Transformations of Intimacy in the Contemporary World* (pp. 107–120). Nashville: Vanderbilt University Press.

Reeser, T. W., & Gottzén, L. (2018). Masculinity and Affect: New Possibilities, New Agendas. *NORMA, 13*(3–4), 145–157.

Riley, D. (1987). The Serious Burdens of Love? Some Questions on Child-Care. In A. Phillips (Ed.), *Feminism and Socialism* (pp. 176–199). Oxford: Basil Blackwell.

Risman, B. J. (1998). *Gender Vertigo: American Families in Transition.* New Haven: Yale University Press.

Robertson, R. P. (2010). Child Sexual Abuse, Masculinity and Fatherhood. *Journal of Family Studies, 18*(2–3), 130–142.

Robinson, V., & Hockey, J. (2011). Embodiment: Masculinity and the Body. In *Masculinities in Transition. Genders and Sexualities in the Social Sciences.* London: Palgrave Macmillan.

Rochlen, A. B., Suizzo, M., McKelley, R. A., & Scaringi, V. (2008). "I'm Just Providing for My Family:" a Qualitative Study of Stay-at-Home Fathers. *Psychology of Men and Masculinity, 9*(4), 193–206.

Romero-Balsas, P., Muntanyola-Saura, D., & Rogero-Garcia, J. (2013). Decision-Making Factors Within Paternity and Parental Leaves: Why Spanish Fathers Take Time Off from Work. *Gender, Work and Organization, 20*(6), 678–691.

Roseneil, S. (2005). Living and Loving Beyond the Boundaries of the Heteronorm: Personal Relationships in the 21st Century. In L. Mackie, S. Cunningham-Burley, & J. McKendrick (Eds.), *Families in Society: Boundaries and Relationships* (pp. 241–258). Bristol: Policy Press.

182 References

Sampson, C., & Atkinson, P. (2013). The Golden Star: An Emotional Repertoire of Scientific Discovery and Legacy. *The Sociological Review, 61*, 573–590.

Scheer, M. (2012). Are Emotions a Kind of Practice (And Is That What Makes Them Have a History)? A Bourdieuian Approach to Understanding Emotion. *History and Theory, 51*, 193–220.

Schofield, A. (2016). Hard Bodies, Soft Hearts: Mixed-Race Men as Muscular Daddies in the Films of Vin Diesel and Dwayne Johnson. In E. Podnieks (Ed.), *Pops in Pop Culture* (pp. 125–140).

Schrock, D., & Schwalbe, M. (2009). Men, Masculinities and Manhood Acts. *Annual Review of Sociology, 35*, 277–295.

Seebach, S. (2017). *Love and Society: Special Social Forms and the Master Emotion.* London: Routledge.

Segal, L. (2007). *Slow Motion: Changing Masculinities, Changing Men.* Basingstoke: Palgrave Macmillan.

Seidler, V. J. (1998). Masculinity, Violence and Emotional Life. In G. Bendelow & S. J. Williams (Eds.), *Emotions in Social Life: Critical Themes and Contemporary Issues.* London: Routledge.

Seidler, V. J. (2006). Gender, Power, Ethics and Love. In V. J. Seidler (Ed.), *Transforming Masculinities: Men, Cultures, Bodies, Power, Sex and Love* (pp. 128–142). London: Taylor and Francis.

Seidman, S. (1991). *Romantic Longings: Love in America, 1830–1980.* Charlottesville/New York: University of Virginia/Routledge.

Selin, H. (2013). *Parenting Across Cultures: Childrearing, Motherhood and Fatherhood in Non-Western Cultures.* New York/London: Springer.

Shapiro, S. G., & Shapiro, R. (2004). *The Curtain Rises: Oral Histories of the Fall of Communism in Eastern Europe.* London: McFarland & Company.

Sharpe, S. (1987). *Falling for Love: Teenage Mothers Talk.* London: Virago.

Shields, A. S. (2002). *Speaking from the Heart: Gender and the Social Meaning of Emotion.* New York: Cambridge University Press.

Shirani, F. (2013). The Spectre of the Wheezy Dad: Masculinity, Fatherhood and Ageing. *Sociology, 47*(6), 1104–1119.

Shirani, F., & Henwood, K. (2011). Continuity and Change in a Qualitative Longitudinal Study of Fatherhood: Relevance Without Responsibility. *International Journal of Social Research Methodology, 14*(1), 17–29.

Sikorska, M. (2016). From "Absent Father" to "Involved Father": Changes in the Model of Fatherhood in Poland and Role of Mothers-"Gatekeepers". In E. Ruspini & I. Crespi (Eds.), *Balancing Work and Family in a Changing Society* (pp. 163–175). New York: Palgrave Macmillan.

Simmel, G. (1984). *On Women, Sexuality and Love*. New Haven: Yale University Press.

Skeggs, B., & Moran, L. J. (2004). *Sexuality and the Politics of Violence and Safety*. London: Routledge.

Smart, C. (2007). *Personal Life: New Directions in Sociological Thinking*. Cambridge: Polity.

Smart, C., & Neale, B. (1999). 'I Hadn't Really Thought About It': New Identities/New Fatherhoods. In J. Seymour & P. Bagguley (Eds.), *Relating Intimacies: Power and Resistance* (pp. 118–141). Houndmills: Macmillan.

Smith-Koslowski, A. (2011). Working Fathers in Europe: Earning and Caring. *European Sociological Review, 27*(2), 230–245.

Streets-Salter, H. (2004). *Martial Races: The Military, Race, and Masculinity in British Imperial Culture, 1857–1914*. Manchester: Manchester University Press.

Swidler, A. (2001). *Talk of Love: How Culture Matters*. Chicago/London: University of Chicago Press.

Theodosius, C. (2006). Recovering Emotion from Emotion Management. *Sociology, 40*(5), 893–911.

Thorne, B. (1993). *Gender Play: Girls and Boys in School*. New Brunswick: Rutgers University Press.

Thurer, S. (1995). *The Myths of Motherhood: How Culture Reinvents the Good Mother*. New York: Penguin.

Turcescu, L., & Stan, L. (2005). Religion, Politics and Sexuality in Romania. *Europe-Asia Studies, 57*(2), 291–310.

Turner, B., & Stets, J. (2005). *The Sociology of Emotions*. Cambridge: Cambridge University Press.

Valentine, G. (1997). My Son's a Bit Dizzy, My Wife's a Bit Soft: Gender, Children and Cultures of Parenting. *Gender, Place and Culture, 4*(1), 37–62.

van Dijik, J. (2013). *The Culture of Connectivity: A Critical History of Social Media*. Oxford: Oxford University Press.

Vandenberghe, F. (2008). Sociology of the Heart: Max Scheler's Epistemology of Love. *Theory, Culture & Society, 25*(3), 17–51.

Verdery, K. (1996). From Parent-State to Family Patriarchs – Gender and Nation in Contemporary Eastern Europe. In K. Verdery (Ed.), *What Was Socialism and What Comes Next* (pp. 61–82). Princeton: Princeton University Press.

Voicu, M. (2008). Religiosity and Religious Revival During the Transition Period in Romania. In B. Voicu & M. Voicu (Eds.), *The Values of Romanians 1993–2006: A Sociological Perspective* (pp. 144–170). Iasi: The European Institute.

184 References

Voicu, M., & Tufiş, P. A. (2012). Trends in Gender Beliefs in Romania: 1993–2008. *Current Sociology, 60*(1), 61–80.

von Scheve, C. (2011). Collective Emotions in Rituals: Elicitation, Transmission, and a "Mattheweffect". In A. Michaels & C. Wulf (Eds.), *Emotions in Rituals and Performances: South Asian and European Perspectives on Rituals and Performativity* (pp. 55–78). London: Routledge.

Waitt, G., & Stanes, E. (2015). Sweating Bodies: Men, Masculinities, Affect, Emotion. *Geoforum, 59*, 30–38.

Wall, K. (2014). Fathers on Leave Alone: Does It Make a Difference to Their Lives? *Fathering, 12*(2), 196–211.

Wall, K., Aboim, S., & Marinho, S. (2011). Fatherhood, Family and Work in Men's Lives: Negotiating New and Old Masculinities. *Recherches Sociologiques et Anthropologiques (Anthropological and Sociological Research), 38*(2), 105–122.

Waller, M. R. (2002). *My Baby's Father: Unmarried Parents and Paternal Responsibility*. Ithaca: Cornell University Press.

Waller, M., & Swisher, R. (2006). Fathers' Risk Factors in Fragile Families: Implications for "Healthy" Relationships and Father Involvement. *Social Problems, 53*(3), 392–420.

Walzer, S. (2010). *Thinking about the Baby: Gender and Transitions into Parenthood*. Philadelphia: Temple University Press.

Wetherell, M. (2012). *Affect and Emotion: A New Social Science Understanding*. London: SAGE Publications Ltd.

Wilkinson, E. (2013). Learning to Love Again: 'Broken Families', Citizenship and the State Promotion of Coupledom. *Geoforum, 49*, 206–214.

Williams, S. (2008). What Is Fatherhood?: Searching for the Reflexive Father. *Sociology, 42*(3), 487–502.

Williams, S. (2011). Chaotic Identities, Love and Fathering. *Folklore: Electronic Journal of Folklore, 48*, 31–54.

Wisso, T., & Plantin, L. (2015). Fathers and Parental Support in Everyday Family Life: Informal Support in Sweden Beyond the Auspices of the Welfare State. *Families, Relationships and Societies, 4*(2), 267–280.

Wouters, C. (1989). The Sociology of Emotions and Flight Attendants: Hochschild's Managed Heart. *Theory, Culture & Society, 6*(1), 95–123.

Young, H. (2007). Hard Man, New Man: Re/Composing Masculinities in Glasgow, c. 1950–2000. *Oral History, 35*(1), 71–81.

Index[1]

A

Ambivalent fathers, 81, 149
Authoritative, 5, 133

B

Bodies, 21, 24, 51, 86, 155
Bodily cues, 55
Body techniques, 51

C

Capitalism, 154
Caregiving, 51, 57, 61, 86, 147
Cartesian divide, 35
Complexes of emotions, 58, 156
Connection, 37, 39n4, 45, 49, 51, 54, 56, 73, 81, 102, 113, 124, 157

Co-sleeping, 43, 44, 65
Culture, 2, 23, 24, 36, 37n2, 86, 94, 102, 103, 125, 127, 138, 146, 149

D

Daughter, 42, 44, 45, 54, 58, 59, 64, 65, 78, 88, 92, 94, 110, 111, 115, 122, 133, 136, 138, 162–167
De-feminize' love, 154
Different, 4, 11, 16, 23, 37–39, 42, 44, 57n14, 64, 65, 72, 73, 81, 88, 89, 92, 94, 96, 104, 106, 111–115, 121, 124, 127, 137, 147–149, 151
Doucet, A., 61, 153

---

[1] Note: Page numbers followed by 'n' refer to notes.

© The Author(s) 2020
A. Macht, *Fatherhood and Love*, Palgrave Macmillan Studies in Family and Intimate Life, https://doi.org/10.1007/978-3-030-20358-0

186 Index

E

Embodiment, 43, 51, 54, 55, 57n14, 61, 86, 92, 111
Emotional reflexivity, 24
Emotional vocabularies, 35
Emotion work, 20n10, 64, 78, 88–90, 106, 121, 148, 152
Everyday, 2, 5, 17, 21, 22, 58, 72, 78, 106, 156, 157

F

Fatherhood, 2, 4, 5, 5n1, 7, 12, 16, 17, 21, 40, 57n14, 58, 61, 62n16, 86n3, 112, 147, 152–154, 156
Father's love, 24
Feel, 37–39, 43, 54, 58, 59, 63, 65, 66, 94, 105, 106, 115, 124, 137, 139, 157
Fluid, 152

G

Gender ideals, 7
Give-and-take, 57, 65, 148
Good, vii, 19, 44, 46, 48, 52, 53, 55, 60, 64, 87, 95, 112, 116, 124, 126–128, 137, 139

H

Hochschild, A. R., 20n10, 63, 92, 125, 128, 129

I

Inequalities, 157
Interactions, 17, 20n10, 22, 41, 42, 44n7, 45, 48, 51, 52, 55, 59, 63, 73, 84, 92, 94, 96, 122, 124, 126, 138, 152, 155
Intimate relationships, 12, 13, 20, 21, 44n7, 82, 123, 127, 147, 154
Involved, 36

L

Language, 22, 35, 36, 55, 65, 138

M

Male power, 22
Masculine identity, 35, 51, 58, 59, 62
Mothers, 24, 44, 60, 61, 82, 86, 111, 114, 121, 122, 129, 130, 153, 155, 161

N

Nurturing, 4, 5n1, 20, 20n10, 43, 62, 78, 84, 114, 116, 130, 140

O

Observations, 22, 41n6, 52, 53

P

Patience, 52, 88, 89, 92, 106
Perform, 58
Power, 4, 16, 19, 24, 37, 39, 45, 62, 65, 82, 93, 93n5, 95, 96, 112, 121–128, 136, 137, 140, 150, 152, 155–157
Processual, 16, 24, 60, 92, 94, 121, 139, 156

R

Ranson, G., 44, 45, 51, 57, 86, 153
Relational force, 157
Risman, B. J., 155

S

Similar, 16, 23, 73, 88, 89, 94, 104, 106, 110, 127, 149, 153, 162
Sinister, 58

Social roles, 157
Stoicism, 19, 58, 59, 61, 62, 64, 71, 78, 84, 116, 139, 145, 150, 152, 154, 155

W

Warm, 62
Worry, 56, 57, 102–104, 106

9783030203603